T0150442

GHOSTS OF WAR

ANDREW FERGUSON

GHOSTS OF WAR

A HISTORY OF WORLD WAR I IN POETRY AND PROSE

The History Press

This book is dedicated to my father, James Duncan Ferguson, who
fought in the First World War, and to all those who served.

Front cover illustration: An infantry attack on the Somme. (© IWM, Q 65408)

First published 2016

The History Press
The Mill, Brimscombe Port
Stroud, Gloucestershire, GL5 2QG
www.thehistorypress.co.uk

© Andrew Ferguson, 2016

British Library Cataloguing in Publication Data.
A catalogue record for this book is available from the British Library.

ISBN 978 0 7509 6769 3

Typesetting and origination by The History Press
Printed and bound in Great Britain by TJ International Ltd

CONTENTS

It can but end in the greatest catastrophe that has ever befallen the continent of Europe at one blow.

Sir Edward Grey, Foreign Secretary, *The Times*, 1 August 1914.

FOREWORD

There are many histories of the First World War which focus in depth upon the causes, the strategy and the action. *Ghosts of War* takes a different approach, telling the story of the global war in an accessible and moving way, bringing the conflict to life in a vivid, dramatic and even sometimes humorous manner through an anthology of poetry and prose.

Most British accounts of the First World War are written from an English perspective. This book restores the balance, recognising and remembering the Scottish contribution to both the fighting and the poetry.

I commend *Ghosts of War* as essential reading for all those who have an interest in the First World War and its poetry, and in particular for those who respect and honour the Scottish contribution.

Nicola Sturgeon
First Minister of Scotland

ACKNOWLEDGEMENTS

The author would like to give his very sincere thanks to Chrissy McMorris, Managing Editor for Military and Transport at The History Press, for her whole-hearted support, to the editor Rebecca Newton for her patience and dedication in translating *Ghosts of War* from a manuscript to the printed book and, indeed, to all the staff of The History Press.

Tribute should also be made to the staff at the Imperial War Museum for their unfailing support and, in particular, to Caitlin Flynn for her invaluable assistance in the procurement of copyright material and to Neera Puttapipat for her assistance in securing the copyright approval for the images selected from the IWM library of photographs.

Credit and thanks are also due to Dr John MacAskill who read a draft of the manuscript and made helpful changes.

The author would also like to express his deep gratitude to his wife Liz for her continued support and encouragement through the conception and birth of *Ghosts of War*.

COPYRIGHT ACKNOWLEDGEMENT

Poems and Prose Extracts

of Mark Bostridge and T.J. Brittain-Catlin, Literary Executors for the Estate of Vera Brittain 1970.

W.D.Cocker: The poem *The Sniper* by W.D. Cocker is included by permission of Brown, Son and Ferguson.

Robert Graves: The poems *Corporal Stare*, *November 11*, *Through the Periscope* and *Two Fusiliers* and extracts from *Goodbye to All That* by Robert Graves are included by permission of Carcanet Press Limited.

Violet Jacob: The poem *To A.H.J.* by Violet Jacob is included by permission of Malcolm Hutton.

John Keegan: The extracts from *The First World War* by John Keegan are included by permission of The Random House Group.

Joseph Lee: The poem *German Prisoners* by Joseph Lee is included by permission of the University of Dundee Archive Services.

Christopher Middleton: The translation by Christopher Middleton of the poem *The Dead* by René Arcos is reproduced with the kind permission of Miranda Middleton and Sarah Poulain-Middleton.

Wilfred Owen: The poems of Wilfred Owen are sourced from *Wilfred Owen: The War Poems* by Jon Stallworthy, published by Chatto and Windus, 1994, and are published with the approval of the Trustees of the Wilfred Owen Estate. The letters of Wilfred Owen are published by permission of the Wilfred Owen Royalties Trust.

Siegfried Sassoon: The poems of Siegfried Sassoon and the extracts from *Memoirs of an Infantry Officer* and *The Complete Memoirs of George Sherston* are copyright Siegfried Sassoon and included by kind permission of the Estate of George Sassoon.

Photographs and Maps

Other than those specifically acknowledged, all photographs have been sourced from the extensive collection of the Imperial War Museum and are published with their approval. The maps have been provided by Nick Rowland FRGS.

GHOSTS OF WAR

When you and I are buried
With grasses over head,
The memory of our fights will stand
Above this bare and tortured land,
We knew ere we were dead.

Though grasses grow on Vimy,
And poppies at Messines,
And in High Wood the children play,
The craters and the graves will stay
To show what things have been.

Though all be quiet in day-time,
The night shall bring a change,
And peasants walking home shall see
Shell-torn meadow and riven tree,
And their own fields grown strange.

They shall hear live men crying,
They shall see dead men lie,
Shall hear the rattling Maxims fire,
And see by broken twists of wire
Gold flares light up the sky.

And in their new-built houses
The frightened folk will see
Pale bombers coming down the street,
And hear the flurry of charging feet,
And the crash of Victory.

This is our Earth baptized
With the red wine of War.
Horror and courage hand in hand
Shall brood upon the stricken land
In silence evermore.

(Ewart Alan Mackintosh. Sent from France, October 1917)

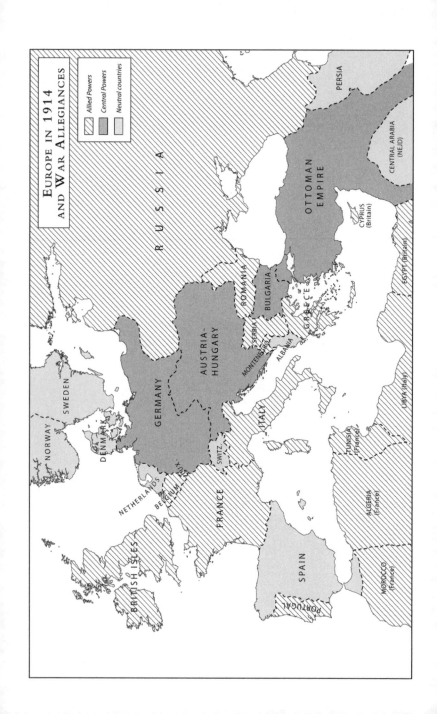

EUROPE IN 1914
AND WAR ALLEGIANCES

Allied Powers
Central Powers
Neutral countries

RUSSIA

OTTOMAN EMPIRE

PERSIA

CENTRAL ARABIA (NEJD)

CYPRUS (Britain)

EGYPT (Britain)

ROMANIA

BULGARIA

SERBIA

MONTENEGRO

ALBANIA

GREECE

GERMANY

AUSTRIA-HUNGARY

ITALY

LIBYA (Italy)

SWEDEN

NORWAY

DENMARK

NETHERLANDS

BELGIUM

LUX.

SWITZ.

FRANCE

BRITISH ISLES

SPAIN

PORTUGAL

TUNISIA (France)

ALGERIA (France)

MOROCCO (France)

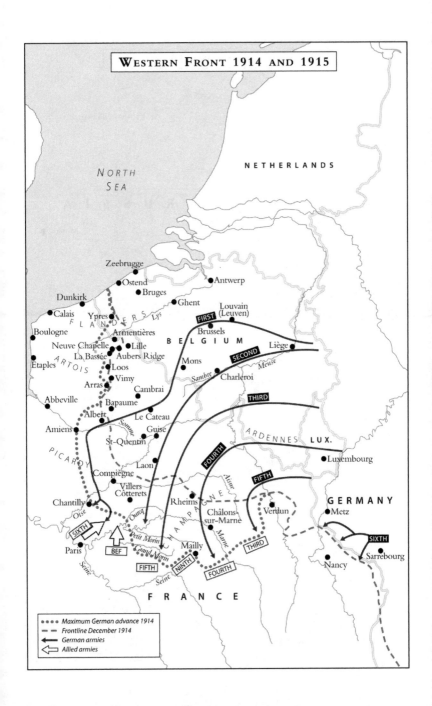

WESTERN FRONT 1914 AND 1915

NORTH SEA

NETHERLANDS

Zeebrugge

Ostend
Bruges
Antwerp

Dunkirk
Ghent

Calais
Ypres
Louvain
(Leuven)

FLANDERS
Lys
FIRST

Boulogne
Armentières
Brussels
BELGIUM
Liège

Neuve Chapelle
Lille
SECOND

La Bassée
Aubers Ridge
Mons
Meuse

Etaples
Loos
Charleroi

ARTOIS
Vimy
Sambre

Arras
Cambrai
THIRD

Abbeville
Bapaume
ARDENNES
LUX.

Albert
Le Cateau

Amiens
Somme
Guise
Luxembourg

St-Quentin

PICARDY
Laon
FOURTH

Compiègne
Aisne
FIFTH

Villers
Cotterets
GERMANY

Chantilly
Rheims
Verdun
Metz

Oise
Ourcq
CHAMPAGNE
Châlons-
sur-Marne

SIXTH
Petit Morin
SIXTH

Paris
BEF
Grand Morin
Mailly
Marne
THIRD
Sarrebourg

Seine
FIFTH
NINTH
FOURTH
Nancy

Seine

F R A N C E

• • • • Maximum German advance 1914
– – – Frontline December 1914
◄── German armies
⬅ Allied armies

THE EASTERN FRONT 1914 - 1917

St Petersburg (Petrograd)

ESTONIA

LATVIA

RUSSIA

Riga

COURLAND

Dvina

Moscow

BALTIC SEA

LITHUANIA

Vilna
(Vilnius)

Minsk

Königsberg

EAST
PRUSSIA

Gumbinnen

Danzig

*Masurian
Lakes*

GERMANY

Tannenberg

Vistula

Warsaw

Lodz

POLAND

Kiev

SILESIA

Lvov
(Lemberg)

Dnieper

Cracow

CARPATHIAN MOUNTAINS

Vienna

AUSTRIA-HUNGARY

Dniester

UKRAINE

Budapest

Odessa

BOSNIA-
HERZ.

Danube

ROMANIA

BLACK SEA

SERBIA

MONTENEGRO

BULGARIA

ALBANIA

Constantinople

GREECE

OTTOMAN
EMPIRE

— — — *Frontline September 1914*
• • • • • *Frontline Armistice 1917*

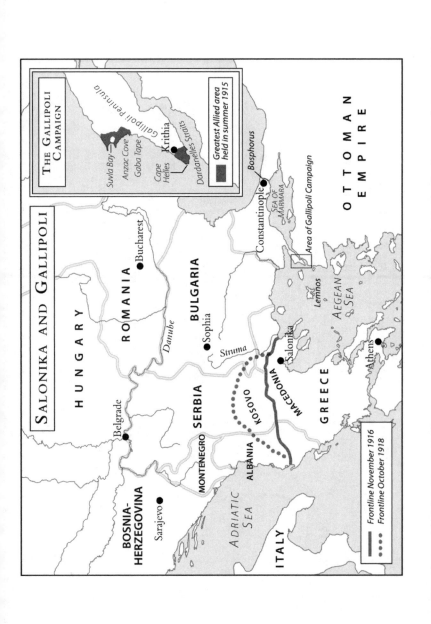

SALONIKA AND GALLIPOLI

THE GALLIPOLI CAMPAIGN

Gallipoli peninsula

Suvla Bay
Anzac Cove
Gaba Tepe
Cape Helles
Krithia
Dardanelles Straits

Bosphorus

Greatest Allied area held in summer 1915

Constantinople

SEA OF MARMARA

Area of Gallipoli Campaign

OTTOMAN EMPIRE

Lemnos

AEGEAN SEA

HUNGARY

ROMANIA

Bucharest

BULGARIA

Sophia

Danube

Struma

Belgrade

SERBIA

KOSOVO

MACEDONIA

Salonika

Athens

GREECE

MONTENEGRO

ALBANIA

BOSNIA-HERZEGOVINA

Sarajevo

ADRIATIC SEA

ITALY

Frontline November 1916
Frontline October 1918

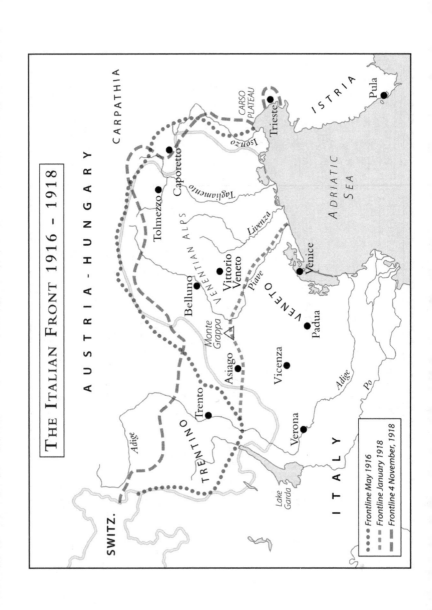

The Italian Front 1916 – 1918

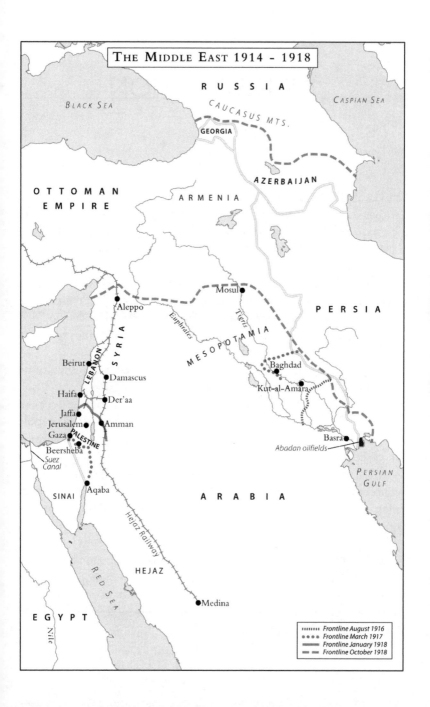

THE MIDDLE EAST 1914 - 1918

BLACK SEA

CASPIAN SEA

R U S S I A

CAUCASUS MTS.

GEORGIA

O T T O M A N
E M P I R E

ARMENIA

AZERBAIJAN

P E R S I A

Mosul

Aleppo

Euphrates

Tigris

M E S O P O T A M I A

Beirut

S Y R I A

Baghdad

L E B A N O N

Damascus

Kut-al-Amara

Haifa

Der'aa

Jaffa

Amman

Jerusalem

P A L E S T I N E

Gaza

Basra

Beersheba

Abadan oilfields

Suez
Canal

P E R S I A N
G U L F

Aqaba

A R A B I A

SINAI

Hejaz Railway

R E D   S E A

E G Y P T

HEJAZ

Nile

Medina

.... Frontline August 1916
●●●● Frontline March 1917
▬▬▬ Frontline January 1918
▬ ▬ ▬ Frontline October 1918

INTRODUCTION

The Great War is, for many, defined by the horror of the stalemate in the trenches dug in the mud of Flanders, but the fighting spread much wider than that. British troops were heavily involved not just in Flanders but also in the ill-fated Gallipoli expedition targeted against the Ottoman Empire, as well as in Mesopotamia and Salonica. The Royal Navy experienced action in the North Sea and in the South Atlantic while also countering the worldwide threat from German U-boats. The countries of the British Empire gave their support, with troops from Australia, Canada, New Zealand and South Africa joining Britain in the fighting, while Indian troops fought in both Flanders and the Middle East.

Germany and Russia became embroiled in a fierce and costly war on Germany's Eastern Front, which would lead to the overthrow of the tsar, while on the southern border of the Central Powers, Austria fought a bitter battle with Serbia before later becoming locked in a protracted struggle with Italy. Even Africa became involved, as a 'proxy' war was fought by the African colonies of the Great Powers.

In 1917 the United States of America joined the conflict, abandoning its neutral stance and declaring war against Germany and, through the size of its forces and its immense industrial capacity, tipping the balance inexorably against a German victory.

The Great War was indeed global. This book, however, aims to highlight the works of the war poets and, in particular, the contribution both to the war and to its poetry made by the Scots. Therefore, it primarily considers the war in Europe – the source of the majority of the war poems – although the conflicts in other parts of the world in what we now call the First World War have not been forgotten.

THE WAR POETS

The First World War is uniquely defined by the number of poets who recorded their thoughts and experiences, providing a moving record of the horrors experienced by the troops in the mud-filled, rat-infested trenches. No war before or since has been so extensively chronicled nor its misery so exposed. There was, of course, no nightly television report to chart the suffering or indeed to record the courage of those who fought, although some poignant cinematic films were taken and, suitably edited, shown in cinemas at home.

The picture portrayed by the war poets is of the folly of war and of the braveness of soldiers asked again and again to 'go over the top' on the orders of unimaginative staff officers who were safely situated in their comfortable billets well behind the lines.

When reading the poems it should always be remembered that poets such as Robert Graves, Wilfred Owen and Siegfried Sassoon were just that – poets. Wilfred Owen wrote shortly before his death, tragically on 4 November 1918 just one week before the Armistice, 'My Subject is War, and the Pity of War', words which would later be inscribed on the monument to the war poets in Westminster Abbey. They did not report on the war nor, indeed, examine its justification – they did, however, portray its pity.

But it was not like this at first. The early poems showed an optimistic patriotism only later replaced by cynicism and despair. This mood was a reflection of that in the country. The chance to enlist was seen as an opportunity for excitement and adventure for many young men, who otherwise faced the prospect of a life of hard work and low pay.

The truth would be somewhat different.

WHO WERE THE WAR POETS?

A number of writers and poets, including John Masefield, Thomas Hardy, Robert Bridges and Rudyard Kipling, were recruited by Sir Edward Grey (Foreign Secretary) and David Lloyd George (Chancellor) shortly after the outbreak of the war to form a Propaganda Bureau, with offices at Lancaster Gate in London. These poets wrote about the war and so, technically, could be considered 'war poets'. For the purposes of this book, however, the generic definition of the term 'war poets' is by and large restricted to those who experienced active service during the war, either as infantry in the trenches or in other branches of the services.

Within this definition, the typical war poet was an officer – middle class, public-school educated and English – and they wrote initially of an England of the leisured class, of tea on manicured lawns and English lanes.

Rupert Brooke

Rupert Brooke, described memorably by Yeats as 'the handsomest young man in England', wrote most of his poems before the war, perhaps achieving fame more through his good looks and his ambivalent sexuality than through the sometimes trite and pretentious sentiments expressed. Brooke only participated briefly in active service in the unsuccessful defence of Antwerp when Churchill, in a typically idiosyncratic gesture, had despatched 8,000 untrained men from the Royal Naval Division to defend the city from the advancing German troops.

Brooke, therefore, has only a tenuous claim to be considered a war poet, although he was amongst the First World War poets to be commemorated in Poet's Corner in Westminster Abbey. Of the sixteen poets thus honoured, just one, Charles Hamilton Sorley, was a Scot. Six of the sixteen died in the war.[*]

In the first of his five war sonnets, *Peace*, Brooke glorifies war and possible death paradoxically as an opportunity to taste life to the full:

---

[*] The sixteen were: Richard Aldington, Laurence Binyon, Edmund Blunden, Rupert Brooke, Wilfrid Gibson, Robert Graves, Julian Grenfell, Ivor Gurney, David Jones, Robert Nicholls, Wilfred Owen, Herbert Read, Isaac Rosenberg, Siegfried Sassoon, Charles Sorley and Edward Thomas.

Peace

Now, God be thanked Who has matched us with His hour,
 And caught our youth and wakened us from sleeping,
With hand made sure, clear eye, and sharpened power,
 To turn, as swimmers into cleanness leaping,
Glad from a world grown old and cold and weary,
 Leave the sick hearts that honour could not move,
And half-men, and their dirty songs and dreary,
 And all the little emptiness of love!

Oh! We, who have known shame, we have found release there,
 Where there's no ill, no grief, but sleep has mending,
  Naught broken save this body, lost but breath;
Nothing to shake the laughing heart's long peace there
 But only agony, and that has ending;
  And the worst friend and enemy is but Death.

(August 1914)

In poems such as *The Old Vicarage, Grantchester* (written while he was in Berlin and evidently full of nostalgia for Cambridge life), with its oft parodied final couplet – 'Stands the Church clock at ten to three? And is there honey still for tea?' – Brooke portrayed a picture of an England which existed before the outbreak of war, but only for a favoured minority. It was a way of life which would have been unrecognisable to the Scots who would later enlist in vast numbers to fight for their country and an equally alien world to those English recruits who served in the ranks, if not to their officers.

For these men life would be very different from Brooke's idyll. Men who worked on the farms or in the industrial factories and the many women in domestic service endured a life of hard, manual labour, working long hours for low pay, with little prospect of escape.

There were, however, already signs of burgeoning unrest. Britain had one of the most restrictive democratic franchises of all the European countries and issues such as the extension of the vote to all adult males, the rise of trade unionism, the increasing militancy of the suffragettes and the Irish Home Rule Movement were threatening the established order. The war would bring about profound social changes, particularly in the role and status of women.

Brooke's sonnets elegantly expressed the concept of self-sacrifice and the seemingly noble act of patriotism in dying for one's country but not, ironically, in living for it. He captured the initial mood of the country and his fulsome patriotism was a gift to the government propaganda machine.

In February 1915 Brooke sailed with the British Mediterranean Expeditionary Force to take part in the Gallipoli landings. He was delighted at the prospect of fighting near the site of ancient Troy but, somewhat anti-climactically, he was bitten by a mosquito during the voyage, developed sepsis and died on 23 April 1915. He was buried on the Greek island of Skyros.

The imminence of action and the prospect of possible death had changed his view of war, reflected in a poem he had begun in April 1915 while on board a ship to Gallipoli in which he shows an appreciation that death is not the glorious achievement of self-sacrifice but a tragic waste of human life:

I Strayed About the Deck

I strayed about the deck, an hour, tonight
Under a cloudy moonless sky; and peeped
In at the windows, watched my friends at table,
Or playing cards, or standing in the doorway,
Or coming out of the darkness. Still
No-one could see me.

                       I would have thought of them –
Heedless, within a week of battle – in pity,
Pride in their strength and in the weight and firmness
And link'd beauty of bodies, and pity that
This gay machine of splendour 'ld soon be broken,
Thought little of, pashed, scattered …

                       Only always
I could but see them – against the lamplight – pass
Like coloured shadows, thinner than filmy glass,
Slight bubbles, fainter than the wave's faint light,
That broke to phosphorous out in the night,
Perishing things and strange ghosts – soon to die
To other ghosts – this one, or that, or I.

The war poets such as Sassoon, Graves and Owen personally experienced the horror of war and, therefore, were able to graphically portray its misery and futility in their writing. Less well known are the Scottish war poets such as Ewart Alan Mackintosh, W.D. Cocker, Roderick Watson Kerr, Joseph Lee, J.B. Salmond, Charles Hamilton Sorley and others who give a Scottish perspective on the war. Of these, arguably the greatest was Sorley, although he was killed too early in the war to leave more than a tantalising glimpse of a poet who could have rivalled Wilfred Owen. Alongside him, as an outstanding but often unrecognised war poet, stands Ewart Alan Mackintosh, whose works encompassed both the tragedy and the 'trench humour' of war.

Ewart Alan Mackintosh

Ewart Alan Mackintosh was born on 14 March 1893 to Scottish parents. He was brought up near the South Downs but often visited Scotland with his father, developing a great love for his homeland. He read Classics at Oxford University and during the holidays would fish the waters and walk the hills of Scotland with his friends. In his poem *Mallaig Bay*, written in 1912, he contrasts unfavourably the soft contours of the Downs with the ruggedness of Skye:

Mallaig Bay

I am sickened by the south and the kingdom of the downs,
    And the weald that is a garden all the day.
And I'm weary for the islands and the Scuir that always frowns,
    And the sun rising over Mallaig Bay.

I am sickened of the pleasant down and pleasant weald below,
    And the meadows where the little breezes play,
And I'm weary for the rain-cloud over stormy Coolin's brow,
    And the wind blowing into Mallaig Bay.

I am sickened of the people that have ease in what they earn,
    The happy folk who have forgot to pray,
And I'm weary for the faces that are sorrowful and stern,
    And the boats coming into Mallaig Bay.

Mackintosh wrote poetry before the war but, as with Owen, his later poetry gained an edge, tempered by his experience in the trenches. Also like Owen, he believed, tragically correctly, that he would die young, writing his disturbing poem *In the Night* in 1912 while at Oxford:

In the Night

Gallant fellows, tall and strong,
Oh, your strength was not for long,
Now within its bed alone
Quiet lies your nerveless bone.

Merry maidens, young and fair,
Now your heads are bleached and bare,
Grinning mouths that smiled so sweet,
Buried deep the dancing feet.

Men and maidens fair and brave
Resting in your darkened grave,
Have you left the light behind,
Will you never feel the wind?

Oh I know not if you may,
But from eve till dawn of day
Terror holds me in my bed,
Terror of the living dead.

Mackintosh volunteered as soon as war broke out, but was initially rejected because of poor eyesight. He applied again and on 31 December 1914 was commissioned as a second lieutenant serving with the 5th Battalion of the Seaforth Highlanders. In July 1915 he was posted to France where the 5th Seaforth formed part of the 51st Highland Division.

Mackintosh had his first experience of the front line in August 1915 when he was inspired to write nostalgically of his time at Oxford:

Oxford from the Trenches

The clouds are in the sky, and a light rain falling,
And throughout the sodden trench splashed figures come and go,
But deep in my heart are the old years calling,
And memory is on me of the things I used to know.

Memory is on me of warm lit chambers,
And the laughter of my friends in the huge high-ceilinged hall,
Lectures and the voices of the dons deep-droning,
The things that were so common once – O God, I feel them all.

Here are the great things, life and death and danger,
All I ever dreamed of in the days that used to be,
Comrades and good-fellowship, the soul of an army,
But, oh, it is the little things that take the heart of me.

For all we knew of old, for little things and lovely,
We bow us to a greater life beyond our hope or fear,
To bear its heavy burdens, endure its toils unheeding,
Because of all the little things so distant and so dear.

(Bécourt, 1915)

Mackintosh was appointed battalion bombing officer shortly after his arrival at the front line. He was responsible for leading raids at night into no man's land to lob a few bombs into the German trenches, or into the listening posts where two or three Germans would be lying in a hole outside the barbed wire attempting to locate British patrols. He wrote of bombing in a pastiche of the Gilbert and Sullivan song, 'A Policeman's Lot is Not a Happy One':

A Bomber's Life

When our enterprising bombers are not bombing,
    And our rifles are not throwing their grenades,
We get tidings that the Gilded Staff are coming,
    And we get the men to work with picks and spades.

When our bombing posts at night-time we're alarming
    For surprises by the ever-ready Hun,
And it's raining and the weather isn't charming,
    Oh, a bomber's life is not a happy one.

Chorus:-
When he's scheming out surprises for the Hun,
Oh, a bomber's life is not a happy one.

First our bombing post in trenches we are placing
    Where the enterprising German might creep in,
Then back homeward for a memo we are chasing
    On a hand grenade deficient of a pin.
When our parties we are personally taking
    Through a salient that's like a rabbit-run,
And our knees with fear of oil-cans both are quaking,
    Oh, a bomber's life is not a happy one.

Chorus:-
When he's scheming out surprises for the Hun,
Oh, a bomber's life is not a happy one.

When we contemplate a little mild aggression,
    Other officers all gather round and say
In tones of unmistakable depression,
    That they'd much prefer it if we'd go away.
When at last, by dint of infinite intriguing,
    They allow a little bombing to be done,
And we find that all our men are off fatiguing,
    Oh, a bomber's life is not a happy one.

Chorus:-
When he's scheming out surprises for the Hun,
Oh, a bomber's life is not a happy one.

Mackintosh's first collection of poems, *A Highland Regiment*, which he dedicated to the officers and men of the 5th Seaforth Highlanders, was published in 1917. *Ghosts of War* was written shortly before he was killed in action on the second day of the Battle of Cambrai in November 1917. In his poem *Anns an Gleann'san Robh Mi Og*, written at the outbreak of war, Mackintosh foretells his own future, as he writes of a soldier on the point of death recalling the boyhood he has left behind:

Anns an Gleann'san Robh Mi Og

In the glen where I was young
Blue-bell stems stood close together,
In the evenings dew-drops hung
Clear as glass above the heather.
I'd be sitting on a stone,
Legs above the water swung,
I a laddie all alone,
In the glen where I was young.

Well, the glen is empty now,
And far I am from them that love me,
Water to my knees below,
Shrapnel in the clouds above me;
Watching till I sometimes see,
Instead of death and fighting men,
The people that were kind to me,
And summer in the little glen.

Hold me close until I die,
Lift me up, it's better so;
If, before I go, I cry,
It isn't I'm afraid to go;
Only sorry for the boy
Sitting there with legs aswung
In my little glen of joy,
In the glen where I was young.

(August 1914)

Charles Hamilton Sorley

Charles Hamilton Sorley was possibly the greatest Scottish war poet but was killed at the age of 20 before he had fulfilled his potential. A collection of his work was published posthumously in 1916.

Sorley was born in Aberdeen in 1895, but when he was 5 years old his father was appointed Professor of Moral Sciences at the University of Cambridge and the family moved south to England. Unsurprisingly, Sorley was not enchanted by the flat Cambridgeshire countryside which contrasted poorly with Aberdeenshire.

He was educated in England at Marlborough College and was an avid student, reading the works of English writers such as Thomas Hardy and John Masefield and also the Greek Classics such as Homer's *Odyssey*, which he read in the original Greek. He felt an affinity with the Wiltshire Downs, appreciating the prominent role they had played in the history of ancient man, as shown in his poem *Stones*:

Stones

This field is almost white with stones
    That cumber all its thirsty crust.
And underneath, I know, are bones,
    And all around is death and dust.

And if you love a livelier hue –
    O, if you love the youth of year,
When all is clean and green and new,
    Depart. There is no summer here.

Albeit, to me there lingers yet
    In this forbidding stony dress
The impotent and dim regret
    For some forgotten restlessness.

Dumb, imperceptibly astir,
    These relics of an ancient race,
These men, in whom the dead bones were
    Still fortifying their resting-place.

Their field of life was white with stones;
    Good fruit to earth they never brought.
O, in these bleached and buried bones
    Was neither love nor faith nor thought.

But like the wind in this bleak place,
    Bitter and bleak and sharp they grew,
And bitterly they ran their race,
    A brutal, bad, unkindly crew:

Souls like the dry earth, hearts like stone,
    Brains like that barren bramble-tree:
Stern, sterile, senseless, mute, unknown –
    But bold, O, bolder far than we!

(14 July 1913)

Sorley was expected by his parents to join the Indian Civil Service, but he developed a social conscience and in January 1913 wrote to them saying that he had decided 'to become an instructor at a Working Man's College or something of that sort' (letter to Professor and Mrs Sorley, quoted in Hilda Spear (ed.), *The Poems & Selected Letters of Charles Hamilton Sorley*, p.84).

In December 1913 he won a scholarship to Oxford University, but as he was not due to take up his place until the following October he decided to leave school early and go to Germany to improve his German. When war came he was studying at the University of Jena, where he was arrested and briefly imprisoned before returning to Britain and enlisting. He applied for a commission in the Territorials, writing, 'Compromise as usual. Not heroic enough to do the really straight thing and join the regulars as a Tommy' (letter to A.E. Hutchison, a school friend, quoted in Spear, *Poems & Selected Letters*, p.91).

His Scottish birth had, from the outset, given him an independent view of the war, and his time in Germany had given him an empathy with the Germans. In his poem *To Germany*, Sorley emphasised the irony that the German on the 'Berlin tram' no more wanted war than his British counterpart on the 'Clapham omnibus':

To Germany

You are blind like us. Your hurt no man designed,
And no man claimed the conquest of your land.
But gropers both through fields of thought confined
We stumble and we do not understand.
You only saw your future bigly planned,
And we, the tapering paths of our own mind.
And in each other's dearest ways we stand,
And hiss and hate. And the blind fight the blind.

When it is peace, then we may view again
With new-won eyes each other's truer form
And wonder. Grown more loving-kind and warm
We'll grasp firm hands and laugh at the old pain,
When it is peace. But until peace, the storm
The darkness and the thunder and the rain.

In August 1914 Sorley was commissioned as a second lieutenant in the Suffolk Regiment. He stayed in England until May 1915, enervated by the monotony of army life, but was then posted to France and in August was promoted to captain. As a result of this promotion his leave was postponed and he was instead posted to the front line. The delay would cost him his life; he was killed by a sniper at the Battle of Loos on 13 October 1915.

His premature death came just as he was reaching maturity as a war poet. As a result, he has left as his legacy only a small collection of war poems. He was described by Robert Graves as 'one of the three poets of importance killed during the war'[*] (Spear, *Poems & Selected Letters*, Preface, p.9).

Siegfried Sassoon

Siegfried Sassoon was born on 8 September 1886. He was the second of three sons of Alfred Sassoon, a member of a wealthy Jewish family, and of Theresa, an Anglo-Catholic member of the Thornycroft family of sculptors. There was no German background – he was named Siegfried because of his mother's passion for the operas of Wagner. However, because of his

---

[*] The others were Isaac Rosenberg and Wilfred Owen.

Germanic name and the prejudice it aroused he would later write under the name George Sherston.

Sassoon had a troubled childhood; his parents separated when he was 4 years old and he was sent away to preparatory school, then Marlborough College, before completing his education at Clare College, Cambridge, where he did not graduate. He was sexually confused and it may have been the combination of suppressed homosexuality and his perceived rejection by his parents which drove Sassoon to continually seek to prove himself, firstly in the hunt and later on the battlefield. As he wrote, he 'had serious aspirations to heroism' (Siegfried Sassoon, *Memoirs of a Fox-Hunting Man*, p.244).

Sassoon did not pursue a career. His father had bequeathed him a small income – enough, but barely enough, for Sassoon to fund his chosen life, which he divided between winters spent fox hunting and summers as a no-more-than-average batsman in the cricket team of the village where he lived with his aunt, a life which he colourfully portrayed in his book *Memoirs of a Fox-Hunting Man*.

With the outbreak of war, Sassoon was caught up in the wave of patriotism and enlisted in the army a few days before war was declared, but was then injured in a riding accident. He was commissioned as a second lieutenant in the Royal Welch Fusiliers on 29 May 1915.

Initially, his war poems reflected the general feeling of patriotism, the belief that it was a just war, that it was a duty – even heroic – to join the fight against aggression. His poem *Absolution* expresses these ideals:

Absolution

The anguish of the earth absolves our eyes
Till beauty shines in all that we can see.
War is our scourge; yet war has made us wise,
And, fighting for our freedom, we are free.

Horror of wounds and anger at the foe,
And loss of things desired; all these must pass.
We are the happy legion, for we know
Time's but a golden wind that shakes the grass.

There was an hour when we were loth to part
From life we longed to share no less than others.

Now, having claimed this heritage of heart,
What need we more, my comrades and my brothers?

(Written April–September 1915)

Sassoon was exceptionally (perhaps perversely) brave, even foolhardy, and was determined to prove his courage, often going out alone on patrol in no man's land. In *Memoirs of an Infantry Officer* (p.18), he wrote:

> Six years before I had been ambitious of winning [horse] races because that had seemed a significant way of demonstrating my equality with my contemporaries. And now I wanted to make the World War serve a similar purpose, for if only I could get a Military Cross I should feel comparatively safe and confident.

Sassoon records that before one attack he was instructed to improve gaps which had been cut in the British barbed wire to enable the troops to pass through in the intended attack. It must be done that night. One problem was that the standard-issue British Army wire cutters were moderately ineffective when used to cut a path through British wire, but totally ineffective against the more substantial German barbed-wire defences. Sassoon had his own wire cutters, recording how while on leave he 'had invaded the Army and Navy Stores and procured a superb salmon, two bottles of old brandy, an automatic pistol and two pairs of wire cutters with rubber-covered handles' (*Memoirs of an Infantry Officer*, p.38). He writes:

> When we did get started I soon discovered that cutting tangles of barbed wire in the dark in a desperate hurry is a job that needs ingenuity, even when your wire-cutters have rubber-covered handles and are fresh from Army and Navy Stores. More than once we were driven in by shells which landed in front of our trench (some of them were our own dropping short); two men were wounded and some of the others were reluctant to resume work. In the first greying of dawn only three of us were still at it. Kendle (a nineteen year old lance-corporal from my platoon) and Worgan (one of the tough characters of our company) were slicing away for all they were worth; but as the light increased I began to realize the unimpressive effect of the snippings and snatchings which had made such a mess of our rubber gloves. We had been working three and a half hours but the hedge hadn't suffered much

damage, it seemed. Kendle disappeared into the trench and sauntered back to me, puffing a surreptitious Woodbine. I was making a last onslaught on a clawing thicket which couldn't have been more hostile if it had been put there by the Germans. 'We can't do any more in this daylight,' said Kendle.

But Sassoon was unconvinced. He continued:

I had made up my mind to have another cut at the wire, which I now regarded with personal enmity, enjoying at the same time a self-admiring belief that much depended on my efforts. Worgan stayed behind with me. Kendle was unwilling to be left out of the adventure, but two of us would be less conspicuous than three, and my feeling for Kendle was somewhat protective. It was queer to be in an empty front-line trench on a fine morning, with everything quite peaceful after a violent early bombardment. Queerer still to be creeping about in the long grass (which might well have been longer, I thought) and shearing savagely at the tangles which had bewildered us in the dark but which were now at our mercy. As Worgan said, we were giving it a proper hair-cut this journey.

He concluded that eventually prudence prevailed and he was ordered back into the trenches:

Soon afterwards we dropped into the trenches and the Manchesters began to arrive (for the intended attack). It had been great fun, I said, flourishing my wire-cutters.   (*Memoirs of an Infantry Officer*, pp.49-52)

His diaries record that he was inspired by the desire to avenge the death of his brother, wounded at Gallipoli, and of brother officers killed in action, to commit almost suicidal acts of courage such that he became known as 'Mad Jack' by his men. In *Sherston's Progress* (p.791), he reflected:

It was the old story; I could only keep going by doing something spectacular. So there was more bravado than bravery about it, and I should admire that vanished self of mine more if he had avoided taking needless risks. I blame him for doing his utmost to prevent my being here to write about him. But on the other hand I am grateful to him for giving me something to write about.

On 27 July 1916 he was awarded the Military Cross. The citation read:

For conspicuous gallantry during a raid on the enemy's trenches. He remained for 1½ hours under rifle and bomb fire collecting and bringing in the wounded. Owing to his courage and determination all the killed and wounded were brought in.

Sassoon later had doubts as to the morality of the war and would become famous as the war poet who, wracked by self-doubt, made a political statement of his concerns.

He survived the war and became literary editor of the *Daily Herald*. In his published books he wrote only of his wartime experiences, as if with the coming of peace his life had ended. After the war he had a number of homosexual affairs before he eventually married and fathered a son. He finally resolved his religious searching by becoming a Catholic.

Robert Graves

Robert Graves was born in 1895 in Wimbledon. His full name was Robert von Ranke Graves, the von Ranke coming from his mother Amalie von Ranke who was the eldest daughter of a German Professor of Medicine at the University of Munich and had come to England at the age of 18 to act as companion to an appropriately named Miss Britain. When she died she left her estate to Amalie who, despite sharing it with her four siblings, retained enough to become an heiress. Amalie had been determined to go to India as a missionary but, on the principle that charity begins at home, married Graves' father, who was a widower with five children. Despite Amalie's principal task being to help with the existing children, she rather improvidently added to her responsibilities by having five children of her own – two girls, then Robert when she was 40, followed by two more boys (Robert Graves, *Goodbye to All That*, p.17).

Graves was educated at a number of prestigious preparatory schools before winning a scholarship to Charterhouse, where he was bullied because of his German name and his unfashionable taste for scholarship, which was abhorrent to the public-school ethos. In reaction to this, he took up boxing and became school welterweight champion. One of the masters at Charterhouse was George Mallory (later to die in an attempt to climb Everest), who introduced Graves to mountain climbing on Snowdon. While at Charterhouse, Graves, more in tune with the public-school ethos, formed a close attachment with a younger boy, Dick, and they corresponded regularly during the early years of the war.

Graves enlisted in the Royal Welch Fusiliers at the outbreak of war. His first collection of poems was published in 1916, written with the realism gained through his experience of war. In *Through the Periscope*, Graves wrote fatalistically of life in the trenches:

Through the Periscope

Trench stinks of shallow buried dead
    Where Tom stands at the periscope,
Tired out. After nine months he's shed
    All fear, all faith, all hate, all hope.

Sees with uninterested eye
    Beyond the barbed wire, a gay bed
Of scarlet poppies and the lie
    Of German trench behind that red –

Six poplar trees ... a rick ... a pond
    Ruined hamlet and a mine ...
More trees, more houses and beyond
    La Bassée spire in golden sunshine.

The same thoughts always haunt his brain,
    Two sad, one scarcely comforting,
First second third and then again
    The first and second silly thing.

The first 'It's now nine months and more
    That I've drunk British beer,' the second
'The last few years of this mad war
    Will be the cushiest, I've reckoned,'

The third 'The silly business is
    I'll only die in the next war,
Suppose by luck I get through this
    Just 'cause I wasn't killed before.'

Quietly he laughs, and at that token
    The first thought should come round again
But crack!
    The weary circle's broken
And a bullet tears through the tired brain.

Graves was seriously injured in the Battle of the Somme by a shell fragment which passed through his lung. He was thought to be dead and a letter was sent to his mother saying he had been wounded and had died of his injuries. However, he survived and was invalided back to Britain. A correction to the earlier and, as it proved, premature announcement of his death was printed in *The Times* very properly 'without charge'.

He returned to France in November but shortly afterwards was diagnosed with bronchitis and was once again invalided home. He recovered physically but had been damaged psychologically and did not return to active service in France. He wrote:

> I thought of going back to France but realised the absurdity of the notion. Since 1916, the fear of gas obsessed me; any unusual smell, even a sudden strong smell of flowers in a garden, was enough to send me trembling. And I couldn't face the sound of heavy shelling now; the noise of a car backfiring was enough to send me flat on my face, or running for cover.   (*Goodbye to All That*, pp.219-20)

After the war and a failed first marriage Graves settled in Majorca where he wrote his autobiography *Goodbye to All That*, in which he gives an evocative account of his experiences in the First World War, the immensely successful *I, Claudius* and its sequel *Claudius the God*, classically portrayed on television, and many other books and poems. He died in 1985.

Wilfred Owen

Wilfred Owen came from a less favoured background than some of his fellow war poets. He was born in 1893, the son of a stationmaster, and his first two years were spent in relative comfort in his grandfather's house in Oswestry; however, on his grandfather's death Owen's parents were forced to move to relatively mean lodgings in Birkenhead. Fortunes for the family gradually improved over the years and in 1907, when his father Tom Owen was appointed assistant superintendent of the Joint Railways, the family moved to Shrewsbury. His life was still far removed from the privileged upbringing of Sassoon and Graves, and although Owen passed the examination for entry to the University of London he did not take up his place as the family could not afford to support him through university.

Owen was very close, perhaps obsessively close, to his mother. He wrote poetry from an early age and, inspired by John Keats, believed that he too would die young. In this, he would be proved right, as he was killed in action at the age of 25, the same age as Keats when he died in Rome from tuberculosis.

Owen was living in France at the foot of the Pyrenees when war broke out, working as an English tutor. He was 21 years old. Perhaps because of the distance, he was initially unaffected by the war, writing, 'I can do no service to anybody by agitating for news or making dole over the slaughter ... I feel my own life all the more precious and more dear in the presence of this deflowering of Europe' (Jon Stallworthy, *Wilfred Owen*, p.109).

A visit to England in May 1915, however, brought him face to face with the moral pressure to volunteer, and after returning briefly to France he eventually enlisted on 21 October 1915 in the Artists' Rifles. In June 1916 he was commissioned as a second lieutenant in the 5th Battalion of the Manchester Regiment.

His initiation to life in the trenches was swift and brutal. Just twelve days after arriving in France he wrote a letter to his mother describing his experience when he had led his platoon not to the front but beyond to hold an advanced post – effectively a dugout in the middle of no man's land:

We had a march of 3 miles over shelled road then nearly 3 along a flooded trench. After that we came to where the trenches had been blown flat out and had to go over the top. It was of course dark, too dark, and the ground was not mud, not sloppy mud, but an octopus of sucking clay, 3, 4, and 5 feet deep, relieved only by craters full of water. Men have been known to drown in them. Many stuck in the mud & only got on by leaving their waders, equipment, and in some cases their clothes.

High explosives were dropping all around, and machine guns spluttered every few minutes. But it was so dark that even the German flares did not reveal us.

Three quarters dead ... we reached the dug-out and relieved the wretches therein ...

My dug-out held 25 men tight packed. Water filled it to a depth of 1 or 2 feet, leaving say 4 feet of air.

One entrance had been blown in & blocked.

So far, the other remained.

The Germans knew we were staying there and decided we shouldn't.

Those fifty hours were the agony of my happy life.

Every ten minutes on Sunday afternoon seemed an hour.

I nearly broke down and let myself drown in the water that was now slowly rising over my knees.

Towards 6 o'clock, when I suppose you would be going to church, the shelling grew less intense and less accurate: so that I was mercifully helped to do my duty and crawl, wade, climb and flounder over No Man's Land to visit my other post. It took me half an hour to move about 150 yards ...

In the Platoon on my left the sentries over the dug-out were blown to nothing ... I kept my own sentries half way down the stairs during the most terrific bombardment. In spite of this, one lad was blown down and, I am afraid, blinded.   (16 January 1917, quoted in Stallworthy, *Wilfred Owen*, pp.156-7)

Owen was injured a number of times – concussed after falling into a shell hole, blown up by a trench mortar – and spent several days sheltering from enemy fire alongside the dead remains of a fellow officer. Perhaps not surprisingly, he suffered from shell shock and was sent to Craiglockhart Hospital where he met Siegfried Sassoon, whose criticism brought the hardened edge to his poetry that now ranks amongst the finest written by the war poets. Owen used his early experience in his poem *The Sentry*, written at Craiglockhart:

The Sentry

We'd found an old Boche dug-out, and he knew,
And gave us hell; for shell on frantic shell
Lit full on top, but ever quite burst through.
Rain, guttering down in waterfalls of slime,
Kept slush waist-high and rising hour by hour,
And choked the steps too thick with clay to climb.
What murk of air remained stank old, and sour
With fumes from whizz-bangs, and the smell of men,
Who'd lived there years, and left their curse in the den,
If not their corpses ...

There we herded from the blast
Of whizz-bangs; but one found our door at last,
Buffeting eyes and breath, snuffing the candles,
And thud! flump! thud! down the steep steps came thumping
And sploshing in the flood, deluging muck,
The sentry's body; then his rifle, handles
Of old Boche bombs, and mud in ruck on ruck.
We dredged it up, for dead, until he whined,
'O sir my eyes, – I'm blind, – I'm blind, – I'm blind.'
Coaxing I held a flame against his lids
And said if he could see the least blurred light
He was not blind; in time they'd get all right.
'I can't,' he sobbed. Eyeballs, huge-bulged like squids',
Watch my dreams still, – but I forgot him there
In posting Next for duty, and sending a scout
To beg a stretcher somewhere, and flound'ring about
To other posts under the shrieking air.

Those other wretches, how they bled and spewed,
And one who would have drowned himself for good –
I try not to remember these things now.
Let Dread hark back for one word only: how,
Half-listening to that sentry's moans and jumps,
And the wild chattering of his shivered teeth,
Renewed most horribly whenever crumps
Pummelled the roof and slogged the air beneath –
Through the dense din, I say, we heard him shout
'I see your lights!' – But ours had long gone out.

On a lighter note, he wrote amusingly, but bitterly, of being an officer in his poem *Inspection*, clearly influenced by Sassoon:

Inspection

'You! What d'you mean by this?' I rapped.
'You dare to come on parade like this?'
'Please, Sir, it's –.' ''Old yer mouth,' the sergeant snapped.
'I takes 'is name, sir?' – 'Please, and then dismiss.'

Some days 'confined to camp' he got,
For being 'dirty on parade'.
He told me, afterwards, the damned spot
Was blood, his own. 'Well, blood is dirt,' I said.

'Blood's dirt,' he laughed, looking away,
Far off to where his wound had bled
And almost merged for ever into clay.
'The world is washing out its stains,' he said.
'It doesn't like our cheeks so red:
Young blood's its great objection.
But when we're duly white-washed, being dead,
The race will bear Field Marshal God's inspection.'

(Written while a patient in Craiglockhart Hospital, August/September 1917)

Owen returned to France and was awarded the Military Cross in October 1918. He was killed in action on 4 November 1918 in the crossing of the Sambre-Oise Canal, just one week before the end of the war. In an ultimate irony, his mother was listening to the church bells ringing to celebrate the Armistice when she received the telegram informing her of her son's death.

1   SETTING THE SCENE

We still have no consensus on how the First World War happened and I suspect that we never will. The possible factors are so many and the questions of how to give each one weight so intractable.

Margaret MacMillan, *Times Literary Supplement*, 22 January 2016.

THE THREE COUSINS

At the outbreak of the war five of the six principal protagonists were still monarchies, a relic of Europe's past in a modernising world. The exception was France, which was a republic. Of the monarchs, three – King George V, Kaiser Wilhelm II and Tsar Nicholas II – were closely related; the first two were grandsons of Queen Victoria and the third, Tsar Nicholas, had married one of Victoria's granddaughters, Princess Alix, who took the name Alexandra on her marriage and, fatally, carried the haemophilia gene. This relationship was more than coincidence. Queen Victoria was called, with some justification, the 'grandmother of Europe', as her consort, Prince Albert, had deliberately set out to ensure peace in Europe through intermarriage of the royal families in the mistaken belief that families don't quarrel.

King George V was the second son of the Prince of Wales, later King Edward VII. He had therefore not been expected to accede to the throne and had entered service in the Royal Navy. With the unexpected death of his brother from pneumonia in 1892 he moved up in the succession stakes, also acquiring his brother's bride-to-be. On the death of his father in 1910 he was crowned king accompanied by his wife, the formidable Queen Mary. He was a severe man with a strong sense of duty who ruled as a constitutional monarch, recognising that the power of decision-making rested with the government, democratically elected, albeit on a restricted franchise. He kept closely in touch with world events and was in regular contact with Foreign Secretary Sir Edward Grey.

Tsar Nicholas II was a shy and autocratic ruler who was closely involved in government and foreign affairs, which he often conducted in opposition to the policies of his government, for whom he had scant respect. Inevitably, this dichotomy often sent a confused and contradictory message to the outside world. Under his direction, Russia had been badly defeated by Japan in the Russo-Japanese War, with the destruction of two of Russia's three naval fleets – first the Pacific Fleet and then the Baltic Fleet, which had made its way around the Cape of Good Hope (the British had forbidden passage through the Suez Canal) only to be destroyed by the Japanese Fleet which had been lying in wait. This defeat caused a considerable loss to the authority of the tsar, and his desire to recapture lost military prestige would influence his decisions in the weeks and months leading up to the war.

Kaiser Wilhelm II was the son of Prince Frederick of Prussia and Princess Victoria, and was Queen Victoria's first grandchild. Interestingly, his mother, Princess Victoria, was Queen Victoria's first-born and had she not been overtaken in the succession stakes by Edward, who came through on the rails as the eldest son, Wilhelm would have inherited the British crown.

Wilhelm had suffered a traumatic breech birth which left him with a withered arm, carefully disguised in early portraits. His mother believed that as heir to the throne he should acquire the appropriate martial abilities and, despite his infirmity and the pain it caused, insisted on his having riding lessons. His physical handicap and his harsh upbringing left him with an inferiority complex, only satisfied in later years by the presence of obsequious courtiers who fanned his vanity. The Kaiser believed, somewhat presumptuously, that he embodied the spirit of his country, writing in a letter to the future King Edward VII, 'I am the sole master of German policy and my country must follow me wherever I go' (letter to the Prince of Wales, quoted in Christopher Clark, *The Sleepwalkers*, p.178). He was a wilful, tactless, bombastic, vacillating and impulsive man who would communicate directly with other heads of state without consultation with his ministers and would threaten military action in a multitude of diverse situations, only to back down in panic if his bluff was called.

These were the three royal cousins. They met occasionally at state funerals and on formal visits but without shared warmth. It has been argued that the First World War was an unnecessary war, driven by the inability of the three cousins, Kaiser Wilhelm II, Tsar Nicholas II and King George V, to resolve their differences or even to meaningfully communicate, although there would be a desperate exchange of telegrams in the last few hectic days of peace. There is merit in this argument, but it overstates their respective powers materially to influence events and ignores the growing appetite for war amongst the principal participants, especially Russia, France, Germany and Austria-Hungary.

GROWING TENSION

From Britain's point of view the increasing economic power of Germany and its militaristic expansion under the Kaiser were seen as direct threats to the empire. Britain relied on the Royal Navy for her protection and in 1906, in order to reinforce her pre-eminence, had launched HMS *Dreadnought*, the first of a new class of battleship which was faster and had heavier armour plating than any other battleship then afloat (100mm against 75mm). It was, however, not just her speed or her strength which made *Dreadnought* such a formidable fighting force, but her awesome weaponry. She had ten 12in guns which could destroy an enemy ship more than 20 miles away from outside the range of the guns of existing battleships, which could be blown out of the water before they could approach close enough to fire their own guns. The Liberal manifesto had promised cuts in the defence budget and, at the time, this was supported by Lloyd George, who proposed a reduction in the building programme for Dreadnought battleships from six to four. The proposed cuts were overruled following a well-orchestrated public campaign, covertly supported by Jackie Fisher, First Lord of the Admiralty, adopting the slogan 'we want eight and we won't wait'. The consequent increase in the Dreadnought building programme was fundamental to the Royal Navy's pre-eminence at the outbreak of the war.

In response, Germany had developed her own 'super battleships', with the declared intention of creating a navy to challenge the supremacy of the Royal Navy and threaten Britain's trade routes with the empire – the source of both her wealth and essential supplies of food, oil and raw materials.

The growth in Germany's military capabilities was coupled with increasing economic power, and the German economy had expanded rapidly after the formation of the new German Empire in January 1871. When Bismarck had taken office in Prussia in 1862, the combined industrial production of the German states represented a meagre 4.9 per cent of world production, putting them in fifth place; Britain, with 19.9 per cent, comfortably led the world. By 1913, however, Britain had dropped to third place and the United States now headed the list, with Germany in second place. World trade showed a similar picture. In 1880 Britain had 22.4 per cent of world trade compared with Germany's 10.3 per cent, but by 1913 Germany had closed the gap with 12.3 per cent against Britain's 14.2 per cent (Clark, *Sleepwalkers*, pp.164–5).

CHOOSING YOUR PARTNER

In 1894, France, still smarting from its defeat in the Franco-Prussian War of 1870 and the loss of Alsace-Lorraine, and fearing further German aggression, signed the Franco-Russian Alliance. Through this mutual defence pact both parties immediately guaranteed to mobilise against Germany should the other be attacked, thus ensuring that any German aggression would instantly result in Germany having to fight on both her western and eastern borders. Germany watched as both France and Russia significantly increased the size of their military forces in the years leading up to the war. To drive home the lesson, France made substantial loans to Russia to finance major improvements to the Russian railway system to allow Russian troops to be mobilised and transported more rapidly to the German border if war were to break out. Germany responded by rearming, arguing with some justification that their rearmament was merely a defensive response to the Franco-Russian Alliance.

The strategic planners saw mobility and manpower as the source of victory in future conflict and not the reliance upon substantial static fortified positions as in the past. This resulted in a peculiar form of arms race intended to maximise the size of one's army and of the reserves available on mobilisation. France had introduced two-year conscription in 1905, stimulating Germany to respond by substantially increasing the size of its peacetime army, only to be trumped by the French who in 1913 extended conscription to three years.

Russia, too, was rapidly expanding the size of its army, and its economy was growing fast. Germany was understandably fearful of this Russian expansion, significantly overestimating both Russia's rate of economic growth and the effectiveness of its military muscle; was there an argument for a German pre-emptive strike before Russia became overbearingly powerful?

But neither the threat implicit in Germany's rearmament nor the challenge from Germany's rapid industrial growth were the principal reasons why Britain signed the Entente Cordiale with France in 1904, following the popular and influential visit of King Edward VII to Paris in 1903, nor indeed why Britain signed the Convention with Russia in 1907 after Russia's disastrous defeat in the Russo-Japanese War. Although these were obviously factors, Britain's primary objective in joining the Triple Entente was to reduce the pressure from the French and the Russians on the outermost extremities of its empire. During the months and years before the outbreak of war, the British followed this policy by maintaining, as far as possible, a friendly relationship with Russia and, accordingly – and perhaps fatally – not responding to approaches from Germany. Britain's worst fear was that there would be a rapprochement between Russia and Germany, which would have left it isolated.

The balance of power had now polarised into two power blocks: the Triple Alliance, linking Germany, Austria and an increasingly reluctant Italy, and the Triple Entente, linking Britain, France and Russia. All of these countries had developed, to a greater or lesser extent, strategic plans for implementation in the event of a European war, and as the political situation worsened these plans would trigger automatic reactions as the dominos fell.

THE SIMMERING BREW

Tensions were also developing within the British political system. At the outbreak of war there were 17 million manual workers working long hours for poor pay and living in crowded, often unsanitary conditions. Voting rights for men were restricted to those owning property, meaning that many men lacked the right to vote. Women had no voting rights at all and the government was facing increasingly violent demonstrations from the suffragettes demanding the right to vote, although the greatest threat to the political system came not from the suffragettes but from the demand for Irish Home Rule.

In the face of these domestic problems, little attention was given to the burgeoning threat of a European war, leading Arthur Nicholson to write in May 1914, 'Since I have been at the Foreign Office I have not seen such calm waters' (quoted in Clark, *Sleepwalkers*, p.314). The British Foreign Office may have been unconcerned, but the temperature was steadily rising.

To further raise the temperature of this simmering brew, British Foreign Secretary Sir Edward Grey, who was a keen fisherman and naturalist - he had written a respected treatise on fly fishing - but a seemingly reluctant politician, added a cocktail of confused messages to the potion. Privately, in talks with the French (very probably in English, as he spoke no French), he confirmed that Britain would come to the support of France in the event of a European war. His public position was, however, very different - to counter the concerns of non-interventionists within the Cabinet Grey repeatedly denied that Britain had any such obligation and explained away combined Anglo-French military manoeuvres as merely contingency plans. As a result, the French were assured of Britain's support if war were to break out but, dangerously and conversely, the Germans were led to believe that Britain would not intervene in any such conflict. As Charles Hamilton Sorley wrote:

> If only the English from [Sir Edward] Grey downwards would cease from rubbing in that, in the days that set all the fuel ablaze, they worked for peace honestly and with all their hearts! We know they did; but in the past their lack of openness and trust in their diplomatic relationships helped to pile the fuel to which Germany supplied the torch.   (Letter to Mrs Sorley dated March 1915, quoted in Spear, *Poems and Selected Letters*, p.96)

The threat of war was developing a momentum which made conflict virtually inevitable and Britain, through the Entente Cordiale with France and the Convention with Russia, could not realistically stay aloof from the politics of Europe. Despite the desire of both the politicians and the people to avoid war, it had become inevitable that should Europe become engulfed by war then Britain would inexorably be drawn into the conflict to prevent a German military conquest of Europe. It is certainly arguable that if Britain had adopted the alternative of standing aside from the conflict and, as would have been probable, France had been defeated by Germany, then Britain would eventually have been forced into a subsequent war against a strengthened Germany in a German-controlled Europe.

2 THE OVERTURE

STIRRING THE ETHNIC SOUP

The Austro-Hungarian Empire had remained a powerful force despite the loss of Italy some fifty years earlier, but the structure was crumbling. Austria had pacified Hungarian nationalism, agreeing in 1866 to recognise Hungary's autonomy within the empire by creating the dual monarchy, but was increasingly threatened by the developing demands for autonomy both amongst its own diverse population and from the countries on its borders.

The empire comprised an ethnic soup. Austria was primarily Germanic, the Tyrol remained Italian while Hungary, although under the political control of the Magyars, had substantial numbers of Slovaks, Romanians and Croats. Within the empire there were also Czechs, Slovenes and Poles, but of all the races it was the Slavs who were seen as the greatest threat to the security of the empire.

Austria had stood aside from the First and Second Balkan Wars of 1912 and 1913, whereby Serbia had roughly doubled in size through the acquisition of Macedonia and Kosovo and increased its population from 2.9 million to 4.4 million (Hew Strachan, *The First World War*, p.6). The Austrians had, with some justification, become disillusioned in their dealings with the Serbs, in particular with their repeated perfidy, and had lost confidence that the threat from Serbia could be dealt with solely through diplomatic channels; perhaps force was the only argument to which the Serbs would listen?

Serbia, for its part, had long had a dream of creating a Greater Serbia by uniting all the Serbian people of the Balkan states, Bosnia-Herzegovina and Croatia – even Serbs in what is now Romania – in one Greater Serbian state. It was recognised that some of these states contained non-Serbian ethnic groups, such as the Croats, but they would soon get used to the idea of Serbian rule. In a foretaste of what would happen at the end of the twentieth century, the Serbians were ruthless in the exploitation of their new peoples. The British Vice Consul in Monastir reported, 'It is already abundantly evident that Moslems under Servian [*sic*] rule have nothing whatever to expect but periodical massacre, certain exploitation and final ruin' (quoted in Clark, *Sleepwalkers*, p.44).

The Serbs had a major obstacle to their dream: they were sandwiched between the Austro-Hungarian Empire and the powerful, although declining, Ottoman Empire, which had formerly ruled the Balkan states. In 1908 Austria had flexed its muscles and formally annexed Bosnia, which had been under military occupation by Austria since 1878 and part of the Ottoman Empire prior to that, but this move had antagonised the Serbs, who saw it as a potential threat both to their independence and to their dream of a Slav state; Bosnia was key to the building of a Greater Serbia. More seriously for Austria, the Russians saw themselves as protectors of the Slavs and felt they had been duped by the Austrian move. The Bosnians, in turn, were no happier, deeply resenting their new and overbearing masters, a resentment exacerbated by the arrogance of Archduke Franz Ferdinand, the heir apparent to Emperor Franz Josef of Austria.

SARAJEVO: JUNE 1914

It was, therefore, perhaps not the most sensible of plans for the archduke and his wife Sophie to visit Bosnia, arriving in Sarajevo in June 1914 on an official visit to watch the troop manoeuvres of the Austrian forces. On the evening before the manoeuvres, the archduke and Sophie had driven into the city on an informal visit to meet the people and browse its shops. Security was relaxed and they were delighted with their reception, but beneath the surface there were underlying tensions arising from the fermenting resentment amongst the Bosnians against their new imperial overlord, a resentment which was fanned by Serbia.

Sophie was encouraged by their warm reception, remarking to a prominent Bosnian parliamentarian how delighted they were with the warmth of the welcome. Dr Sunaric replied presciently, 'Your Highness, I pray to God that when I have the honour of meeting you again tomorrow night, you can repeat those words. A great burden will be lifted from me' (Vladimir Dedijer, *The Road to Sarajevo*, p.10, quoted in Max Hastings, *Catastrophe*, p.xxxiv).

The following day, 28 June, the imperial couple were due to make a formal visit to Sarajevo, an inauspicious date for such a visit, as it had been on 28 June 1389 that the defeat in Kosovo of the Serbian Army by the forces of the Ottoman Army had brought an end to Serbian independence. By the close of day they would both be dead, shot by an assassin as they toured the city in an open-topped car.

Gavrilo Princip was a Bosnian who believed that Bosnia should become part of a Greater Serbia, but that this would only be achieved through violence. The unpopular Archduke Franz Ferdinand was the unfortunate target chosen. Princip, together with six other potential assassins, had been armed with automatic pistols and bombs, along with cyanide capsules in case of capture, by the Serbian terrorist group popularly called the 'Black Hand' – its proper name was 'Union or Death', or in Serbian, the rather less catchy '*Ujedinjenje ili smrt*'. The first assassin threw a bomb at the car, which bounced off, killing two of the attending staff but leaving the archduke and his wife unharmed. The archduke gave the order to his driver to continue the tour but, crucially, after the formal proceedings he asked him to take them to the hospital to see the officers who had been wounded in the attack. Unfortunately, this change of plan had not been communicated to the driver and as he struggled to turn – the Gräf und Stift Double Phaeton had no reverse gear – the car was, by mischance, near to where Princip was standing. He fired and killed Sophie outright. The archduke died minutes later; his last words were moving: 'Sophie, Sophie, don't die, stay alive for our children' (quoted in Clark, *Sleepwalkers*, pp.372–5).

This violent act initiated a series of reactions which led inexorably to war. The catalyst was Austria's response.

THE AUSTRIAN ULTIMATUM

Austria's initial reaction to the outrage was to punish Serbia with a military invasion. It is possible that if they had moved immediately Russia would have stood aside and the war would have been restricted to a local squabble between Austria and Serbia.

Austria's bellicose reaction was not, however, supported by the Hungarian half of the dual monarchy and a more structured response was demanded. The Austrians, belatedly recognising the possibility that any move against Serbia might antagonise Russia, sought the support of their alliance partner Germany in any future conflict and sent an emissary to the Kaiser, receiving in return an unrestricted pledge of support – the infamous 'blank cheque'.

On 2 July the participants in the assassination confessed, confirming Serbia's complicity, whether official or unofficial. Austria had long believed that the Serbs needed to be taught a lesson: the assassination of Franz Ferdinand now provided the excuse. Accordingly, on 23 July the Austrian government issued a forty-eight-hour ultimatum to Serbia, making outrageous demands upon the Serbian government in a document described by Winston Churchill in a letter to Clementine as 'the most insolent document of its kind ever devised' (quoted in Clark, *Sleepwalkers*, p.456).

Serbia immediately sought the support of the tsar. Russia, who saw itself as the guardian of Slav interests, pledged its support to Serbia and authorised the 'partial' mobilisation of its forces, possibly not with aggressive intent but in the hope that a show of strength might prevent war. Tragically the dominos were beginning to fall. Serbia, emboldened by the Russian offer of support, issued a reply which, in the words of Christopher Clark in his excellent work *The Sleepwalkers*, was 'perfectly pitched to convey the tone of voice of reasonable statesmen in a condition of sincere puzzlement, struggling to make sense of outrageous and unacceptable demands' (p.466).

While conciliatory in tone, the reply from Serbia admitted little and offered less. It was imperiously disregarded by Austria. Events now moved with shattering speed. On 27 July Grey attempted to convene a four-power conference to resolve the dispute. The Kaiser and Tsar Nicholas also attempted to stem the move to war, exchanging messages pledging to take all steps to avoid the escalation of the conflict but, tragically, it was all too late. The crisis had developed a momentum of its own.

On the morning of 28 July 1914, Emperor Franz Joseph signed Austria's declaration of war against Serbia, blithely ignoring the very real possibility that Russia would in turn declare war in support of Serbia. Although the Kaiser recognised that Serbia had been conciliatory in its response, even writing on his copy of the Serbian reply that 'this does away with the need for war' (Clark, *Sleepwalkers*, p.522), he was bound by Germany's commitment to support Austria-Hungary and now had no choice but to honour that pledge; German forces were mobilised in support of Austria.

The dominos now fell faster. Russia ordered a general mobilisation of its forces on 30 July, not just against Austria but against Germany as well, including the mobilisation of its Baltic Fleet. Germany responded by demanding that Russia rescind the order, failing which it would have no alternative but to declare war on Russia. Britain was kept informed of this demand and at 1.30 a.m. King George V was woken and, in his dressing gown, prevailed upon to send a telegram to the tsar urging Russia to halt their mobilisation, but with no response. The die was cast.

The assassination had been an insignificant event – sad, but hardly of world-shattering importance – but like the famous example of the butterfly fluttering its wings, the ramifications of the murders would bring four years of suffering, not just to Europe but to the world, with as many as 10 million soldiers dead and probably twice that number physically or mentally damaged (Catriona MacDonald and E.W. McFarland (eds), *Scotland and the Great War*, p.30).

The world would never be the same. There would be revolution in Russia, the power of the Austro-Hungarian Empire would be destroyed and the United States would emerge as the leading world power. Britain would change from a supremely confident world power with an empire and significant overseas assets to a country with shrunken influence and extensive overseas debts, while the cosy social order which had protected the lifestyles of the upper class and the affluent middle classes would be shattered. Serbia, the initial cause of the crisis, became almost an irrelevance in what became a global conflict.

THE SCHLIEFFEN PLAN: GERMANY DECLARES WAR

In 1905 an ageing German general had drawn up a plan for a European war. General Count Alfred von Schlieffen realised that Germany's main enemies were France and Russia and that if one was attacked the other would be bound by treaty obligations to join the battle, requiring Germany to fight on both a western and eastern front. The Schlieffen Plan relied upon the assumption that it would take the Russians at least six weeks to mobilise, giving vital time to neutralise the threat from France. Accordingly, the plan was for Germany to launch an immediate all-out assault on France, invading not directly but by swinging north in an arc through Belgium, with the objective of outflanking the French defences and capturing Paris within six weeks. With France defeated, one half of the German forces would then be moved east to counter the anticipated Russian attack.

There were fatal flaws in the Schlieffen Plan. Firstly, it was based upon the assumption that the Russians would take six weeks to mobilise. Secondly, the plan relied on the rapid movement of vast numbers of troops through Belgium and France. The reality would be exposed when war eventually did come and Germany's 1st Army faced the prospect of a march of 200 miles from the German border to Paris, with endless columns of men marching for mile after mile, day after day, supported by horses laboriously pulling the artillery, the field kitchens and all the other paraphernalia of war (John Keegan, *The First World War*, p.87). Thirdly, and crucially, the plan relied upon the assumption that Britain would not enter the war.

On 1 August, in the absence of a Russian response to its ultimatum, Germany declared war on Russia. Germany recognised that France was bound by the Entente to support Russia and that it was inevitable she would enter the fray and so – following the precepts of the Schlieffen Plan as modified by Helmuth von Moltke, who was now Chief of the General Staff – began its campaign against France, with the objective of defeating the French before the Russians had time to complete the mobilisation of their forces.

The necessary planning had been carried out. Railway lines had been laid across Germany, terminating at little-known destinations on the frontier to enable rapid mobilisation of troops. There was a slight technical difficulty in that the northern route to France passed through Belgium, but the solution was simple if harsh – 'let us pass through or we will invade', was Germany's threat to Belgium. This decision, which would fundamentally affect the conduct of the war, was made by the military without consulting the politicians, who might have pointed out the danger that an invasion of Belgium might precipitate Britain's entry into the war in honour of her treaty obligations.

Early on the morning of Sunday, 2 August, trains carrying the German Army were heading west, transporting more than 2.1 million men and 100,000 horses on 20,000 trains to Germany's border with France and Belgium (Margaret MacMillan, *The War that Ended Peace*, p.298).

On the British side of the Channel, however, the government still watched and waited, impotent as Europe moved inexorably towards war. There was anguished discussion within the British Cabinet as to whether Britain should go to the aid of France in recognition of the non-binding Entente between the two countries, or whether it should stand aside from the developing conflict.

3 THE CURTAIN RISES

GERMANY INVADES BELGIUM:
BRITAIN DECLARES WAR

We are on the eve of horrible things. I wish you were nearer my darling: wouldn't it be a joy if we could spend Sunday together? I love you more than I can say.

> Henry Asquith, British Prime Minister. Letter written to his mistress,
> Venetia Stanley, on 4 August 1914 – the day war was declared.

Venetia Stanley

As evidenced by his letter, the imminent prospect of catastrophe did not deter the British prime minister from enjoying his own personal *entente cordiale*, demonstrating a sense of priorities which would have probably been endorsed by Britain's French allies. Asquith's first wife had died from typhoid fever in 1891 and in 1894 he married Margot Tennant, the daughter of the Scottish chemicals magnate Sir Charles Tennant, but in 1912 he had become infatuated with Venetia Stanley, a close friend of his daughter Violet. He wrote to Venetia daily, describing in detail the inner secrets of government and the conduct of the war, writing in three years a total of 560 letters, thereby creating an invaluable record of the thinking at the heart of the British government (Richard Freeman, *'Unsinkable': Churchill and the First World War*, p.115).

The Move to War

While the prime minister was regretting time not spent with Venetia, Europe was moving swiftly and with seeming inevitability towards all-out war.

On 3 August 1914 the King of Belgium made a direct appeal to Britain to come to the aid of his country. Unlike the informal Entente Cordiale with France, Britain had entered into a formal treaty obligation to defend the neutrality of Belgium if attacked. Accordingly, when German forces swept into Belgium on 4 August, Britain had no honourable choice but to deliver an ultimatum to Germany to withdraw or face war. Germany failed to respond by the deadline, which had been set at 11 p.m. on 4 August 1914, and so Britain declared war on Germany. Winston Churchill, as First Lord of the Admiralty, sent an immediate message to all ships of the Royal Navy, 'Commence hostilities against Germany'.

Many felt war had been avoidable. An article in the Liberal newspaper *The Nation* on 1 August stated, 'There has been no crisis in which the public opinion of the British people has been so definitely opposed to war as it is at this moment,' and yet only a week later the view in the same paper was:

> There are great masses of opinion in this country which hoped that this country might have avoided intervention. But the feeling is unanimous that the struggle must now be carried on with the utmost energy, not indeed until Germany is crushed, but until German aggression is defeated and German militarism broken.   (Quoted in David Roberts (ed.), *Minds at War*, p.34)

The Invasion of Belgium

What had changed public opinion? It was not the declaration of war that tipped the British public in favour of war but the atrocities which had been committed – or were reported to have been committed – by the invading German troops during the invasion of Belgium.

The War Convention held at the Hague in 1907 had set down certain 'rules' for war, including the stipulation that it was not permissible to enter neutral countries with armed forces and that resistance to any such invasion was not to be treated as a hostile act. The Germans repudiated this convention and as they advanced they seized hostages to 'guarantee' the good behaviour of Belgian citizens, executing civilians in reprisal for any assumed resistance. Belgian villages were ruthlessly destroyed, culminating in the devastation of much of the old university town of Louvain where buildings were looted and then deliberately set on fire. German soldiers poured petrol on its fine library and then set it alight, destroying its collection of over 200,000 books, including a number of priceless manuscripts. Innocent citizens were beaten up or killed and centuries of culture and learning were wilfully destroyed.

Hundreds of thousands of refugees fled from Belgium in the first two months of the war, many of whom came to Britain, and many more were deported as slave labourers to Germany. The truth was harsh enough, but it was embroidered by stories of Belgian girls raped and mutilated and Belgian babies bayoneted. British public opinion was outraged. The war was a just war – a fight against evil and against aggression.

The Mood in Britain

The initial mood in Britain was buoyant as the troops were waved off to fight. The war would be over by Christmas. Brooke expresses this idealised view of war in his sonnet *The Soldier:*

The Soldier

If I should die, think only this of me:
    That there's some corner of a foreign field
That is for ever England. There shall be
    In that rich earth a richer dust concealed;
A dust whom England bore, shaped, made aware,
    Gave, once, her flowers to love, her ways to roam,
A body of England's, breathing English air,
    Washed by the rivers, blest by suns of home.

And think, this heart, all evil shed away,
    A pulse in the eternal mind, no less,
Gives somewhere back the thoughts by England given;
    Her sights and sounds; dreams happy as her day;
And laughter, learnt of friends; and gentleness,
    In hearts at peace, under an English heaven.

(Written in November and December 1914)

Brooke writes of the honour of dying in the defence of an idealised England, although it is hard to visualise your hardened Glaswegian, or indeed a Geordie or a Cockney, empathising with this romanticised portrait of an *England*, not a Britain, for whom they were being asked to fight. This dichotomy is captured in the recruitment poster entitled *Your Country's Call*, which depicts a kilted soldier pointing to an archetypal English village with thatched cottages, underscored with the caption, 'Isn't this worth fighting for?' (see photograph p. 171).

Ewart Alan Mackintosh – To a Private Soldier
Brooke was writing with the idealism of one who would never experience life
in the trenches. Mackintosh, who did, gives a very different view in his poem
To a Private Soldier:

To a Private Soldier

The air is still, the light winds blow
Too quietly to wake you now.
Dreamer, you dream too well to know
Whose hand set death upon your brow.
The shrinking flesh the bullets tore
Will never pulse with fear again;
Sleep on, remembering no more
Your sudden agony of pain.

Oh, poor brave smiling face made naught,
Turned back to dust from whence you came,
You have forgot the men you fought,
The wounds that burnt you like a flame;
With stiff hand crumbling a clod,
And blind eyes staring at the sky,
The awful evidence of God
Against the men who made you die.

You have forgotten, sleeping well,
But what of them? Shall they forget
Your body broken with the shell,
Your brow whereon their seal is set?
Does earth for them hold any place
Where they will never see the flies
Clustered about your empty face
And on your blind, accusing eyes?

Good-night, good sleep to you. But they
Will never know good night again,
Whose eyes are seeing night and day,
The humble men who died in vain.

Their ears are filled with bitter cries,
Their nostrils with the powder smell,
And shall see your mournful eyes
Across the reeking fires of hell.

'YOUR KING AND COUNTRY WANT YOU'

The patriotic feeling that swept the country is perhaps best expressed not by stilted poems on the lines of Henry Newbolt's *Vitai Lampada* (the torch of life), which starts with, 'There's a breathless hush in the Close tonight, Ten to make and the match to win', and ends with the exhortation to 'Play up! play up! and play the game!', but by the popular music-hall song 'Your King and Country Want You' by Paul Rubens, which was intended to be sung by women to encourage their men to enlist:

Your King and Country Want You

We've watched you playing cricket
And every kind of game
At football, golf and polo
You men have made your name
But now your country calls you
To play your part in War
And no matter what befalls you
We shall love you all the more
So come and join the forces
As your fathers did before.

Oh! We don't want to lose you
But we think you ought to go
For your King and Country
Both need you so
We shall want and miss you
But with our might and main
We shall cheer you, thank you, kiss you,
When you come back again.

J.P. Ede – Counted For
This buoyant mood is captured in a jocular poem, *Counted For*, by Private
J.P. Ede of the Royal Army Medical Corps:

Counted For
[second verse omitted]

Five-and-fifty sprightly lads
    Are standing on parade,
The section's roll is quickly called
    And not a man has strayed.
Then five-and-fifty pairs of heels
    Together smartly click,
'Mid murmurs from admiring throngs
    'Phew! Section Five is slick!'

Six men in deep humility,
    Before 'tis seven o'clock,
Go down on their knees to scrub
    Th' administrative block;
For seven successive morns they writhe
    In anguish sore to see,
But on the eighth each man falls sick
    With chronic housemaid's knee.

A score of men are marched 'two deep'
    Towards the comp'ny's mess,
And what they find awaiting there
    Appals them, I confess.
For while the bitter wintry air
    Coagulates their blood,
They peel the epidermis
    From the soil-beladen 'spud.'

But five-and-fifty hungry lads
    Complete their tasks at length,
And swiftly glide to breakfast

To recover wasted strength.
There bully beef and bacon
    They attack with frantic glee,
Or stab the sulky 'submarine,'
    And wash it down with tea.

Many a wife in days to come
    When strife at length is o'er,
Complacently will sit and watch
    Her hubby scrub the floor.
And as he slices carrots
    And removes potato eyes,
She'll murmur 'War is, after all,
    A blessing in disguise.'

William Cameron – Speak Not to Me of War!

Not everyone was in favour of war. William Cameron does not qualify as a war poet, as herein defined, because he was not a participant but a journalist contributing to the Socialist newspaper *Forward*. He was opposed to the war and wrote movingly of a mother's loss in his poem:

Speak Not to Me of War!

Speak not to me of sword or gun,
    Of bloody war and strife;
Laud not the inhuman brutes who've won
    And spilt their brother's life.
See yonder bloody corpse-strewn plain,
    Where man has butchered man;
Then write upon your scroll of fame:
    Write 'glorious' if you can!

See yonder lonely woman weep,
    The heart-felt silent tear;
It slowly trickles down her cheek
    For one she loved so dear!
Come, ask the reason of her sigh,

Why weeps she! What's her care!
She mourns a slaughtered son, that's why
    Show me the glory there!

KITCHENER'S ARMY

Lord Kitchener of Khartoum had an impressive war record in Sudan and as the victorious commander in the Boer War. On 3 August 1914 Kitchener was in Dover on his way back to Egypt where he was consul general and de facto governor. However, it was not to be. Asquith, who had become prime minister on the resignation (due to ill health) of Campbell-Bannerman on 3 April 1908, had other ideas and despatched a messenger, who reached Kitchener just before he embarked, delivering to him a summons to return to London where he was appointed Secretary of State for War. It was a popular appointment.

Lord Kitchener was one of the few who realised that the war would not 'be over by Christmas'. Britain, at the outset of the war, had only a small standing army of 247,000 men of whom roughly half were stationed overseas in the empire. Kitchener realised that recruits were urgently needed to increase the size of the British Army to counter that of Germany, which in peacetime numbered 1 million, but on mobilisation of reserves would rise to 3 million or more.

Kitchener had modest ambitions, aiming to raise a 'New Army' of 100,000 volunteers, but the feelings of patriotism engendered by such songs as 'Your King and Country Want You' encouraged more than 2 million to volunteer within just eighteen months. This New Army represented a huge gamble by Kitchener, as a vast number of unproven and militarily inexperienced men had to be trained, equipped and, as far as possible, prepared for the hardship of life in the trenches and for the horrors of the battlefield. It was an experiment which had never before been attempted in the middle of a war and on such a scale.

The New Army was joined by recruits from the empire – Australians, Canadians and New Zealanders – and from the colonies; 230,000 troops from India fought in Flanders in the first months of the war, and overall well over 1 million Indian troops fought in the various conflicts around the world.

At its peak, the British Expeditionary Force (BEF) totalled just over 2 million, although more than 5.7 million served throughout the war.

Kitchener did not believe in a conscripted army, but considerable public pressure was put on men to enlist and 2.45 million did in fact volunteer, some more voluntarily than others. Conscription was not introduced until January 1916, but by the end of the war more than 3.25 million men had been conscripted. The strength and resilience of the BEF is often thought to derive from the fact that it was a volunteer force, but by the end of the war the number who volunteered had been outnumbered by those who had been conscripted by 800,000.

Ewart Alan Mackintosh - Recruiting

Mackintosh's poem *Recruiting* was inspired by a poster which attempted to shame men into enlisting. Mackintosh begins by painting an unflattering picture of the civilians who were encouraging men to fight while safely at home themselves and then rewrites the poster as it should have read:

Recruiting

"Lads, you're wanted, go and help"
On the railway carriage wall
Stuck the poster, and I thought
Of the hands that penned the call.

Fat civilians wishing they
"Could go out and fight the Hun."
Can't you see them thanking God
That they're over forty-one?

Girls with feathers, vulgar songs –
Washy verse on England's need –
God – and don't we damned well know
How the message ought to read.

"Lads! You're wanted! Over there"
Shiver in the morning dew,
Many poor devils like yourselves
Waiting to be killed by you.

Go and help to swell the names
In the casualty lists.
Help to make a column's stuff
For the blasted journalists.

Help to keep them nice and safe
From the wicked German foe.
Don't let him come over here!
"Lads, you're wanted – out you go"

There's a better word than that,
Lads, and can't you hear it come
From a million men that call
You to share their martyrdom.

Leave the harlots still to sing
Comic songs about the Hun,
Leave the old fat men to say
Now we've got them on the run.

Better twenty honest years
Than their dull three score and ten.
Lads, you're wanted. Come and learn
To live and die with honest men.

You shall learn what men can do
If you will but pay the price,
Learn the gaiety and strength
In the gallant sacrifice.

Take your risk of life and death
Underneath the open sky.
Live clean or go out quick –
Lads you're wanted. Come and die.

Alfred Lichtenstein - Leaving for the Front

In the bitter symmetry of this unnecessary war the German recruits showed a similar fatalism. In his poem *Leaving for the Front*, written on 7 August 1914, Alfred Lichtenstein gives the German perspective, realistically accepting the likelihood of death. Seven weeks later, just as he had foretold, he was dead:

Leaving for the Front

Before I die I must just find this rhyme.
Be quiet, my friends, and do not waste my time.

We're marching off in company with death.
I only wish my girl would hold her breath.

There's nothing wrong with me. I'm glad to leave.
Now mother's crying too. There's no reprieve.

And now look how the sun's begun to set.
A nice mass-grave is all that I shall get.

Once more the good old sunset's glowing red.
In thirteen days I'll probably be dead.

(Translated from the German by Patrick Bridgwater)

THE HUMAN COST

A total of 743,000 British soldiers were killed in action, registered as missing, or died from their wounds during the Great War, together with a further 192,000 from the empire and Commonwealth (Martin Gilbert, *The First World War*, p.541), memorably commemorated by the poppies planted in the moat of the Tower of London in November 2014. A further 150,000 were taken prisoner and 1.6 million wounded. Even these bald statistics, bad as they are, understate the effect on the families of brothers who were badly maimed by artillery shells or whose faces had been shot away, husbands with one leg amputated or sons with lungs irrevocably damaged by gas.

Britain was not the only country to suffer. By the time the war had ended France had lost 1.4 million men, Germany 1.8 million and the Austro-Hungarian Empire a further 1.3 million. Russian losses, not accurately determined, probably exceeded 1.7 million (Gilbert, *First World War*, p.541).

Siegfried Sassoon - Does it Matter?
Siegfried Sassoon wrote movingly of injuries suffered in battle in his poem *Does it Matter?*:

Does it Matter?

Does it matter? - losing your legs?
For people will always be kind.
And you need not show that you mind
When the others come in after hunting
To gobble their muffins and eggs.

Does it matter? - losing your sight?
There's such splendid work for the blind;
And people will always be kind,
As you sit on the terrace remembering
And turning your face to the light.

Do they matter? - those dreams from the pit? ...
You can drink and forget and be glad,
And people won't say that you're mad;
For they'll know that you've fought for your country
And no one will worry a bit.

(Written at Craiglockhart Hospital, 1917)

The Effect on Scotland
For Scotland the figures are even bleaker. At the end of the war 585,000 Scots were serving in the army, 72,000 in the Royal Navy and 33,000 in the Royal Flying Corps and Royal Air Force, totalling 690,000 out of a total population of 4.8 million. The exact number of Scots who served is difficult to determine because many Scots served in non-Scottish regiments (MacDonald and McFarland, *Scotland*, p.20).

The cost was cruel. In a sealed casket at the Scottish National Memorial in Edinburgh are the Rolls of Honour which list the Scots who died in the Great War. One hundred and forty-seven thousand Scots* are estimated to have died in the war, of whom 85,000 are listed on the memorial tablets of the Scottish infantry regiments; 11,000 men who served with the Royal Scots, including 600 officers; 9,000 with the Gordon Highlanders; and 10,000 with the Black Watch (MacDonald and McFarland, *Scotland*, p.1).

Many had been recruited into the 'pals' regiments – men recruited from the same towns, villages, workplaces or leisure clubs to serve together. The intention was to have friends and brothers serving alongside each other, relying on the bonding of kindred souls to inspire comradeship and to encourage commitment. The downside was that these same towns and villages could be decimated by the loss of life from just one battle.

Famous amongst the pals were the Heart of Midlothian football team who, joined by a large numbers of their supporters, enlisted en masse after a home match at Tynecastle on 26 November 1914, with the majority joining the 16th Battalion Royal Scots (Derek Young, *Scottish Voices from the Great War*, p.27). The 16th Battalion fought in the Battle of the Somme, advancing further on the first day than any other battalion but at a loss of nearly 600 killed, missing or wounded. Three Hearts footballers were killed that day alone, amongst them Harry Wattie, in his time one of Scotland's finest inside forwards. His body was never found.

*   The number of Scots who died in the First World War is the subject of argument amongst eminent historians, with Sir Hew Strachan claiming the figure is overstated.

4 ACT ONE: THE OPENING OF HOSTILITIES

THE BRITISH EXPEDITIONARY FORCE

On 4 August the German Army crossed the border and swept through Belgium towards France, but first they had to break through the series of defensive fortifications which had been expensively constructed by the Belgians. The fortress of Liege consisted of a number of independent forts arranged in a circle, protected by deep ditches. It had been designed to withstand the heaviest artillery then known, but the builders had not allowed for the new monster German howitzers, whose massive shells stripped the armour plating from the walls and shredded the thick concrete walls. The Belgians, defending heroically, were being overwhelmed and it was essential that British reinforcements arrived as soon as possible if France was not to fall. The BEF had been devised just for this purpose – to deliver a rapid response to a perceived or actual threat.

The Haldane Reforms
The BEF had been the brainchild not of a soldier but of a politician – Viscount Haldane who, although trained as a lawyer, had been appointed in 1905 as the Secretary of State for War. In common with the new Foreign Secretary, Sir Edward Grey, Haldane had recognised the need for Britain to be able to despatch a trained professional army at short notice should the threat of a European war materialise.

He established two armies: the first a regular army of roughly 250,000 troops, which would provide the basis of the BEF; the second a home-based Territorial Force, planned to eventually reach 300,000 men, consisting of fourteen infantry divisions and fourteen cavalry brigades based on the county regiments. This regular army was pitifully small in comparison to the armies of Germany, France and Russia, reflecting the British defence strategy which relied upon the Royal Navy to protect Britain from invasion and to preserve Britain's vital supply lines from the empire.

Haldane was also instrumental in introducing officer training corps in the public schools and universities – providing the training ground for the young officers of the First World War – and for creating the Advisory Committee for Aeronautics, which brought a scientific approach to the development of the burgeoning aircraft industry that would have a dramatic influence on the later stages of the war.

Haldane's reforms were critical to Britain's ability to respond swiftly to the German threat, and the rapid mobilisation of the BEF would prove crucial in stemming Germany's seemingly inexorable advance through northern Belgium, thereby preventing the threatened collapse and defeat of France within the opening weeks of the war.

The Men in Charge

Three men would prove fundamental to the conduct of the war. They were brave men who had served the British Army with distinction in India, Sudan and the Boer War. They had battlefield experience and proven leadership qualities and had demonstrated personal courage. They were also opinionated, pig-headed, unimaginative and disloyal to each other. They were Lord Horatio Kitchener, Field Marshal Sir John French and General Sir Douglas Haig.

Lord Kitchener of Khartoum had been appointed the Secretary of State for War at the outbreak of hostilities. He gained his fame – and his title – by defeating the Mahdi at the Battle of Omdurman in 1898. The Mahdi were followers of Muhammed Ahmad who, after the defeat of the British under General Gordon in the siege of Khartoum, had, in an interesting parallel with today, established a religious state in Sudan that imposed harshly interpreted Sharia law. Although heavily outnumbered by the dervish army, Kitchener commanded a professionally trained army with modern rifles, machine guns and artillery and inflicted a heavy defeat, with the Mahdi losing 10,000 killed and 13,000 wounded, at a cost of only forty-seven British soldiers.

Sir John French was appointed commander-in-chief of the BEF. As a boy he had intended to join the Royal Navy, but persistent seasickness persuaded him to change his allegiance to the army. He enlisted in 1870 and four years later was commissioned as a lieutenant in the King's Royal Irish Hussars, a regiment famous for its tradition of enjoying a good claret with breakfast. He fought with distinction in Sudan, India and the Boer Wars and was a capable soldier, but was arguably over-promoted when he was given command of the BEF in 1914. Outwith his military career, he enthusiastically embraced a second career as a serial adulterer.

Haig had been born in Edinburgh and had fought with distinction in India and the Boer Wars before being given command of I Corps of the BEF (Smith-Dorrien commanded II Corps). Haig would, in due course, replace French as commander-in-chief of the BEF. A competent commander, he would prove obdurate in persisting with a strategy based on attrition, despite the horrendous loss of men it entailed. In fairness, he was not alone in being slow to appreciate the fundamental difference between the static war on the Western Front and the mobility of previous wars – characterised by forced infantry marches and the dynamic use of cavalry – or, indeed, to recognise the impact on the fighting of the massive power of the newly developed artillery. However, he was guilty of severely underestimating the effectiveness of the machine gun.

The Structure of the British Army

As the war developed and the size of the British forces increased dramatically, they were organised into a number of armies, each of which comprised between two and five corps. A corps would consist of three infantry divisions, each of 15,000–20,000 men, together with the requisite support functions such as transport and artillery. The division, predominantly infantry, was the smallest unit that could operate independently. Each division consisted of three brigades with artillery support and each brigade comprised between three and five battalions, not necessarily from the same regiment, so that a division could include men from a number of different regiments. An infantry battalion would comprise, initially at least, around 1,000 men in four companies and would be commanded by a lieutenant colonel, with a major as second in command.

The company, comprising roughly 250 men, would be commanded by a major or, more usually, a captain. The company, in turn, comprised four platoons, each under the command of a lieutenant or second lieutenant assisted by a sergeant. A number of the war poets served as second lieutenants, who would be expected to take over command of a company if the senior officers were killed or wounded – as would happen to Wilfred Owen (Kevin Munro, *Scotland's First World War*, p.107).

The Scottish Contribution

An estimated 20,000 of the roughly 250,000 men in the regular army were Scots. There were ten Scottish regiments, each with its own depot comprising barracks, stores and training areas, as well as providing a home for the regimental honours. All these depots were located in Scotland, with the exception of the King's Own Scottish Borderers, which was appropriately located on the border, but on the English side at Berwick-upon-Tweed.

Each consisted of two line infantry battalions, one of which was stationed at home, but not necessarily in barracks, while the other was on active service overseas serving the empire. For example, when war broke out, the 2nd Battalion Royal Scots was stationed in Plymouth whereas the 1st Battalion was stationed in India. Each regiment would also have men based at the regimental barracks to provide reserves as required. The home-based battalions were the first to go to France, forming a part of the first four divisions of the BEF, followed closely by the battalions who had been serving overseas.

Cheering crowds lined the streets as the regiments marched off to war. In Edinburgh, the pipers played as the 1st Cameron Highlanders marched out from Edinburgh Castle to the railway station for embarkation to Southampton and then by boat to France. The streets and the station were crowded with well-wishers cheering their departure, and these scenes were repeated throughout Scotland as the various regiments mustered and departed. At the same time, the Territorial regiments were being mobilised to provide home defences and for further training to provide reserves, if needed (Munro, *Scotland's First World War*, p.107).

Scots responded positively to the call to war and many signed up to fight inspired by the call to patriotism, seeking the chance of some excitement or looking for an opportunity to escape the poverty of life in the inner cities. More than a quarter (26.9 per cent) of eligible Scots volunteered to serve, compared with just less than a quarter (24.2 per cent) in England and Wales (MacDonald and McFarland, *Scotland*, p.20). Some would lie about their age but, although evidently too young, would be accepted by the recruiting sergeant and examining doctor – surely not in any way influenced by the bounty paid for each man enlisted?

Robert Irvine was perhaps typical:

When Lord Kitchener's pointing finger was on every hoarding throughout the country – 'Your King and Country Needs You' – I was one of the innocents who was enmeshed in the web of patriotism at the First World War. I was only a shop assistant at the time, and on reflection I think it was more that I wanted to escape from the humdrum life behind a grocer's counter and see a bit of the country.   (Quoted in Young, *Scottish Voices*, p.24)

Charles Murray – A Sough o' War

Charles Murray was born in Aberdeenshire in 1864 but had worked as a mining engineer in South Africa. He had fought in the Boer War and served in the Great War as a lieutenant colonel with the South African Defence Force. He summed up the mood in Scotland in the summer of 1914 in his poem *A Sough o' War*, in which he portrays the gentle sough (rustle) of the summer wind turning into the dreadful harvest of war, challenging Scots to enlist:

A Sough o' War

[first verse only]

The corn was turnin', hairst was near,
  But lang afore the scythes could start
A sough o' war gaed through the land
  An' stirred it to its benmost heart.
Nae ours the blame, but when it came
  We couldna pass the challenge by,
For credit o' our honest name
  There could but be the ae reply.
    An' buirdly men, fae strath an' glen,
      An' shepherds fae the bucht an' hill,
    Will show them a', whate'er befa',
      Auld Scotland counts for something still.

The Impact of the War Upon Scotland

The effect of the war upon the many Scots not serving in the armed forces would be profound. Many Scots worked in shipbuilding and the munitions factories, in the steelworks and the coal mines. It was a remarkable contribution for a small country. Three of the largest shipbuilders, John Brown, Fairfield and William Beardmore, were designated as naval dockyards and their workers were prohibited from volunteering to preserve the skill base.

Even when conscription was introduced in 1916 this exemption remained. These three yards produced four battlecruisers, ten light cruisers, two aircraft carriers, twenty-nine submarines and eighty-five destroyers. In total, more than 450 warships were built on the Clyde, together with hundreds of other ships for the Royal Navy and the merchant marine (Munro, *Scotland's First World War*, p.64).

The impact was as great for women. By the end of the war there would be 31,000 women working in Scottish munitions factories producing artillery shells in huge numbers, while in Dundee the jute factories produced sandbags at the rate of millions per month for use in the trenches of the Western Front (MacDonald, *Scotland and the Great War*, p.23).

Mobilisation

Mobilisation of the BEF was rapid. By 17 August over 80,000 men had arrived in France, accompanied by 30,000 horses but just 300 field guns. Horses were a key constituent of all armies, not just as mounts for the cavalry but to transport supplies and artillery, and they had been rapidly and ruthlessly requisitioned, albeit with generous compensation. The mission of the BEF was to provide support to the badly pressed French forces by taking up a position on the French left flank to defend the north of the line protecting the Channel ports and blocking the way to Paris. The BEF would prove vital in stemming the German advance, but the British contribution was dwarfed by the numbers which would be mobilised by the other major combatants – 3 million Austro-Hungarians, 4 million French, 4.5 million Germans and nearly 6 million Russians (Gilbert, *First World War*, p.37).

Britain had immense confidence in the quality of its army. Although dwarfed in size by the conscript armies of France and Germany, the British Army was a trained, professional volunteer army, later described in the official history of the war as 'the best trained, best organised and best equipped British Army that ever went forth to war' – a somewhat optimistic view, as there were serious shortages of heavy artillery, high-explosive shells and machine guns. The Kaiser was somewhat less complimentary of this 'trained, professional army', reputedly giving his generals the order to 'walk over French's contemptible little army'. Although no record exists of any such order, the survivors of the regular army would, in later years, refer to themselves as the Old Contemptibles.

The Lee-Enfield .303 Rifle

The standard rifle used by the British was the Lee-Enfield, named after its designer James Paris Lee and its place of manufacture, the Royal Small Arms Factory at Enfield. The design of the rifle caused the striker to be cocked on the closing stroke of the bolt, enabling a faster rate of fire than with other types of rifle. The rifle had a magazine holding ten rounds and British riflemen were trained to fire ten or more aimed rounds a minute, initially giving the impression to the Germans that they were faced with machine-gun fire.

The rifle was equipped with a bayonet for close-quarter fighting. Sassoon writes of being inculcated into the finer aspects of the use of a bayonet while in the 4th Army School in Flixécourt. In his *Memoirs of an Infantry Officer* (pp.11-12), he wrote:

A gas expert from G.H.Q. would inform us that 'gas was still in its infancy'. (Most of us were either dead or disabled before gas had had time to grow up.) An urbane Artillery General assured us that high explosive would be our best friend in future battles, and his ingratiating voice made us unmindful, for the moment, that explosives often arrived from the wrong direction.

But the star turn in the schoolroom was a massive sandy-haired Highland Major whose subject was 'The Spirit of the Bayonet.' Though at the time undecorated, he was afterwards awarded the D.S.O. for lecturing. He took as his text a few leading points from the *Manual of Bayonet Training*:

'To attack with the bayonet effectively requires Good Direction, Strength and Quickness, during a state of wild excitement and probably physical exhaustion. The bayonet is essentially an offensive weapon. In a bayonet assault all ranks go forward to kill or be killed, and only those who have developed skill and strength by constant training will be able to kill. The spirit of the bayonet must be inculcated into all ranks, so that they go forward with that aggressive determination and confidence of superiority born of continual practice, without which a bayonet assault will not be effective.'

He spoke with homicidal eloquence, keeping the game alive with genial and well-judged jokes. He had a Sergeant to assist him. The Sergeant, a tall sinewy machine, had been trained to such a pitch of frightfulness that at a moment's warning he could divest himself of all semblance of humanity. With rifle and bayonet he illustrated the Major's ferocious aphorisms, including the facial expression. When told to 'put on a killing face,' he did so, combining it with an ultra-vindictive attitude. 'To instil fear into the opponent' was one of the Major's main maxims. Man, it seemed, had been created to jab the life out of Germans. To hear the Major talk, one might have thought that he did it himself every day before breakfast. His final words were: 'Remember that every Boche you fellows kill is a point scored to our side; every Boche you kill brings victory one minute nearer and shortens the war by one minute. Kill them! Kill them! There's only one good Boche, and that's a dead one!'

Sassoon continues:

Afterwards I went up the hill to my favourite sanctuary, a wood of hazels and beeches. The evening air smelt of wet mould and wet leaves; the trees were misty-green; the church bell was tolling in the town, and smoke rose from the roofs. Peace was there in the twilight of that prophetic foreign spring.

But the lecturer's voice still battered on my brain. 'The bullet and the bayonet are brother and sister.' 'If you don't kill him, he'll kill you.' 'Stick him between the eyes, in the throat, in the chest.' 'Don't waste good steel. Six inches are enough. What's the use of a foot of steel sticking out at the back of a man's neck? Three inches will do for him; when he coughs, go and look for another.'

THE BRITISH ARRIVE IN FRANCE

The Battle of the Frontiers

France had its own version of the Schlieffen Plan – Strategic Plan XVII. This was predicated upon France taking the initiative in the event of a European war by attacking Germany to the south. The objective was emotive: to recapture the territory of Alsace-Lorraine, which had been lost to Germany after the Franco-Prussian War in 1871. This had been foreseen by the Germans, who had positioned its forces to counter such a thrust.

Adhering to the principle of attack, the French commander, General Joffre, ordered the cavalry to charge the German lines, only to be met rather unsportingly by accurate and deadly fire from German infantry. The French infantry, wearing the same long blue coats and red trousers that their predecessors had worn forty years earlier, fared somewhat better, and by 7 August had re-captured the 'lost' territories of Alsace-Lorraine as the Germans obligingly fell back. The French prematurely celebrated the capture of Mulhouse before, six days later, the Germans launched a massive counter-attack and forced the French to retreat back across the frontier with their tails between their legs. This was a serious reverse that General Joffre sensibly hid, not just from the French public but from his political masters (Max Hastings, *Catastrophe*, pp.165–8).

Undeterred, on 11 August Joffre ordered a second major assault. Mulhouse was recaptured, but this time the local population was less enthusiastic, as they feared reprisals if and when the Germans returned. Again the Germans retreated, luring the French into a trap. On 20 August the Germans at last stood firm, fighting from prepared defensive positions against the attacking French forces. More than 40,000 French advanced over open ground to be greeted by murderous fire. The Germans pressed home their advantage and the French were once again forced to retreat. Successive attacks by the French along the frontier resulted in further heavy losses (Hastings, *Catastrophe*, pp.171–6).

By 23 August the Battle of the Frontiers, as it is now known, had ended. The French had expensively realised that all-out attack was not the answer. French casualties exceeded 250,000 men, of whom 75,000 had been killed. Remarkably, French morale did not collapse (Hastings, *Catastrophe*, p.199).

The Arrival of the British Expeditionary Force

The French had contributed to their misfortune through their Strategic Plan XVII, but by attacking the German positions to the south they had crucially left the route to the north open, allowing the German invasion force to move rapidly through Belgium and into France.

It is arguable, indeed probable, that had the BEF not been mobilised so rapidly to strengthen the French defences in the north then the German armies would have broken through and reached Paris in six weeks as planned, resulting in the collapse and surrender of France.

The BEF were mobilised at depots across Britain and taken by train to Southampton and then by ship to France, where they boarded French trains for transport to the battlefields. Officers travelled in passenger compartments in reasonable comfort, but the men were put into freight wagons which were labelled to carry '40 Hommes – 8 Chevaux'; they were more comfortable for the '*chevaux*' than the '*hommes*'. The wagons were cramped and unheated, the only saving grace being that they crawled along at 4mph or so and men could jump down and stretch their legs before they re-joined the train.

The Retreat from Mons

The BEF was soon in action, reaching the Belgian town of Mons where they were directed by the French commander to dig in along the banks of the canal to prevent the Germans crossing. Sir John French arrived to brief Haig and Smith-Dorrien, his two corps commanders, whom he helpfully advised to advance, hold the line or withdraw, as conditions demanded, before getting back into his car and driving away.

Surprisingly, no charges were laid to destroy the various bridges over the canal so that, despite facing a barrage of murderous rifle fire, advancing Germans were able to cross the canal, forcing the BEF to withdraw across the border into France. At Le Cateau, in a deliberate misunderstanding of his orders, General Sir Horace Smith-Dorrien, commanding II Corps, made a brave stand, for a while stemming the seemingly inexorable German advance, despite his flank becoming exposed by the untimely withdrawal of I Corps under the command of Haig. After determined resistance, II Corps was forced to join the general retreat (Gilbert, *First World War*, pp.59-60). Of the 80,000 British troops who had formed the first tranche of the BEF, 15,000 were casualties in the retreat from Mons, either killed, wounded or captured (Hastings, *Catastrophe*, p.257).

In *The Times* of 25 August, Arthur Moore wrote in the 'Mons Despatch', 'I have seen the broken bits of many regiments. We have to face the fact that the British Expeditionary Force, which bore the great weight of the blow, has suffered terrible losses and requires immediate and immense reinforcement.' After just three weeks of fighting, the harsh realisation of the immensity of the task ahead was revealed to Britons at home. Four days later the appeal by Kitchener for 100,000 more men was featured in *The Times*.

The First Battle of the Marne

Despite their fierce resistance, the BEF, together with French and Belgian forces, were forced by the advancing Germans to retreat to a new defensive position on the River Marne to protect Paris. The First Battle of the Marne, fought from 6-9 September, was critical in slowing the seemingly inexorable German advance. The French dug in, backed by their 75mm quick-firing field guns, which could fire up to twenty rounds a minute. The fighting was fierce, confused, desperate and bloody. Sergeant I.F. Bell of the 2nd Battalion Gordon Highlanders wrote of the attack:

On rushing the trench and leaping into it, I found that the dead were lying three deep ... I slipped into the rear of the trench, to cut across and meet the lads as they emerged from the communication trench, but had only gone about six yards when I received what in the regiment was called the 'dull thud.' I thought I had been violently knocked on the head, but, feeling I was not running properly, I looked down and discovered that my right foot was missing.

He was picked up by the advancing German soldiers and carried to a forward medical station where he was given aid. Although in great pain, he wrote of the scene around him:

All the way from the trench to the barn I saw British dead, mostly Highlanders – Black Watch, Camerons and Gordons – and as they lay there in their uniforms, I thought how young and lonely they looked.   (Quoted in Young, *Scottish Voices*, p.67)

The retreat continued until the Allied forces had been forced back to the River Aisne, where at last the retreat was stemmed and the Allies were able to launch a counter-attack. It was in this battle that the bravery of the Scottish regiments was first recognised with the award of two Victoria Crosses: the first to Private Ross Tollerton of the 1st Camerons for his courage in bringing a wounded officer to safety, despite being under fire and wounded himself, and the second to Private George Wilson, 2nd Highland Light Infantry, who captured single-handed a German machine-gun position (Trevor Royle, *The Flowers of the Forest*, p.62).

In the fighting so far, the casualties had been enormous – the French had lost half a million men, of whom 300,000 had been killed, while the Germans had lost nearly a quarter of a million men (Keegan, *First World War*, p.146).

The Germans now made one last effort to destroy the Allied defences and to open the road to Paris and victory. The plan chosen to break the stalemate was to outflank the Allied defences and cut the British off from the Channel ports, not just preventing the supply of essential reinforcements and equipment but also removing an escape route were the BEF to be defeated. A desperate race took place, the so-called 'Race to the Sea', as the German Army tried to outflank the Allied armies and the British forces raced to prevent them.

THE FIRST BATTLE OF YPRES
(19 OCTOBER–22 NOVEMBER 1914)

I told the men to keep under cover and detailed one man, Ginger Bain, as 'lookout.' After what seemed ages Ginger excitedly asked, 'How strong is the German army?'

I replied 'Seven million [sic].'

'Well,' said Ginger, 'here is the whole bloody lot of them making for us.'

Sergeant I.F. Bell, 2nd Battalion Gordon Highlanders. Quoted in Young, *Scottish Voices*, p.6.

The Germans sensed a weakness in the Allied lines near Ypres, a lovely old Flanders town about 30 miles east of Dunkirk. Here the BEF would face a massive German onslaught in the First Battle of Ypres, in what would prove to be a defining moment of the early part of the war.

When the BEF reached Ypres they were greeted by the sight of thousands of refugees fleeing the town. On 21 October the troops began to dig in, forming part of a trench network that would eventually stretch over 400 miles from the sea to the borders of Switzerland. The land around was low-lying, and over the months and years of the war the combination of persistent, heavy artillery bombardment, the constant movement of troops, their horses and motorised vehicles, and the incessant rain would turn it into a sea of mud. Death or severe injury was arbitrary and instantaneous. German shrapnel (artillery shells filled with balls of shot) would land in the trenches and then explode, scattering up to 400 metal balls which killed and maimed indiscriminately.

The remnants of the BEF were battle-scarred and exhausted, haggard and unshaven. And yet these mud-spattered men were the only Allied defence against the rampaging German Army. Defeat would deal a severe blow to both the Allied cause and to British morale and would leave France open to the invading German armies.

The Germans threw immense resources at the British defences, sending into battle large numbers of new and unblooded recruits, who suffered heavy losses in what became known in Germany as 'the massacre of the innocents'. On 30 October the London Scottish became the first Territorial battalion to go into action on the Messines Ridge. Seven hundred and fifty men, inspired by the pipes, attacked the German lines, but bravery was no defence against German machine guns and only 350 survived (Royle, *Flowers*, p.55).

On 31 October General Falkenhayn ordered the assault to be renewed. The Gordon Highlanders were amongst a number of British units that were virtually wiped out in the desperate rearguard action, as the British line held until a brave counter-attack by the men of the Worcestershire Regiment, charging with fixed bayonets towards the German lines, drove the German troops back and saved the day.

Fierce fighting continued through November, but by the end of the month both sides were exhausted and gratefully accepted the onset of winter, which brought a temporary pause to the fighting. The seemingly inexorable German advance had been halted, but the cost had been severe. The BEF had suffered 80,000 casualties – 16,000 killed, 48,000 wounded and a further 16,000 taken prisoner or missing – half of the 160,000 men of the BEF who had, by then, been despatched to France (Keegan, *First World War*, p.146).

The British had succeeded in repelling the attack, although outnumbered by the attacking German forces, and this superiority of defence over offence would continue until the last months of the war. Haig, however, believed the Germans had failed because they had not pushed hard enough and his conviction that victory would come to the side that persevered longest would influence his tactical thinking throughout the war, encouraging him to continue to attack long after the momentum had been lost.

As a side note, a young Austrian, believing that the merging of the two nationalities in the Austro-Hungarian Empire had tarnished the purity of Austrian nationality, had moved to Munich in 1913 at the outbreak of war and enlisted in a Bavarian regiment. He fought at the First Battle of Ypres and was awarded the Iron Cross, Second Class. He was later wounded at the Battle of the Somme and in 1918 was awarded the Iron Cross, First Class. His name would later become infamous – it was Adolf Hitler.

LIFE IN THE TRENCHES

The war on the Western Front now become static as the opposing German and Allied armies dug themselves into trenches separated by just 100–300yd of no man's land. The combined efforts of all the combatants would result in the construction of roughly 25,000 miles of trenches stretching from the Channel to the Swiss border, long enough to reach once around the world.

Siegfried Sassoon - A Working Party
Sassoon wrote his poem *A Working Party* on the front line during his first tour of duty in the trenches. He vividly portrayed the conditions in the trenches, the constant mud and water and the ever-present fear of death from a sniper through a moment's inattention or from the indiscriminate explosion of an artillery shell:

A Working Party

Three hours ago he blundered up the trench,
Sliding and poising, groping with his boots;
Sometime he tripped and lurched against the walls
With hands that pawed the sodden bags of chalk.
He couldn't see the man who walked in front;
Only he heard the drum and rattle of feet
Stepping along barred trench boards, often splashing
Wretchedly where the sludge was ankle-deep.

Voices would grunt 'Keep to your right – make way!'
When squeezing past some men from the front-line:
White faces peered, puffing a point of red;
Candles and braziers glinted through the chinks
And curtain-flaps of dug-outs; then the gloom
Swallowed his sense of sight; he stooped and swore
Because a sagging wire had caught his neck.

A flare went up; the shining whiteness spread
And flickered upward, showing nimble rats
And mounds of glimmering sand-bags, bleached with rain;
Then the slow silver moment died in dark
The wind came posting by with chilly gusts
And buffeting at corners, piping thin.
And dreary through the crannies; rifle-shots
Would split and crack and sing along the night,

And shells came calmly through the drizzling air
To burst with hollow bang below the hill.

Three hours ago he stumbled up the trench;
Now he will never walk that road again:
He must be carried back, a jolting lump
Beyond all need of tenderness and care.

He was a young man with a meagre wife
And two small children in a Midland town,
He showed their photographs to all his mates,
And they considered him a decent chap
Who did his work and hadn't much to say,
And always laughed at other people's jokes
Because he hadn't any of his own.

That night when he was busy on his job
Of piling bags along the parapet,
He thought how slow time went, stamping his feet
And blowing on his fingers, pinched with cold.
He thought of getting back by half-past twelve,
And tot of rum to send him warm to sleep
In draughty dug-out frowsty with the fumes
Of coke, and full of snoring weary men.

He pushed another bag along the top,
Craning his body outward; then a flare
Gave one white glimpse of No Man's Land and wire;
And as he dropped his head the instant split
His startled life with lead, and all went out

(Written 30 March 1916)

The construction of trenches reflected national stereotypes. The German trenches were well constructed and they had the advantage of choosing the line of their trench system, which was built with the primary purpose of protecting their defensive position. Accordingly, they used the lie of the land to best advantage, building on higher ground to provide a better field of fire against attacking troops (as an incidental benefit it also enabled better drainage, preventing the trenches from turning into a quagmire with the unremitting rain). The German trenches were usually deeper than those of the British, with extensive use of strengthening timber, and they were supported by shellproof, well-ventilated dugouts constructed out of reinforced concrete to give protection against artillery attack.

The Germans applied a scientific approach to the design of their trench system, often creating a second or third line of trenches to provide strength in depth. The trenches were built in a zigzag pattern, which meant a whole trench would not be vulnerable to crossfire if it was overrun. They also created a system of redoubts, which enabled withering enfilade fire from machine guns across the lines of any attacking forces. To complete the defences they used heavier gauge barbed wire, which proved resistant to British wire cutters and survived the artillery fire intended to 'cut the wire' before any attack. This combination made a decisive breakthrough by Allied troops through a frontal assault a virtual impossibility.

The French predictably sought more comfort, often furnishing their trenches with items plundered from the local houses to include such luxuries as beds, stoves and tables, and even, exceptionally, clocks and ornaments.

The first British trenches had been primitive, constructed on the premise that the trenches would only be occupied temporarily before a successful break through the German lines, and gave some protection against sniper fire but none against the German artillery shells – men could only huddle in the trenches waiting for the screech of the incoming shells. Later the British trench system consisted of three lines of trenches. The front face of the forward trench would have a fire 'step' and the sides were usually constructed of sandbags with duckboards laid on the floor. During daylight hours the constant threat of snipers made occupation of the front-line trenches hazardous and accordingly they would be lightly manned and only occupied in force at dawn and dusk, or if an attack was planned or an enemy attack anticipated.

From the forward or 'firing' trench, small trenches, known as 'saps', were driven towards the German lines to provide listening posts, grenade-throwing positions or machine-gun posts. The second line consisted of support trenches to which troops could withdraw when the front line was under bombardment, and the third line was occupied by the reserve force from which troops could launch a counter-attack if the front line of trenches was captured. The three lines were linked by communication trenches. Although excellent in theory, the whole system was, in practice, vulnerable to artillery attack.

Wilfred Owen - Asleep

Wilfred Owen's poem *Asleep*, which he wrote 'as from the trenches' while he was in Shrewsbury in 1917, gives a vivid picture of life – and death – in the trenches:

Asleep

Under his helmet, up against his pack,
After so many days of work and waking,
Sleep took him by the brow and laid him back.

There, in the happy no-time of his sleeping,
Death took him by the heart. There heaved a quaking
Of the aborted life within him leaping,
Then chest and sleepy arms once more fell slack.

And soon the slow, stray blood came creeping
From the intruding lead, like ants on track.

Whether his deeper sleep lie shaded by the shaking
Of great wings, and the thoughts that hung the stars,
High-pillowed on calm pillows of God's making,
Above these clouds, these rains, these sleets of lead,
And these winds' scimitars,
-Or whether yet his thin and sodden head
Confuses more and more with the low mould,
His hair being one with the grey grass
Of finished fields, and wire-scrags rusty-old,
Who knows? Who hopes? Who troubles? Let it pass!
He sleeps. He sleeps, less tremulous, less cold,
Than we who wake, and waking say Alas!

It is almost impossible to envisage what life was like for the British soldiers huddled in their trenches. Overarching everything would be the stench of death and decay. If an artillery shell landed in a trench its effect would be arbitrary; of two soldiers talking together, one could be blown to bits while the other survived. Men killed by artillery fire or the chance shot of a sniper would sometimes lie where they had fallen, so it was not unknown to find a man's arm or leg in the watery mud underneath the duckboard at the foot of the trench. Graves writes in *Goodbye to All That* (p.98) of the horrors of trench warfare:

June 9th. I am beginning to realize how lucky I was in my gentle introduction to the Cambrian trenches. We are now in a nasty salient, a little to the south of the brick-stacks, where casualties are always heavy. [A salient was a part of the trench protruding forward into no man's land and therefore threatened by enemy fire not just from the front but from both sides.] The company had seventeen casualties yesterday from bombs and grenades. The front trench averages thirty yards from the Germans. Today, at one part, which is only twenty yards away from an occupied German sap, I went along whistling 'The Farmer's Boy', to keep up my spirits, when suddenly I saw a group bending over a man lying at the bottom of the trench. He was making a snoring noise mixed with animal groans. At my feet lay the cap he had worn, splashed with his brains. I had never seen human brains before; I somehow regarded them as a poetical figment. One can joke with a badly-wounded man and congratulate him on being out of it. One can disregard a dead man. But even a miner can't make a joke that sounds like a joke over a man who takes three hours to die, after the top part of his head has been taken off by a bullet fired at twenty yards' range.

And above all, there was the mud. The water table in Flanders was often only 3ft or so below the surface and any drainage ditches or channels which had formerly drained the land were soon blocked or destroyed by artillery fire. As a result, part of the British trench system was often built above ground using a parapet of clay-filled sandbags. Sometimes the trenches had been built using existing drainage channels and sometimes they had been dug anew, but, in either case, when it rained the trench became waterlogged and filled with deep, enveloping mud. The winter cold was biting and exposure was a killer as the temperature fell well below zero. Thirst was always a problem – water was carried to the front in petrol cans and the taste of petrol would even permeate through the brew-up of tea.

Private Thomas Williamson of the Royal Scots Fusiliers wrote movingly of being trapped and gradually sucked down into the quagmire of mud:

I went a few steps and suddenly my feet disappeared beneath the mud. I made valiant struggles to get out but the more I struggled, the deeper I sank. I was now beginning to panic as I realised like a flash of lightning that I was in a bog. The more I struggled the deeper I sank. Beads of perspiration were streaming down my face with my efforts to free myself. A terrible fear gripped my heart. I was now up to my knees and I knew I dare not try to struggle any more. I could feel the terrible suction around my feet ... What a death, what an end, to die and not get a fighting chance. Oh the agony of it; I was nearly mad. I was beginning to sink deeper. I was up to the waist, and I knew that I was now slowly but surely approaching my end.

I peered into the blackness, and at last a despairing thought came to me. I began to shout for help ... No answer came. I cried again to God: 'O God have mercy on me.' I shouted until I thought my lungs would burst. Then suddenly I saw a very small light, roughly speaking about two hundred yards away. I renewed my cry for help and I shouted until I was utterly exhausted. The lights then came nearer and I made a supreme effort to shout again.

I then heard a faint cry 'Hullo there, where are you?' They heard me – I was almost fainting. I looked up to where I knew God was in heaven and it was speechless thankfulness. I could not speak.

It was then that I saw dimly the figures of two men, with farm lamps. A rope came whizzing through the air; it dropped short but the second time it was just past my head, and I managed to get hold of it and put it round my body. I was dragged through the mud and stinking water with my head and face almost submerged. I was in such a state I could only stutter, 'thank you lads, you saved my life.' I had been rescued by two lads of the King's Liverpool Regiment.   (Quoted in Young, *Scottish Voices*, pp.113–14)

Williamson was lucky. Others were sucked inexorably down to die a dreadful death, gradually suffocated by the mud, their bodies submerged under a shroud of mud only to reappear later in some dreadful reincarnation.

Strangely, one of the greatest killers in the war was not the machine gun or the impersonal artillery shell but disease brought on either by the appalling conditions or by the infection of open wounds. Sanitary conditions in the trenches were worse than rudimentary. Latrines were basic, and dysentery, cholera and typhus were rampant. Antibiotics had not been discovered and the treatment of wounds was primitive. Trench foot, leading to gangrene and eventual amputation, was common. Feet would swell up to two or three times their size and would go completely dead. You could stick a bayonet into your foot and not feel a thing, but when – and if – the swelling went down the true agony began. Men would scream out with the pain, which was only alleviated when the foot or leg was amputated.

And there has been no mention of the rats and the lice. The trenches swarmed with rats, which devoured the detritus of battle. Men remained unwashed in the same clothes for many days, providing a fertile breeding ground for body lice, and infestation was common. The lice would lie in the seams of clothes and in the deep furrows of woolly pants and suck the blood of the soldiers as they tried to rest, providing constant and maddening irritation. The satisfaction of crushing one between your fingers brought only a temporary respite and the discovery of a new harvest of lice eggs in one's clothes was a harbinger of future misery.

Ewart Alan Mackintosh – Ode to a French Regiment
Mackintosh had a good sense of humour and wrote a number of lighter poems including his *Ode to a French Regiment*, which referred to taking over a trench from the French and 'finding they had left behind more Stores than we had bargained for' – the trench was infested with lice:

Ode to a French Regiment

Dear Allies, whom we were relieving,
    When we came to the line from our rest,
We came to you fondly believing
    You would take us and give us your best.
You gave us your wine in full measure,
    Your rum and your coffee was nice,
And as an additional pleasure
        You left us your lice.

Oh, lice full of vigour and beauty,
    That rove where the rich blood was spilt,
Do you really believe it your duty
    To make your abode in my kilt?
Do you honestly thing my suspender
    A fit place to take your repose,
And prey on your country's defenders
        Instead of her foes?

Are you really French vermin, I wonder,
   Or when the new trenches were won
Did they count in the tale of their plunder
   The fleas and the lice of the Hun?
Do no thoughts of my vengeance appal you
   When at night to the battle you rise,
Are you patriots, or shall I call you
         Mere traitors and spies?

Nay, then I shall slay you, preferring
   To think you the breed of the Boche,
Who leap from your trenches preparing
   To feed on the vitals of Tosh.
When the iron of the tailor is singeing
   The pleats of the kilt that was mine,
I like to think you will die singing
   The Watch on the Rhine.

[Mackintosh was known as 'Tosh' to his fellow officers and men.]

THE BATTLE OF THE FALKLANDS
(8 DECEMBER 1914)

Strangely, one of the few naval battles of the First World War took place
thousands of miles away in the South Atlantic, but its origins were even
further away – in the Far East. The German East Asiatic Squadron was sta-
tioned at its base at Tsingtao in China, which had been seized from China
in 1897 as part of Germany's policy of increasing its global reach. Germany
had a powerful fleet in the Far East, numerically equivalent to the Hong
Kong-based Far East Fleet of the Royal Navy, but with the addition of the
armoured cruisers *Scharnhorst* and *Gneisenau*, which were more modern
and better equipped.

   Britain had become concerned at the threat which Russia posed to its
empire and, in particular, to British interests in Central Asia and the Far
East, and therefore in 1902 had entered into a defensive alliance with
Japan which itself possessed a powerful navy, including fourteen battle-
ships. With the outbreak of war, Japan was seen as a powerful counter to

the perceived German threat in the Far East, and so on 6 August 1914 Sir Edward Grey asked the Japanese for naval support.

This was Japan's opportunity. It had long wanted to expand territorially and on 23 August Japan declared war on Germany and launched an attack on Tsingtao. In a startling precursor to the capture of Singapore in the Second World War – was the lesson not learnt? – the Germans had created strong defences to protect Tsingtao against attack from the sea but, rather unfairly, the Japanese attacked from the landward side through an amphibious landing in China. On 7 November the German garrison surrendered and, objective achieved, the Japanese went home.

The outcome was that the German fleet was deprived of its Far Eastern base, potentially critical at that time, as warships were still predominantly coal fired and required to call into coaling stations every eight to ten days to replenish fuel supplies. Vice Admiral Maximilian Graf von Spee decided he would make a virtue out of necessity and set course for South America to operate as a marauding battle squadron, threatening and destroying British shipping. He knew that Chile was favourably disposed towards Germany and would provide his ships with much-needed coal. Consequently, by the autumn of 1914 the German East Asia Squadron, comprising the armoured cruisers *Scharnhorst* and *Gneisenau* and three light cruisers *Nürnberg*, *Dresden* and *Leipzig*, was stationed off Chile.

The British South Atlantic Squadron, under the command of Rear Admiral Sir Christopher Cradock, set out in pursuit. The squadron consisted of the ageing battleship HMS *Canopus*, two armoured cruisers, HMS *Good Hope* and HMS *Monmouth*, and four light cruisers. The *Canopus*, with its 12in guns, was the only ship with sufficient firepower to threaten the German ships, but she was too slow and was left behind in the chase to find the German fleet.

Cradock located the German fleet on 1 November. The British had the sun behind them, and thus an advantage, but the advantage was lost when, crucially, von Spee stayed out of range of the British guns until the sun had set. Instead, the British ships were themselves highlighted against the red of the setting sun. Although severely outgunned – both of the German armoured cruisers had eight 8in guns, while only the *Good Hope* had guns that could match their range (and of these only two) – and facing ships with greater speed and with battle-hardened crews, Cradock, in the best Nelsonian tradition, ordered the fleet to attack. It proved a brave but foolhardy action, as the German fleet were able to stay out of the range of the British guns while mercilessly pounding the British armoured cruisers. Cradock died with the sinking of his flagship *Good Hope*, which was hit before she had fired her guns. HMS *Monmouth*, although badly holed, refused to surrender but was also destroyed when she was shelled at close quarters by the cruiser *Nürnberg*. Only HMS *Glasgow* managed to escape destruction and was able to warn HMS *Canopus*.

Although unsuccessful, the British action did in the end prove decisive, as it left the German fleet short of coal and ammunition. Von Spee made the fateful decision to assault Port Stanley in the Falklands to replenish his stocks from the coaling station and ammunition store on the islands – fateful, because he erroneously assumed the islands were undefended, but the Royal Navy had got there first. Reinforcements had been despatched from the Grand Fleet to deal with this irritation in the South Atlantic. These comprised the battlecruisers HMS *Inflexible* and HMS *Invincible*, armed with eight 12in guns and capable of 25 knots, the armoured cruisers HMS *Carnarvon*, HMS *Cornwall* and HMS *Kent*, and the light cruiser HMS *Bristol*. They were joined by HMS *Glasgow* and HMS *Canopus*.

With this change in relative strengths, the German admiral had to make a rapid alteration to his plan and the German fleet fled westward, pursued by the British battlecruisers, which had a 5-knot advantage in speed over the German ships. Within three hours they were in range and able to open fire on the fleeing Germans. Despite closing to within range of their guns, the German ships were outgunned and outfought; the *Scharnhorst* and *Gneisenau* were both sunk, as were the *Nürnberg* and the *Leipzig*. Only the *Dresden* escaped, until she too was sunk in March 1915.

The German fleet was destroyed, and with it went the threat from the marauding von Spee and his squadron; the Royal Navy had confirmed its control of the ocean. Germany's campaign to destroy Britain's Merchant Fleet and prevent the supply of vital food and resources now depended upon the German U-boat fleet. Ironically, despite this defeat the name of the German vice admiral was commemorated in the pocket battleship *Admiral Graf Spee*, which was scuttled in Montevideo Bay in the Second World War after being trapped by the British ships HMS *Ajax*, HMS *Achilles* and HMS *Exeter* in the Battle of the River Plate.

THE CHRISTMAS TRUCE
(24 DECEMBER 1914)

The ordinary soldier knew quite well in his heart that at bottom Fritz was much such another as himself.

Captain E.C. Crosse, senior chaplain on the Western Front. Quoted in Malcolm Brown, *The IWM Book of the First World War*, p.81.

The war was 5 months old and the two armies had reached stalemate; the fighting troops were locked in their trenches, mired in mud, cold and frightened and separated only by a few yards of no man's land. Was there, in truth, much separating the soldiers who manned the German and the Allied trenches?

It was generally accepted that there could be no new offensive until the spring and as a result the edge had been taken off the fierce tempo of earlier fighting. Soldiers in the opposing armies experienced the same hardships and in some parts of the line this shared suffering created a feeling of empathy between the soldiers.

It was with this background that the almost unbelievable happened. It was Christmas Eve 1914; there was a hard frost and the ground was frozen. Men's breath blew clouds in the cold air. The night was still and quiet and the normally persistent smell of rotting flesh from the corpses in no man's land faded in the chill. In the German trenches, a few flickering lights from the candles that had been placed on improvised Christmas trees could be seen. Schnapps and cigarettes were cautiously exchanged with the British. And then in the still, cold air, a single voice was heard:

> Stille Nacht! Heilige Nacht!
> Alles schlaft; einsam wacht
> Nur das traute hoch heilige Paar.
> Holder Knab'im lockigen Haar,
> Schlafe in himmlischer Ruh!
> Schlafe in himmlischer Ruh!

> Silent Night! Holy Night!
> All is calm, all is bright,
> Round yon Virgin Mother and Child!

> Holy Infant, so tender and mild,
> Sleep in heavenly peace!
> Sleep in heavenly peace!

The British soldiers responded with 'The First Noel' and 'O Come All Ye Faithful', in which the Germans joined singing the Latin version, '*Adeste Fideles*'.

Christmas Day saw an unofficial truce with both sides moving in full view of each other. Tradition records that in one section of the front a Seaforth Highlander produced a football and, using hats or helmets for goalposts, an informal football match took place. The result is not known, but fortunately the impromptu match was not decided on penalties! Sergeant Saunders of the 6th Battalion Gordon Highlanders wrote:

> Christmas Day in the trenches! And of all extraordinary days, it took the bis-cuit. An order was passed along the line not to shoot. A few minutes later I saw the Germans getting up out of their trenches. I was with the Captain and the Colonel. We rushed along to see the men didn't shoot and found our men getting out of the trenches as well, and I'm dashed if they didn't walk out, meet the Germans and stand shaking hands and chatting to them like old friends. On Christmas and Boxing Days we wandered about all over in full view of the Germans. It all seemed most peculiar.

In some parts of the line the impromptu truce continued. Sergeant Saunders described New Year's Eve:

> There was no firing until midnight or thereabouts when a few volleys were fired into the air to welcome in the New Year. We got a crowd together and sang 'Auld Lang Syne' and 'God Save the King'. The Germans sang some songs and played 'God Save the King' on the mouth organ and everyone shouted 'Happy New Year!' Then the Pipe Major came along and played; he had come down especially. We fortunately were able to give him a drop of rum. This morning the men are wandering about all over getting brown bread and other things from the Germans. It doesn't look as if they are short of food.

He continued:

And so the days went on till the afternoon of 3rd January, when a German Officer and an orderly approached our lines and enquired for an officer. I heard the request and scrambling out of the trench I went out to meet them. We saluted and the orderly acting as interpreter informed me that higher command had given orders for the normal conditions of war to be resumed ... Only a few stray shots were fired that day, but orders for volley fire were received next day and along the line from the 2nd Gordons through the 6th Gordons a ripple of fire spread like a 'feu-de-joie,' the muzzles of the rifles in approved text book fashion being held well in the air.   (Quoted in Young, *Scottish Voices*, pp.69-70)

The military top brass feared this spirit of fraternisation could spread and on Boxing Day the General Staff, British 7th Division, 'issued orders saying that such unwarlike activity must cease' (*Gun Fire: A Journal of First World War History*, quoted in Gilbert, *First World War*, p.119). The generals were right to be worried. The war might come to an unofficial end, and what would *that* do for the generals' careers?

The extraordinary truce was over. The natural humanity of the men serving in the front-line trenches was overridden by the commands of those safely situated well behind the lines.

Ewart Alan Mackintosh - Carol of the Innocents

In his poem, which had been written on Christmas Eve 1913, Mackintosh contrasts the joyful news of Christ's birth with the horror of the Slaughter of the Innocents ordered by King Herod to eradicate the perceived threat from the birth of the holy baby destined to become the King of the Jews. It could just as well relate to the slaughter of millions of innocent men in a needless war:

Carol of the Innocents

As I look upon the sky
And watch the clouds come driving by,
I know when for a moment's space
I see a laughing baby's face,
It is the Innocents that ride
Across the sky at Christmastide.

Above the world they dance and play,
And they are happy all the day,
And welcome on the joyous morn
A little king among the born.
God looks upon them as they go,
And laughs to see them frolic so.

Their little clouds are stained with red
To show how shamefully they bled,
And all above the world they sing
A carol to their childish king.
It is the Innocents that ride
Across the sky at Christmastide.

AUSTRIA'S WARS

For the Austrians, events did not go well. Despite its militaristic ambitions Austria was poorly prepared for war. Their army was ill-trained and inadequately equipped, with outdated field artillery and without a pool of trained reservists who could be conscripted into the conflict. It was only fit for the purpose of a Balkan war.

This was the key flaw in Austria's strategy, which was based on the hypothesis that Austria could concentrate all its resources upon a regional war against Serbia assuming that, as had happened before, Russia would stand aside from the conflict. Russia had, however, built up its military forces and was prepared to flex its muscles in support of the Slav peoples.

Austria had a fall-back plan if Russia did declare war and that was to rely upon Germany to protect its eastern flank. This was in direct conflict with the Schlieffen Plan, which required Germany to concentrate its forces in a pre-emptive strike against France before Russia had time to mobilise and only to attack Russia after the defeat of France.

Nevertheless, following the expiry of its 'impossible' ultimatum, and confident in the support of Germany, on 28 July Austria recklessly declared war on Serbia. As a direct consequence, Russia gave the order to mobilise its armies on 30 July. Austria was now faced with fighting on two fronts, not one, and this conflicted not just with its military capacity but with the mobilisation of its armies that had been focused on an invasion of Serbia.

The Austrian Campaign Against Serbia

The Austrian command was, as a result of Russia's intervention, forced to split its forces, despatching the Austrian 5th Army, supported by the 6th, to attack Serbia. The Austrians were not only outnumbered but badly commanded and were fighting a Serbian Army battle-hardened from the Balkan Wars. Despite these shortcomings, the Austrians fought their way to Belgrade, which was captured on 2 December, but only at an immense cost.

The Austrians were determined to deliver a punishing blow to the Serbs and waged the war with an unprecedented ferocity, killing not only soldiers but also unarmed civilians – men, women and children – in a brutal foretaste of the Nazi atrocities in the Second World War. Victims were shot, bayoneted or even locked into barns and burnt alive. John Reed, an American war correspondent, wrote of the Austrian occupation of Sabac:

> The soldiers were loosed like wild beasts in the city, burning, pillaging and raping. We saw the gutted Hotel d'Europe and the blackened and mutilated church where three thousand men, women and children were penned together without food or water for four days, and then divided into two groups – one sent back to Austria as prisoners of war, the others driven ahead of the army as it marched south against the Serbians.   (Quoted in Gilbert, *First World War*, p.111)

The Serbians fought a fierce, defensive battle and as the weather worsened the Austrians, whose 6th Army had already been destroyed and the 5th under pressure, were forced to withdraw, leaving 60,000 Austrians behind as prisoners of the Serbs. The expedition to punish the Serbs had turned into a massive self-inflicted disaster, brought about by the incompetence of the Austrian military commanding a poorly trained army with outdated equipment that was ill-suited to the demands of modern warfare.

The Austrian Campaign Against Russia

Austria, somewhat ambitiously, had simultaneously invaded Russia to get its retaliation in before Russia had fully mobilised, and to capture a part of Russian territory (now Poland) which acted as a 'wedge' between Germany and Austria-Hungary. This proved a costly mistake.

The war soon exposed the deficiencies in the Austrian military. Its army had very little artillery, their rifles were obsolete and whereas the other combatants had embraced the transport opportunities offered by the railways, Austria still relied on tried and tested horse-drawn carts.

The two armies met at Lemberg, now Lvov in Poland, and fought to a standstill. The Russians now played their trump card, a second army, but in a farcical absence of secure communication the Russian signals were sent unencrypted, enabling the Austrian commander Conrad von Hötzendorf to learn of the impending arrival of the second Russian army and get his retreat in first. Men and horses which had toiled away dragging all the Austrian guns and equipment in the optimistic invasion of Russian territory just a few weeks before now had to drag them back through heavy mud to their native Austria.

Within just four months Austria had been virtually destroyed as a fighting entity, with casualties reaching an astonishing 957,000 men, over twice the army's pre-war strength (Strachan, *First World War*, p. 31). Austria had suffered not one but two humiliating defeats, and without its German ally the war for Austria would have been over.

THE RUSSIAN CAMPAIGN

The Russians were the first to make a move, mobilising not in six weeks, as the Schlieffen Plan had assumed, but in ten days an immense army of 4.5 million men with a further 2 million in reserve – an army strong enough, they believed, to crush the German forces. On 19 August 1914 they launched a two-pronged attack around the Masurian Lakes to encircle the German forces. The downside with this plan was that by so doing the Russians fatally divided their forces.

The Russian 1st Army in the north advanced into Germany where it comprehensively defeated the outnumbered German forces in the Battle of Gumbinnen, using artillery to mow down the German troops as they advanced in line across open ground. The Germans were forced to pull back, but Russian commander General Rennenkampf, spurred on by military success but short of essential supplies, failed to press home the advantage.

In the south, General Samsonov, who commanded the Russian 2nd Army, also advanced into German territory as the second arm of the pincer. He learnt of the success of the Russian 1st Army and determined to cut off the defeated Germans to complete a historic victory. In a desperate move, the ineffective German commander, General Prittwitz, was summarily removed and replaced by 60-year-old General Paul von Hindenburg, with Erich Ludendorff as his Chief of Staff. The Germans learnt of the movement of the Russian forces through the interception of unencrypted military messages and rapidly responded to the threat by drafting in extra troops.

The first day's fighting on 24 August was fierce. In the evening the German centre withdrew, encouraging the overconfident Samsonov to resume the attack the next day by advancing in the centre, only to receive withering German fire from both flanks. The German 8th Army finally destroyed the Russian 2nd Army with a massive artillery assault on 27 August in a battle that the Germans called the Battle of Tannenberg, in somewhat belated revenge for the defeat in 1410 of the Teuton Knights by the Poles near the village of that name. By 30 August, 90,000 Russian troops had been captured and a further 50,000 killed or wounded. General Samsonov killed himself rather than live with the disgrace of defeat (Keegan, *First World War*, p.163).

The German troops were now rapidly loaded onto trains and transported north to confront the Russian 1st Army, attacking them on 5 September in the Battle of the Masurian Lakes. Once again the Russians suffered a horrendous defeat as their troops retreated in panic, many to die in the swamps surrounding the lakes. Another 100,000 Russian soldiers were killed, wounded or captured. In less than a month, the Russians had lost a quarter of a million men. The war was barely a month old.

5 ACT TWO: THE WAR IN 1915

THE WESTERN FRONT

By the beginning of 1915 the BEF had sufficiently expanded to be reorganised into the 1st Army commanded by Haig, the 2nd Army commanded by Smith-Dorrien and a cavalry division commanded by Allenby, but the British forces remained small in comparison with the forces of France and Germany. Sir John French recognised the virtual impossibility of breaking through the enemy defences without substantial reinforcements, instead adopting a defensive posture to protect his army from further losses. The French persisted with Gallic enthusiasm in their policy of daring all-in attack, losing 50,000 men in February and March for the gain of just 500yd.

Neuve Chapelle

Encouraged by the arrival of significant numbers of Canadian and Indian troops and not to be outdone in futility, Sir John French decided that a victory was necessary, if not for the war then certainly for his career, and on 10 March launched an attack at Neuve Chapelle using the newly arrived Indian Expeditionary Force. The key to success would be speed and surprise, with the attack preceded by an intense thirty-five-minute artillery bombardment to soften the enemy position before the advancing British and Indian troops would break through the German lines.

The battle was movingly described by Corporal Alex Thompson, 4th Battalion Black Watch:

> There was a silence – a few guns fired – then – with a roar that shook the earth – every gun in the district opened fire. The crash of that awful salvo must have struck terror into the hearts of the enemy even more than to us who were more or less prepared for it. Daylight was beginning to strengthen

and we could see the fresh troops that had been brought up, making ready to go forward to the attack. Still the awful roar of countless guns continued and indeed to me it seemed it would never stop.

He goes on to describe the attack:

The [Seaforth] Highlanders went forward in three long, straight lines. There was no sign of haste – it might have been a parade ground instead of the bloodiest battle-field of the war. A whistle blew and down went every man flat on the ground. A few seconds elapsed then another whistle went and as one man the Seaforths rose once more and swept towards the battered and broken German lines, disappearing shortly in the edge of the wood.   (Quoted in Young, *Scottish Voices*, p.117)

After four hours of fierce fighting the village of Neuve Chapelle was captured and the German trenches were overpowered, but the attacking troops then came under fire from the left flank where the German forces had been spared the artillery bombardment. To reinforce this initial success it was imperative that it be supported by a second wave but, unbelievably, this decision could not be made on the battlefield and had to be referred up the chain of command from battalion to brigade to division to headquarters and then back again, and this in the days before effective radio communication when orders could only be transmitted by runner. Vital hours were therefore wasted before the second wave of men were sent in, by which time the early initiative was lost and, crucially, the Germans had been given time to bring in reserves.

The British artillery was now running out of shells, the advance had lost its impetus and darkness was coming. French blamed his failure to reinforce the initial breakthrough on the lack of shells and wrote a letter to his mistress (war was not allowed to encroach upon his recreational pastimes) complaining that any spare shells and men were being sent to Gallipoli, that Kitchener was incompetent and should be sacked, and that his French allies were subject to unpredictable interference by the politicians. In truth, the main reason for the eventual failure of the assault had been the absence of effective and rapid communication between the front and headquarters and the resultant loss of critical time. A salient 2,000yd wide and 1,200yd deep had been captured. The cost: 7,000 British and 4,000 Indian casualties.

This would be one of the last occasions on which Indian troops were used in action on the Western Front, although they fought at Festubert and Loos. They were considered unsuited to the demands of Flanders, but would later serve with distinction in Mesopotamia in a form of warfare more appropriate to their traditions.

Murdo Murray - *The Dead in the Field*

Murdo Murray was born in 1890 on the island of Lewis. He enlisted in the 4th Seaforth Highlanders when war broke out and crossed to France in February 1915. His first taste of war was at the Battle of Neuve Chapelle, when his battalion of the Seaforth Highlanders suffered heavy casualties in the first two days. He wrote in Gaelic and in English:

Na Mairbh san Raoin
(The Dead in the Field)

Eagerly they went across the fields of strife
   Who lie there stretched in everlasting quiet;
Warm was the tender breath of love from their heart's wealth
   Before death's black deluge flooded and engulfed it.
In obeisance to those who fell in the battle's heat,
   Beside them quietly, silently dig a grave
And in their battle attire there bury them
   Where they fell down, death to the enemy in their cry.
Silently lift them, who won fame for glorious deeds,
   And with fond regard lay down their heads in the rest
Time will not end through the eternity of their course;
   Close up the dwelling, and leave the lovely daisy
To sing their virtue in the sweet breath of wind;
   And raise a cross as a memorial over warriors gone.

THE WEAPONS OF WAR

Artillery Shells

The most frightening weapon, and that which inflicted the most casualties, was the artillery shell that would arrive virtually without warning and could burst asunder both the trench in which a soldier was sheltering and his best mate to whom he was talking. A conventional shell would be heard coming and gave about two seconds to take avoiding action, but the so-called 'whizz-bangs' arrived virtually without warning, leaving blackened flesh, scattered body parts and a blood-lined trench. Seventy per cent of casualties were caused by artillery.

Lieutenant Sotheby of the Argyll and Sutherland Highlanders, but attached to the Black Watch, wrote movingly of the effect of German shrapnel:

> So terrific is the explosion that at forty feet up, each shrapnel bullet makes a hole as big as a cricket ball in the ground. It contains over four hundred bullets usually ... One shell fell close to our Sergeant Major who was going to put up a notice for a trench. He heard the shell coming, crouched up against the trench, but it burst only ten yards from him, and the poor chap received most of the effect of it. I won't describe his condition. The other shells buried several and a piece of one entered a dug out and tore one man's side clean away. He died without a murmur, I believe ... the other two fellows we dug up after ten minutes from their entombment. They were a ghastly sight from not being able to breathe ... another man received from one of the shells a large piece right into his stomach, it doubled him up. He too will die, I'm afraid.   (Quoted in Young, *Scottish Voices*, pp.92–3)

Shortage of shells was a perennial complaint of the British High Command and indeed of all the combatants. In Britain it would, in time, indirectly lead to the fall of the Asquith government.

The Machine Gun

The Maxim gun was invented by Sir Hiram Maxim in 1894 as an improvement on the earlier Gatling gun. His invention became an instant success and many countries, including Germany, manufactured the Maxim gun under licence, ironically from the British Vickers company. The British Army was slow to adopt the machine gun – perhaps it was seen as an ungentlemanly way of killing when compared with the glamour of a cavalry charge – and initially battalions were limited to just two machine guns.

Conversely, Germany had immediately recognised the significance of the new invention and had 12,000 when the war began. They had studied the use of the machine gun in battle, determining it was most effective if used to provide enfilading fire. Machine guns would be set up on each flank of the ground over which attacking troops were advancing and would fire in an arc, creating a murderous 'killing zone'. A German soldier described the ensuing slaughter of a British attack advancing in line abreast:

> We were very surprised to see them walking. We had never seen that before ... The officers went in front. I noticed one of them walking calmly, carrying a walking stick. When we started firing we just had to load and reload. They went down in their hundreds. You didn't have to aim. We just fired into them.   (Quoted in Roberts (ed.), *Minds at War*, p. 118)

The Sniper

The ever-present danger was being shot by an enemy sniper. One instant of inattention, one moment of looking over the parapet or not keeping down when crossing the communication trenches and that moment could be your last. In *Goodbye to All That* (p.83), Graves wrote of his first time in the trenches and of his particular dislike of rifle fire:

> The guide gave us hoarse directions all the time. 'Hole right.' 'Wire high.' 'Deep place here, sir.' 'Wire low.' The field-telephone wires had been fastened by staples to the side of the trench, and when it rained the staples were constantly falling out and the wire falling down and tripping people up. If it sagged too much, one stretched it across the trench to the other side to correct the sag, but then it would catch one's head.
>
> We now came under rifle-fire, which I found more trying than shellfire. The gunner, I knew, fired not at people but at map-references – crossroads, likely artillery positions, houses that suggested billets for troops, and so on. Even when an observation officer in an aeroplane or on a church spire directed the guns, it seemed random, somehow. But a rifle-bullet, even when fired blindly, always seemed purposely aimed. And whereas we could usually hear a shell approaching, and take some sort of cover, the rifle-bullet gave no warning at all.

W.D. Cocker - The Sniper

The single shot from a trained sniper could cause a mother to lose her son, a wife her husband or a girl her sweetheart. Its effect was arbitrary and impersonal, as W.D. Cocker's poem emphasises. Cocker was born in Rutherglen and had worked before the war for the *Daily Record*. He was 32 when war broke out and initially served with the 9th Highland Infantry and then from 1915 with the Royal Scots. He was taken prisoner in 1917. He wrote of his experiences as a prisoner of war, but is best remembered for his poem *The Sniper*:

The Sniper

Two hundred yards away he saw his head;
    He raised his rifle, took quick aim and shot him.
Two hundred yards away the man dropped dead;
With bright exulting eye he turned and said,
    'By Jove, I got him!'
And he was jubilant; had he not won
    The meed of praise his comrades haste to pay?
He smiled; he could not see what he had done;
    The dead man lay two hundred yards away.
He could not see the dead reproachful eyes,
    The youthful face which Death had not defiled
But he had transfigured when he claimed his prize.
    Had he seen this perhaps he had not smiled.
He could not see the woman as she wept
    To hear the news two hundred miles away,
Or through his every dream she would have crept,
    And into all his thoughts by night and day.
Two hundred yards away, and bending o'er
    A body in a trench, rough men proclaim
Sadly, that Fritz, the merry, is no more.
    (Or shall we call him Jack? It's all the same.)

THE SECOND BATTLE OF YPRES
(22 APRIL–27 MAY 1915)

On the Western Front both armies still believed that a powerful thrust would break the stalemate, create a gap in the enemy lines and lead to ultimate victory. For the Germans, the best opportunity of achieving a breakthrough was thought to be at Ypres where, if the Allied lines could be broken, a way would be opened for their forces to reach Paris and defeat the French.

At daybreak on 22 April the Germans launched the assault, beginning with a massive German bombardment on the French lines, after which a greenish fog was seen drifting across the battlefield carried by the gentle winds blowing from the German lines. This was Germany's secret new weapon – chlorine gas – which was released as the taps were opened on 6,000 canisters of liquid chlorine. Gas, the Germans believed, would break the stalemate.

The chlorine rolled across the battlefield until it reached the French lines where Algerian troops fighting in the French Army were the first to experience the horror of a gas attack. The effect was immediate and dramatic. Soldiers fought for breath as the chlorine stripped the lining from the victim's lungs, choking him as he tried desperately and agonisingly to breathe. A day later the Germans released more gas, this time against Canadian troops fighting with the French. The results were just as immediate and just as horrific. The Germans, wearing primitive gas masks, then advanced through the gap that had opened in the Allied lines but, crucially, did not press home their advantage. On 24 April a further gas attack was launched, this time against British troops.

The Use of Gas

Chlorine was easy to detect through its colour and characteristic smell, but it was brutally effective, severely damaging the lungs. The symptoms were a splitting headache, a terrific thirst and the coughing-up of a greenish froth; the victim either died or suffered permanent lung damage. Phosgene, first used in December 1915, was far more lethal than chlorine and, smelling of musty hay, was harder to detect. But the most effective was mustard gas, introduced by the Germans in July 1917. Mustard gas was hard to detect and would linger over the battlefield, causing casualties over a longer period. Although not always fatal, it caused horrendous yellow blisters and inflamed the respiratory system, leaving the victims in such pain that they often had to be strapped to their beds until death came as a release.

The use of gas released from cylinders suffered from the drawback that its effectiveness was subject to the vagaries, and more particularly the direction, of the wind and it was later delivered using artillery shells. It is estimated that in the latter part of the war one in four of all shells fired contained gas.

The use of gas offended the basic principles of humanity but was symptomatic of the depths to which the combatants would sink in order to gain an edge and to win the struggle. Its effects were both physical and psychological.

Counter-Attack

Sir John French ordered his commander, General Smith-Dorrien, to counter-attack to reclaim the ground lost, but Smith-Dorrien demurred as the Canadians had suffered horrific losses. French was incandescent, accused Smith-Dorrien of defeatism and ordered a counter-attack. Fifteen thousand British and Indian troops died.

On 27 May the Second Battle of Ypres ended.

Walter Scott Stuart Lyon - I Tracked a Dead Man Down a Trench

Walter Lyon was born in North Berwick and educated at Balliol College, Oxford, before becoming an advocate. He enlisted in 1914 as a lieutenant in the 9th Battalion, Royal Scots. Lyon was killed during the Second Battle of Ypres.

I Tracked a Dead Man Down a Trench

I tracked a dead man down a trench,
    I knew not he was dead.
They told me he had gone that way,
    And there his foot-marks led.

The trench was long and close and curved,
    It seemed without an end;
And as I threaded each new bay
    I thought to see my friend.

I went there stooping to the ground.
    For, should I raise my head,
Death watched to spring; and how should then
    A dead man find the dead?

At last I saw his back. He crouched
    As still as still could be,
And when I called his name aloud
    He did not answer me.

The floor-way of the trench was wet
    Where he was crouching dead:

The water of the pool was brown,
    And round him it was red.

I stole up softly where he stayed
    With head hung down all slack,
And on his shoulders laid my hands
    And drew him gently back.

And then, as I had guessed, I saw
    His head, and how the crown –
I saw then why he crouched so still,
    And why his head hung down.

THE EASTERN FRONT

Germany had recognised that the war on the Western Front had reached a stalemate and the decision was made to strengthen their defensive system. The first line of the German trenches had been deliberately positioned on high ground to give an effective field of fire, with the second line constructed on the reverse slope and thus protected from the Allied artillery. Three miles was considered the psychological and physical limit that attacking infantry could reach, encumbered as they were by heavy battle gear, and Falkenhayn therefore ordered the construction of a second defensive line of trenches 3 miles behind the front line, where reserves would be in place to launch a counter-attack should the front line be penetrated by enemy attack.

Siegfried Sassoon – Counter-Attack
Written in 1917 while at Craiglockhart, and based on a draft written in July 1916, Sassoon graphically describes such a counter-attack:

Counter-Attack

We'd gained our first objective hours before
While dawn broke like a face with blinking eyes,
Pallid, unshaved and thirsty, blind with smoke.
Things seemed all right at first. We held their line,
With bombers posted, Lewis guns well placed,

And clink of shovels deepening the shallow trench.
 The place was rotten with dead; green clumsy legs
 High-booted, sprawled and grovelled along the saps
 And trunks, face downward, in the sucking mud,
 Wallowed like trodden sand-bags loosely filled;
 And naked sodden buttocks, mats of hair,
 Bulged, clotted heads slept in the plastering slime.
 And then the rain began, – the jolly old rain!

A yawning soldier knelt against the bank,
Staring across the morning blear with fog;
He wondered when the Allemands would get busy;
And then, of course, they started with five-nines
Traversing, sure as fate, and never a dud.
Mute in the clamour of shells he watched them burst
Sprouting dark earth and wire with gusts from hell,
While posturing giants dissolved in drifts of smoke.
He crouched and flinched, dizzy with galloping fear,
Sick for escape, – loathing the strangled horror
And butchered, frantic gestures of the dead.

An officer came blundering down the trench:
'Stand-to and man the fire-step!' On he went ...
Gasping and bawling, 'Fire-step ... counter-attack!'

Then the haze lifted. Bombing on the right
Down the old sap: machine guns on the left;
And stumbling figures looming out in front.
'O Christ, they're coming at us!' Bullets spat,
And he remembered his rifle ... rapid fire ...
And started blazing wildly ... then a bang
Crumpled and spun him sideways, knocked him out
To grunt and wriggle: none heeded him; he choked
And fought the flapping veils of smothering gloom,
Lost in a blurred confusion of yells and groans ...
Down, and down, and down, he sank and drowned,
Bleeding to death. The counter-attack had failed.

Germany Transfers its Attention to the Eastern Front

With the Western Front protected by this strong defensive network, Germany could concentrate her powerful war machine upon the Russians with the objective of delivering a knockout blow that would force Russia to come to the table for peace talks, taking her out of the war. Germany, secure on its Eastern Front, could then devote all its energy and resources to defeating the Allied troops on the Western Front.

Fourteen German divisions and 1,000 heavy artillery guns were moved across the country by troop trains to link with the Austrian forces. The Russian troops were poorly led and poorly armed – there were not enough rifles, so soldiers would have to arm themselves with the rifles of dead comrades – and they had little enthusiasm for the war. On 1 May 1915, after an intense bombardment including gas shells, the German Army broke through the Russian lines in the centre. Within a week the Russians had suffered 70,000 men killed or wounded, with another 140,000 taken prisoner (Strachan, *First World War*, p.139).

The Germans under Hindenburg then launched a massive two-pronged pincer attack to entrap the retreating Russian Army, but the long supply line – the Germans had no access to a rail network – meant that each time the jaws of the trap sprang shut the Russians managed to escape. By mid October the Russians had retreated 300 miles and their total losses since May totalled 1.4 million men, of whom more than half had been taken prisoner – an indication of the poor state of morale amongst the Russian soldiers (Strachan, *First World War*, p.139). The scale of the retreat added to Russia's problems, as huge numbers of guns and artillery shells were captured by the Germans leaving the Russian Army desperately short. But each mile they retreated was left devastated, therefore denying the advancing Germans vital food and supplies.

Paradoxically, the speed and extent of the German success prevented them from achieving their objective of enforcing peace upon the Russians as the German supply lines were too long to support the immense forces needed to protect the territory they had won.

Marina Tsvetayeva – A White Low Sun

The despair of the Russian people is captured in the poem *A White Low Sun* by Marina Tsvetayeva, a Russian poet who asks why so many must die:

A White Low Sun

A white low sun, low thunderclouds; and back
Behind the kitchen-garden's white wall, graves.
On the sand, serried ranks of straw-stuffed forms
As large as men, hang from some cross-beam.

Through the staked fence, moving about, I see
A scattering: of soldiers, trees and roads;
And an old woman standing by her gate
Who chews on a black hunk of bread with salt.

What have these grey huts done to anger you,
My God? And why must so many be killed?
A train passed, wailing, and the soldiers wailed
As its retreating path got trailed with dust.

Better to die, or not to have been born,
Than hear that plaining, piteous convict wail
About these beautiful dark eyebrowed women.
It's soldiers who sing these days. O Lord God.

(Translated from Russian by David McDuff and Jon Silkin)

The Russian Counter-Attack

The Russians were now fighting to protect their motherland and their resistance stiffened. During the winter the Russians regrouped, conscripting huge numbers of peasant farmers to replace the troops who had been lost. Essential supplies of food were delivered to the troops, but at the expense of harsh suffering amongst the civilian population, with food shortages causing simmering discontent. Britain provided Russia with urgently needed military equipment, including 1,000 aeroplanes and aeroplane engines, 250 artillery guns, 27,000 machine guns and 1 million rifles together with ammunition and explosives (Gilbert, *First World War*, p.108).

In the spring of 1916 Russia was asked by the Allies to launch an attack upon the German armies in the east in order to create a diversion that would be synchronised with the planned Allied attack on the Somme. Accordingly, in June 1916 the Russians, under Brusilov, made a surprise attack on the Austrian lines. After an intense bombardment the Russian Army broke through and advanced deep into occupied territory, recovering western Ukraine and even securing a foothold in the Austro-Hungarian Empire. The strategic impact was immense; the Germans were forced to send further men to their eastern front and the command structure was changed, with Ludendorff being given control not just of the German forces on the Eastern Front but also of the Austro-Hungarian troops.

However, this last foray proved to be the death rattle of the Russian war effort. The Russian people, starved and disillusioned, had lost the will to fight and political events would now dominate, eventually leading to the overthrow of the tsar in March 1917.

ITALY (EVENTUALLY) ENTERS THE WAR (23 MAY 1915)

Life in the trenches, though hard, is nothing compared to an assault. The assault is what makes war a calamity. For a soldier, death is a normal event and you are not afraid to die. But the awareness of imminent death, the certainty that death is inevitable, make the hours leading up to an assault a tragedy.

Emilio Lussu, *A Soldier on the Southern Front*, translated by Gregory Conti, p.129.

Italy, although a member with Germany and Austria of the Triple Alliance, had prevaricated. The Italian government, guided by the shrewd and experienced 70-year-old Giovanni Giolitti, did not want war as they feared, with justification, that the Italian Army was not trained or equipped to fight a modern war.

A few firebrands, led by Benito Mussolini with his newly founded paper *Il Popolo d'Italia*, thought that war would be a rite of passage for the nation newly created after the *Risorgimento*. To change policy a popular uprising was required and the fiery poet Gabriele D'Annunzio was to provide the catalyst. He made an inflammatory speech which inspired huge numbers of Italians to take to the streets to demand that Italy should go to war and, as a result, brought down the moderate government of Prime Minister Salandra. Giovanni Giolitti was asked by the king to form a new administration, but with his house under threat and his life in danger from the firebrands he declined. Moderation was out of fashion. Italy would go to war.

Italy had unfulfilled territorial ambitions to seize the lands occupied by Italian speakers, including the South Tyrol and Trieste, which remained within the Austro-Hungarian Empire. The pragmatic question was which side would be best for Italy to support in order to achieve these objectives. Germany promised the Italians most of what they wanted – to the fury of the Austrians – but the Allies offered more, not just generous promises of territory but guns and equipment.

Italy made its choice and on 23 May 1915 entered the war on the side of the Allies, declaring war on Austria-Hungary but very sensibly not on Germany, with whom she had extensive economic ties, perhaps with the bizarre hope that direct conflict with the powerful German Army could be avoided.

Italy at War

The decision for Italy to go to war was not a success. Strategically, an invasion from the south should pose a threat to Austria and the Central Powers, but in practice Austria was protected from Italian attack by the mountains that define the border. The Italians had hoped that by the time they entered the war Austrian strength would have been sapped by the Russian and Serbian attacks, but they had left it too late; the Russians were in retreat and the Serbs had enough troubles of their own. The Austrians, therefore, could concentrate their efforts on the Italians.

Although Italy had nominally an army of 1 million men, only 300,000 were regulars, with the remainder being largely untrained peasants from the sun-drenched south, ill-prepared to fight in the snow and cold of the Alps. To cap this, there were only enough rifles for 700,000 men and there was little heavy artillery support.

There was only one place where the Italians could attack the Austrian front with any hope of success and this was in the north-east. Italy's plan was to force a crossing of the River Isonzo, which meanders to the Adriatic just across the Austrian border, and then to storm the Carso, a treeless limestone plateau which rises towards the mountains where the Austrians had well-defended positions on the ridge. They never got that far as there was an inherent defect in the plan. To cross the River Isonzo the Italians needed to neutralise the Austrians on the ridge on the far side, but to neutralise the Austrians they needed to cross the River Isonzo.

Giuseppe Ungaretti - San Martino del Carso

Giuseppe Ungaretti was born in Alexandria in Egypt in February 1888. After spending some time in Paris he moved to Milan at the outbreak of the war and enlisted in the Italian Army. He started his first book of poetry, *Il Porto Sepolto* (*The Buried Harbour*), on his first day in the trenches on Monte San Michele in the Carso. He wrote:

> I spent those nights lying in mud, opposite the enemy who was positioned higher than us and who was a hundred times better armed. In the trenches, almost always in those same trenches, because we stayed on San Michele even during breaks, the battles went on for a year.   (*Giuseppe Ungaretti, Selected Poems*, edited by Andrew Frisardi, p.264)

San Martino del Carso

Di queste case
non é rimasto
che qualche
brandello di muro

Of these houses
nothing remains
but a few
scraps of wall

Di tanti
che mi corrispondevano
non é rimasto
neppure tanto

Of the many
who were like me
none remain
none at all

Ma nel cuore
nessuna croce manca

But in my heart
no cross is missing

É il mio cuore
il paese piu straziato.

My heart is there
in that most desolate land.

(27 August 1916. Translated from Italian by the author)

Four times in 1915 the Italians tried to break the Austrian lines and four times they were repulsed, losing, in all, 280,000 men. This was not going to plan, but fortunately for the Italians the Austrians fared no better and their attacks also failed. There were, in all, twelve battles of Isonzo. It was stalemate, but a cold, crushing stalemate; Flanders in the mountains, but instead of trenches in the mud the soldiers were digging in amongst Alpine rocks and glaciers at an altitude sometimes as high as 3,000m (10,000ft).

Emilio Lussu describes in his book, *A Soldier On the Southern Front*, his experiences between May 1916 and July 1917 as an officer in the Sassari Brigade, which had been exclusively recruited from Sardinia and was fighting the Austro-Hungarian army on the Asiago plateau in North East Italy. It is a story of tragedy, of repeated assaults upon impenetrable defences, of incompetent commanders and of an army fuelled by brandy. In one touching episode, a friend is arguing that the outcome of the Trojan Wars would have been very different if Hector had drunk brandy. Emilio Lussu wrote:

> I've forgotten a lot of things about the war, but I'll never forget that moment. I was watching my friend smile between one mouthful of smoke and another. A single gunshot rang out fom the enemy trench. He bowed his head, the cigarette still between his lips, and from a newly formed red spot on his forehead, a thin line of blood came streaming out. Slowly he folded in on himself and fell on my feet. I lifted him up, dead.   (Lussu, *A Soldier*, translated by Conti, pp.86-7)

The Italians Retreat

In October 1917 the Germans added six of their divisions into the equation to prevent the threatened collapse of Austria-Hungary, moving secretly with nine Austrian divisions and heavy artillery through the Alps to launch an attack on the Italian lines. The breakthrough was complete and the Italian front line collapsed. There were 320,000 Italian casualties: 40,000 killed or wounded and 280,000 taken prisoner. A further 350,000 decided '*Basta! Basta!*' and deserted (Strachan, *First World War*, p.251).

Faced with a German invasion of their heartland and under a new commander, Italian resistance stiffened. With the support of French and British troops, including two Scottish battalions – the 2nd Battalion King's Own Scottish Borderers and the 2nd Battalion Gordon Highlanders (Royle, *Flowers*, p.123) – the Italians managed to hold a new defensive line 60 miles back on the River Piave, repulsing a final, desperate assault by the Austrians in June 1918 when 100,000 Austrians were lost for no territorial gain.

It was now time for Italy to take the initiative. The Central Powers were crumbling and on 29 October 1918 the Italians counter-attacked, cutting the Austrian Army in two. By now, the Austrians had lost both an empire and the will to fight and 500,000 Austrians were killed, captured or wounded before an armistice was signed on 4 November between Austria and Italy.

Italy had suffered losses of 615,000 killed, in addition to the hundreds of thousands wounded or taken prisoner (Gilbert, *First World War*, p.541). And for what? Just in time, the Italians had rescued glory from defeat, but all their sacrifice was in vain because when the terms of the Treaty of Versailles were agreed the Allies conveniently forgot the territorial promises they had made. Italy was awarded just the South Tyrol and Trieste - territories they might have received anyway had they stayed neutral.

WAR BY PROXY - THE WAR IN THE COLONIES

African Adventures: The Background

Germany had come late to building an empire. North Africa had come under the control of the French, Britain had secured India and Russia controlled Central Asia. All that was left were a few peripheral countries in Africa. Accepting the crumbs off the imperial table, Germany had secured four colonies in Africa: German South West Africa (now Namibia), German East Africa (now Tanzania), Kamerun (now Cameroon) on the Gulf of Guinea, and a small colony in West Africa called Togoland.

As a result, at the outbreak of war all but two countries in Africa - Liberia and Ethiopia - were colonies of the major European powers, primarily Britain, France, Germany and Belgium. These African colonies suddenly found themselves at war with each other as proxies for their European rulers, even though they had no quarrel with each other. In what was essentially a European war, as many as 2 million Africans became involved, either as soldiers or as porters transporting essential supplies. Because much of the fighting took place inland, logistics were a major problem. All supplies had to be carried by porters but, as they also needed to be fed, the longer the lines of communication, the more food was required by the porters and less food got through to the troops. Disease and poor diet meant that the death rate amongst the porters was as high as one in five.

The Fate of the German Colonies: Togoland, Kamerun and German South West Africa

The principal British objective in Africa was the wireless station at Kamina in Togoland, which formed an integral part of Germany's wireless network. This was seized and destroyed within three weeks of the outbreak of war, following an invasion by British troops (Strachan, *First World War*, p.84).

South Africa had only recently recovered from the deeply divisive Boer Wars and initially faced rebellion against its plan to invade German South West Africa in support of Britain and its own territorial ambitions. Nevertheless, it rallied to the British cause and despatched an army into German South West Africa, accepting its surrender in July 1915 (Strachan, *First World War*, p.86).

Kamerun, a much larger country, equivalent in size to France and Germany combined, proved more difficult to capture. However, after an initial setback British-led forces, with naval support, seized the colonial capital, Douala, on 27 September. British and French troops then pushed into the mountainous region, but German resistance was not subdued until eighteen months later with the surrender of the last remaining German outpost in February 1916. This left German East Africa (Keegan, *First World War*, pp.225–6).

German East Africa

The forces of German East Africa, under the command of the charismatic Paul von Lettow-Vorbeck, provided more stubborn resistance. Lettow-Vorbeck's first act on the outbreak of war was to reject the advice of the civilian governor, who wanted to claim neutrality for German East Africa in order to protect, as he saw it, the benefits of colonialisation. He then fought a long and successful guerrilla campaign against the British forces. With no supplies he was forced to live off the land; his weapons were captured from the British.

Lettow-Vorbeck proved such a thorn in the side of the British that in March 1916 General Jan Smuts, a former Boer commander but now South Africa's leading general, was despatched with over 73,000 troops, including 13,000 South African troops, to deal with the German force of just 3,000 Europeans and 11,000 Askari. Steadily, Smuts pushed them back, although never quite cornering them, until in January 1917 he was recalled to London to represent South Africa in the Imperial War Cabinet.

Although Smuts claimed victory, the reality was that his advance had been stalled by the rains. It would be April before his successor resumed the chase. Lettow-Vorbeck now followed his instincts as a Prussian officer and, instead of fighting a guerrilla war, faced his enemy in battle, most notably in October 1917 in the Battle of Mahiwa when the British suffered casualties of 2,700 men while the German forces suffered casualties of only 600 (Strachan, *First World War*, p.92).

Despite this success, Lettow-Vorbeck was becoming short of manpower and desperately short of ammunition, but although his effectiveness as a fighting force was severely diminished he led his depleted force into Portuguese East Africa and into northern Rhodesia. The signing of the Armistice brought an end to his war; he surrendered on 25 November, two weeks after the war had ended in Europe. He had never been defeated.

Lettow-Vorbeck had, over the four years, lost just 100 Germans in the fighting, together with a further 3,000 Africans killed or dying from disease. The British had lost 3,000 British and Indian troops with a further 20,000 African porters and labourers dying from disease (Gilbert, *First World War*, pp.505–6). He was the only German general in the First World War who had occupied British territory when he entered northern Rhodesia in September 1918. But in a sense he had failed. His objective in fighting had been to draw British resources away from the European battlefield, but Britain had left the fighting in the main to the troops of the empire.

In a rather touching postscript, Lettow-Vorbeck became impoverished after the Second World War and it was Smuts who, hearing of his hardship, arranged for a pension to be paid to his former enemy.

THE DARDANELLES CAMPAIGN
(19 FEBRUARY 1915–9 JANUARY 1916)

The Dardanelles campaign is one of the most pitiful, tragic, and glorious episodes in British history.

John Buchan, *A History of the Great War*, Volume II, p.2.

Turkey Makes its Choice
Both Britain and Germany were aware of the strategic importance of securing Turkey, then known as the Ottoman Empire, as an ally.

From a British viewpoint, Turkey occupied a strategically important posi-
tion, as it controlled the Dardanelles, the gateway from the Mediterranean
to the Black Sea, and, consequently, was both a route for Russia's Black
Sea Fleet to reach the Mediterranean and the access whereby the Allies
could ship desperately needed supplies to Russia. The Ottoman Empire
also controlled the Middle East and therefore threatened both Britain's
supplies of oil and the Suez Canal, Britain's link with its empire in the east.
On the positive side, a Turkey linked with the Allied cause would bring pres-
sure to bear on the southern borders of the Central Powers.

Germany had also recognised the strategic importance of Turkey. It
wanted to weaken the countries of the Triple Entente by attacking their over-
seas possessions, but it had no spare resources to devote to such a project,
nor could it embark on any direct intervention because of Britain's control
of the seas. Germany decided the practical alternative would be to encour-
age Muslims to rise against their European masters – there were 100 million
Muslims in the British Empire, principally India, and a further 20 million in the
French North African colonies. The country that could lead such a Muslim
revolt was Turkey. In an attempt to advance their relationship, Germany had
offered the Ottoman Empire the services of General Liman von Sanders to
assist in reorganising and strengthening the Turkish military forces before the
outbreak of war. His advice would prove invaluable.

Britain was building two of the new Dreadnought-class battleships for
the Turkish Navy, but on 29 July 1914, amid the developing tension, Britain
unilaterally seized the vessels, as it was contractually entitled to do. The Turks
were, understandably, not best pleased and reacted positively to Germany
when they were offered in their stead two German cruisers, the battlecruiser
Goeben and the light cruiser *Breslau*. These had escaped from the Royal
Navy blockade in the Mediterranean to reach Turkey; their escape was
helped in no small part by the confusion engendered in the mind of Admiral
Milne, commander of the Royal Navy's Mediterranean Fleet, by frequent
and often conflicting signals from Churchill, who could not resist the impulse
to micro-manage in his role as First Lord of the Admiralty.

The Ottoman Empire had long felt threatened by the Russian presence
on the Black Sea and, fearing a Russian attack, decided to get its retaliation
in first by using its navy – and its two German cruisers – to attack Russia's
Black Sea ports on 29 October 1914. On 14 November 1914 the Ottoman
Empire, or what was left of it by the outbreak of the war, declared a 'holy
war' on Britain and the other countries of the Entente.

The Genocide of the Armenian People

The new breed of Young Turks believed that the true Turkish heartland extended beyond the Caucasus to include the peoples of Azerbaijan, Turkestan and Afghanistan. The war presented the opportunity to incorporate these people within a pan-Turkish state, and an attack was launched on the Russians in the Caucasus, fatally just before the onset of winter. This attack was initially successful, but the Turkish Army was woefully equipped for the fiercely cold temperatures (as low as −20°) and the 3rd Ottoman Army was virtually destroyed when the Russians counter-attacked in January 1915. The Turks lost 75,000 men, not primarily through the fighting but through the cold and the lack of supplies and effective medical care.

The Turks needed someone to blame for this damaging blow to their prestige. On 30 December the tsar had visited the front, encouraging the Armenian people to rise against the Turks. He had promised them a 'brilliant future', but he had effectively sealed their fate, as the Turks chose to blame the Armenians for their defeat, believing, unfairly, that they were in league with the Russians (Gilbert, *First World War*, p.108).

Turkey had long had a sizeable Armenian population of 1.75 million but, following the crushing defeats the Ottoman Empire had suffered in the Balkan Wars of 1912 and 1913 when it had lost much of its territory, millions of Turks had been dispossessed and had moved into the lands occupied by the Armenians, putting pressure on the indigenous population.

The competition by the displaced Turks for land and the belief that the Armenians had collaborated with the Russians conspired to encourage Turkey, from April 1915, to begin a systematic genocide of the Armenian people, which continued over the next seven months. It has been estimated that between 600,000 and 1 million Armenians died, either massacred or dying from starvation as, expelled from their homes, they trekked through the country in the hope of finding safety, begging for food while vultures circled overhead waiting to pick the flesh from the rotting corpses of those who had died in the exodus. It was one of the worst war crimes of the First World War (Gilbert, *First World War*, p.167).

The genocide was condemned at the time by the Allied powers, but there was little they could do to protect the Armenians, and the massacre is now largely ignored through the pressures of realpolitik as Turkey becomes a potential recruit to the European Union and a bulwark against the so-called Islamic State.

The Gallipoli Campaign

On 2 January 1915 the Russian commander-in-chief had sent a message to London asking for a diversionary attack to relieve the pressure from Turkish forces in the Caucasus. The war in Europe had reached a stalemate and a new initiative was required. Winston Churchill, First Lord of the Admiralty, thought he had the answer both to Russia's request and to the stalemate. Churchill's idea was to bring pressure on Turkey with the objectives of diverting precious German troops from the Western Front, opening a route for Britain to deliver essential supplies to Russia and encouraging Romania and Bulgaria to join the Allies and attack Austria from the south. If successful, Austria could be destroyed and Germany isolated, under attack from the Russians in the east and the Serbs, Romanians and Bulgarians from the south. The stalemate would be broken. It was an ambitious plan, but its execution was fatally flawed.

The proposal was for the Royal Navy to force a passage through the Dardanelles (Hellespont, to the ancient Greeks) – the 3-mile-wide strait dividing Turkey from Europe – enabling the fleet to sail from the Aegean to the Sea of Marmara from where it would threaten Constantinople, the capital of Turkey. If Constantinople was captured, Turkey would fall and there would be a powerful inducement for the uncommitted countries of Greece, Romania and Bulgaria to join the Allied cause. The intention was to break the stalemate of trench warfare in the mud of the Western Front, but tragically the result was to replicate it with a stalemate of trench warfare in the heat and dirt of Gallipoli.

The plan was deceptively simple. Royal Navy ships would first bombard and destroy the Turkish fortifications and then ground troops would be landed to defeat the Turkish forces and free the straits for the navy to sail through. Kitchener expressed doubts from the outset as to the possible success of the operation, believing the British Army had enough on its hands on the Western Front and could ill afford to divert precious troops and munitions to support Churchill's dream. The First Sea Lord, Lord Fisher, was also sceptical as to the potential success of this somewhat hare-brained scheme, but the decision was carried by the forceful personality of Churchill, who 'was prepared to force his opinion against the experts' (John Buchan, *A History of the Great War*, Volume II, p.5).

There were two drawbacks to this seemingly simple plan, neither of which were fully appreciated by the British High Command. The first was that the passage through the Dardanelles was strongly defended by strategically situated Turkish fortified positions. There is a kink in the straits about 14 miles from the mouth where the channel, at this point less than a mile wide, makes a sharp turn northward for a few miles. This part of the straits was heavily defended by Turkish forts, making any attempt to force a passage extremely hazardous. The second drawback was that the waters of the Dardanelles had been heavily mined. There would be a third drawback – the choice of the man to lead the operation.

General Sir Ian Hamilton

Kitchener chose General Sir Ian Hamilton to head the Allied Expeditionary Force. Hamilton was born in Corfu to Scottish parents but had spent his childhood in Argyll. He had served with distinction in the Gordon Highlanders in the First Afghan War and in the Boer Wars, for which he had been knighted and recommended for the Victoria Cross for bravery. Unusually for a general, he was interested in painting, music and poetry, but more relevantly to the success of the venture Hamilton had no experience of commanding a seaborne landing and had taken no part in the planning of the campaign. Amazingly, he was also not given any up-to-date maps.

Military Disaster

On 19 February 1915 the combined British and French fleet set sail. It comprised battleships, cruisers and destroyers, but was crucially deficient in effective minesweepers. Action commenced with a heavy bombardment of the Turkish forts to eliminate their threat before eighteen battleships tried to force their way through the straits. In a situation reminiscent of the Western Front, the bombardment proved ineffective in silencing the Turkish forts and the fleet immediately came under heavy Turkish fire.

To counter the enemy fire, four battleships moved through the line to direct their guns at close range upon the Turkish forts. Of these, the French battleship *Bouvet* was hit almost immediately by shells and then by a mine. Able Seaman Cemm, serving in the battleship HMS *Prince George*, wrote:

> The *Bouvet* passed under our stern, and had gone about three or four hundred yards away from us, when we saw her heel over and turn upside down and she sank in two and a half minutes, taking the best part of her crew with her. Where the *Bouvet* sank, there was a huge upheaval of water, caused by the air escaping from the sunken ship.　　(Quoted in Brown, *IWM Book*, p.160)

Two Royal Navy battleships, HMS *Ocean* and HMS *Irresistible*, were also sunk by mines and two further French battleships, the *Suffren* and the *Charlemagne*, and the Royal Navy battleship HMS *Inflexible* were crippled by the heavy Turkish gunfire. The minesweepers, under heavy fire from the shore-mounted Turkish artillery, could not clear the straits of mines and the combined French and Royal Navy Fleet was forced to beat an undignified retreat, retiring to lick its wounds and to pass the baton to the army.

Although the expedition was appearing not so much a 'disaster about to happen' as a disaster which had already happened, the British military top brass were not deterred. The army would force a landing and take the Turkish positions. Reinforcements were demanded and despatched, but the delay gave the Turks, advised by von Sanders, plenty of time to strengthen the fortifications, laying down swathes of barbed wire, digging defensive trenches and bringing in extra artillery and another six divisions comprising 84,000 men.

To attack these positions the British General Sir Ian Hamilton had a force of 70,000 troops, including 30,000 relatively unblooded soldiers from Australia and New Zealand, but crucially very little artillery. The plan was to rely on the navy to soften the enemy through a preliminary bombardment, but after two more ships had been sunk by German submarines the navy withdrew, leaving just a few destroyers with 4in guns to provide artillery support.

The date chosen for the assault was 25 April 1915. Two sites were selected for the landings: Cape Helles at the southernmost end of the peninsula and Gaba Tepe further up the coast.

Anzac Cove

The men of the 1st Australian Division of the Australian and New Zealand Army Corps (ANZAC) landed at Ari Burnu, soon renamed by the men 'Anzac Cove'. They rowed desperately towards the landing beach under murderous Turkish fire. When the boats grounded, the men waded ashore, waist-deep in the sea, with bullets flying all around and trying to avoid the corpses on the seabed. When they reached the beach it seemed a far from ideal place to have chosen to land a seaborne invasion; it was a narrow, pebbly beach under the shadow of an almost vertical cliff of loose sandstone covered in thick growth. They were right; they should have landed a few miles to the south on a beach adjoining the headland of Gaba Tepe.

Despite this, the attacking forces, reinforced by further landings of Australian and New Zealand troops, managed to reach the ridge, which they held under intense Turkish shelling and targeted sniping and without any supportive shelling from the ships offshore, but they didn't succeed in driving the Turks off the main ridge. The ANZACs fought bravely, but hopelessly.

The British Troops Fared Little Better

The landing of the British troops near Cape Helles was equally shambolic. The landing craft could not make the shore so soldiers jumped into the sea with full kit, with many drowning. The invading troops then tried to force their way through the barbed wire and up the beaches under intense fire from Turkish positions based on the ridge behind. They dug in with little protection from the murderous Turkish machine guns which swept the beach with a hail of bullets. During the day they suffered from thirst in the burning heat, while at night they shivered in the intense cold, and the ever-present flies that swarmed over the rations brought rampant dysentery. The ground between the British trenches and the Turkish Army became littered with unburied bodies putrefying in the hot sun, but despite heavy losses and appalling conditions the troops held on.

Further Attacks and Further Losses

There was bitter fighting throughout the summer without any progress. Scottish troops incurred heavy losses in the June offensive. The 7th Royal Scots Territorial Battalion ('Leith's Own') had already suffered when they had left Leith by troop train to Liverpool. The train was near Gretna Green when it was involved in a high-speed collision with a stationary passenger train on 22 May, only to then be hit by the Glasgow express, which ploughed at full speed into the wreckage. It is the worst ever crash on the British rail network, with an estimated 226 killed and a further 246 injured. At a roll-call held after the accident only sixty-five Royal Scots were present from the roughly 500 who had boarded the train.

The battalion, after receiving reinforcements, eventually reached Gallipoli in mid June 1915 just after the 4th Royal Scots Territorial Battalion from Edinburgh; they landed on Cape Helles. Almost immediately, on 28 June 1915, these two unblooded Territorial battalions of the Royal Scots, joined by the 7th Scottish Rifles, were launched in an unsupported frontal assault on the precipitous cliffs, upon which the Turkish forces were entrenched and from which the Turkish snipers and artillery wreaked grievous damage.

Losses in the two Territorial battalions totalled 337 killed or missing and a further 300 wounded. In an appalling comment on the tragedy, Major General Egerton declared that he welcomed the use of the untried Territorials as it was a good way of 'blooding the pups' (MacDonald and McFarland, *Scotland*, p.113).

Private William Begbie of the 7th Battalion Royal Scots was wounded in the attack. He wrote:

> The enemy bombarded our trenches from 9.00 a.m. until 11.00 a.m. They scored many direct hits on our lines and we suffered many casualties before we even left our trenches. At last the hour came and at the words 'Over you go, lads' the troops gave vent to one resounding cheer and swarmed over the parapets into the perils of the open ground.

At first, the Turks retreated in the face of this determined onslaught but then rallied together. Private Begbie continued:

> By this time the Turks, having recovered from their panic, delivered such a terrific fire that our Company fell in bundles and halfway across Major Sanderson dropped and Captain Dawson and Lieutenant Thomson were killed as they neared their goal. By now, men were falling on my left and right. I then felt as if a horse had kicked my right thigh. I fell down and later, when I got up again, I had no feeling in my leg and fell again.
>
> Trying to move, I heard bullets striking the ground so I lay still. I didn't feel very much pain but the sun, which was by this time high in the sky, threw down intense heat on the sand which was crawling with insects of every shape and size. The worst thing was the craving for water – our mouths were so parched by the heat and sand that our tongues swelled.   (Quoted in Young, *Scottish Voices*, p.127)

Begbie was sent to hospital in Alexandria. Once he had recovered from his wounds he returned to Gallipoli on 24 July. He was 16 years old.

Defeat

On 6 August Sir Ian Hamilton ordered a second all-out assault on the Turkish positions involving a night attack at Suvla Bay. The landing was initially successful, with a bridgehead secured, but the attack was not pressed home, enabling the Turks to bring in reinforcements and reverting to a third area of stalemate. It was winter before the inevitability of defeat was accepted and the few remaining troops were evacuated, the last men leaving on 9 January 1916. It was one of the worst failures in the history of the British Army.

Twenty-eight thousand British soldiers died during the campaign, along with 10,000 French, 8,700 Australians and 2,700 New Zealanders (Strachan, *First World War*, p.121). There were a further 250,000 casualties and huge numbers who suffered from dysentery or other diseases.

The Australian press termed the expedition a disaster, which they blamed upon the incompetent leadership of the British command. Hamilton was recalled in October 1915 and precipitately, but probably fairly, sacked, ending his military career. It could, however, be asked whether Kitchener had chosen the right commander.

The political fallout was also dramatic. The First Sea Lord, Jackie Fisher, who opposed 'further depletions of our Home resources for the Dardanelles' and considered Churchill 'a bigger danger than the Germans' (quoted in Strachan, *First World War*, p.164), had resigned on 15 May in protest at the way Churchill interfered in the running of the Admiralty and increasingly usurped their authority. Churchill himself was demoted from First Lord of the Admiralty and resigned from the government in November 1915 to command an infantry battalion of the Royal Scots Fusiliers. Asquith himself was not immune to the pressures. In May, hit privately by the impending marriage of Venetia to Edwin Montagu and publicly by the resignation of Fisher, Asquith was in no condition to resist the demand of the leader of the Conservative Party, Bonar Law, for the formation of a coalition government, spelling the end of a Liberal government in Britain.

Siegfried Sassoon – To My Brother
Hamo Sassoon, Siegfried's younger brother, was fatally wounded at Gallipoli and buried at sea on 1 November 1915:

To My Brother

Give me your hand, my brother, search my face;
Look in these eyes lest I should think of shame;
For we have made an end of all things base.
We are returning by the road we came.

Your lot is with the ghosts of soldiers dead,
And I am in the field where men must fight.
But in the gloom I see your laurell'd head
And through the victory I shall win the light.

THE WAR IN THE AIR

The First Zeppelin Attack: 19-20 January 1915

Count Ferdinand von Zeppelin had begun the design of the first Zeppelin in 1890, developing the concept of the non-rigid airship which was, at the time, little more than an elongated balloon. His design was revolutionary, as it comprised a light but rigid frame structure with individual 'compartments' that contained the individual gas bags filled with hydrogen gas to provide the lift. A gondola was slung underneath, manned by the crew who wore padded boots to avoid igniting a spark and turning the machine into a raging fiery inferno.

The first flight of a Zeppelin took place in 1900 and was a modest success, achieving a speed of nearly 20mph before it was damaged on landing. More than twenty Zeppelins were manufactured before the outbreak of the First World War, some of which were used to give passenger flights.

The strategic possibility of using the Zeppelin in a military role was recognised by the Germans, and a number of Zeppelins were ordered by the German Navy at the instigation of Admiral von Tirpitz, while the German Army commandeered three of the Zeppelins that had been operating commercial flights. Zeppelins were first used against targets in France and on the Eastern Front, but then the Kaiser authorised the use of Zeppelins to bring the war to Britain in attempt to distil panic amongst civilians and thus break the resolve of the British people.

The first raid in Britain was on 19 January 1915 when two Zeppelins released their cargo of incendiary bombs on Great Yarmouth and random villages in Norfolk using the practical but low-tech method of dropping them over the side of the gondola. This raid highlighted one of the major defects of the Zeppelins in that they were very susceptible to wind and therefore difficult to navigate – bombs often landed on villages and residential areas rather than the intended target, making civilians the main casualties. The intended target of this raid had been Humberside.

In April a Zeppelin reached Edinburgh in an attempt to attack the Rosyth naval base, where Vice Admiral Sir David Beatty was based with his Battlecruiser Fleet, but succeeded only in bombing Castle Rock. A second Zeppelin attacking from the south was similarly off target, destroying a family home in Edinburgh. A further raid was even further off target, with bombs dropped on a field near Arbroath.

Despite their inherent inaccuracy, or perhaps because of it, the Zeppelins instilled fear in the British public as these cigar-shaped monsters – up to 600ft long and containing 800,000 cubic feet of gas, later increased to over 1 million cubic feet to gain extra height – glided through the night sky like huge liners carrying their cargo of incendiary bombs, flying at a height of 10,000ft, where they were out of the range of anti-aircraft fire and impervious to the attacks of British fighters.

Zeppelins were used throughout 1916, initially against military targets but later targeted on civilians in London and other British cities.

The First Airship is Shot Down

Surprisingly, although the gas used to provide the airship with buoyancy was highly inflammable hydrogen, this was not ignited by standard bullets or anti-aircraft shells. This all changed with the invention in 1916 of the incendiary bullet. On 2 September 1916 a fleet of sixteen Zeppelin and Schutte (a Zeppelin lookalike) airships, loaded with incendiary bombs and explosives, launched a raid on London. The British intercepted their radio messages and ten aircraft were sent up to attack them.

The first to take off was William Leefe Robinson in a BE2c, a small single-engine biplane that had been developed by the Royal Aircraft Factory at Farnborough. The night was foggy, but at around 1 a.m. he spotted an airship caught in the glare of searchlights as it bombed the London docks. He lost contact as he tried to gain height but then spotted another airship bombing North London. He flew alongside the airship, riddling its length with incendiary bullets, which had been designed first to puncture the hydrogen-filled bags to mix the hydrogen with oxygen and then to ignite this now dangerously inflammable mixture. On his third attack the airship burst into flames and crashed. This was the first time a Zeppelin-type airship had been shot down by a British aircraft, an exploit for which Leefe Robinson was awarded the VC, and it was a turning point in the struggle against the airship. By the time the use of Zeppelins had virtually ceased in 1917, more than seventy airships had been shot down out of a total of 115 that had been used in attacks on British targets.

The Red Baron

The first aeroplanes to be used in the war were unreliable biplanes used primarily for observation, target spotting in support of the artillery and photography, using a camera that was contained in a sturdy mahogany box fixed to the fuselage. It was, after all, only five years since Louis Blériot had crossed the Channel in his epic thirty-six-minute flight.

At the outbreak of the war, Britain and France had roughly 100 aeroplanes each while Germany had 200. By the end of the war the combined production of Britain, France and the United States totalled 11,000 aircraft a month, compared with just 2,000 a month by Germany, and their use had changed from reconnaissance and photography to aerial combat and bombing attacks on strategic enemy targets.

Initially, combat between pilots was cumbersome, with guns being fired out of the cockpit to avoid damaging the propeller, but this was transformed in 1915 when Fokker in Germany developed a mechanism to synchronise the firing of the gun with the revolutions of the propeller so that the pilot could aim his aircraft at the enemy aeroplane and fire through the propeller. This significantly increased the probability of hitting and destroying the target. In March 1916, the British Sopwith fighter was fitted with a Vickers machine gun, synchronised to fire through the propeller. The number of aircraft mushroomed and aerial dogfights took place daily in the skies as fast, manoeuvrable biplanes were used to hunt and shoot down enemy aircraft. The glamorous role of the fighter pilot was born.

One of the most famous of these was the Red Baron – Baron Manfred von Richthofen. In September 1916 the Red Baron shot down his first kill. As his skill became more widely known, the Baron, in his iconic red-painted fighter, was given leadership of four squadrons of fighter planes. He had achieved eighty kills before he recklessly pursued a Royal Air Force Sopwith Camel over the British lines in April 1918 and was shot down by a Canadian pilot, who dived down and attacked him from the rear. Richthofen managed to land his Fokker triplane, but when the aircraft was reached he was dead. In a touching tribute to his skill and reputation he was buried with full military honours by the pilots of the Royal Air Force who had formerly been his enemies, with a wreath that bore the words, 'To our gallant and worthy foe'. The Royal Air Force, the world's first air force, had been created on 1 April 1918 through the merger of the Royal Flying Corps and the Royal Naval Air Service.

German Bombers Attack Britain's Cities

The war was still largely waged by soldiers at the front and by the sailors, but in June 1917 the horror of war was again unleashed on the British civilian. The 13 June was a peaceful summer's day, but the peace was suddenly shattered by the drone of aeroplanes. Fourteen German Gotha biplane bombers were on their way to bomb Britain. The bombers were much more manoeuvrable than the Zeppelins and were less effected by the wind and so more likely to hit their target, in this case, London.

The bombs fell on the London docks and Liverpool Street Station, but one landed on a school, detonating in the basement where fifty children were sheltering, killing eighteen. The raid caused outrage as innocent children became the victims of war.

Bombing raids continued until May 1918 and, although casualties were not high in comparison with those at the front, the impact on civilian life was fearful as the sound of the warning sirens forced people to take cover from an impending attack. The British retaliated by developing bombers to attack German airfields and industrial sites.

Jeffery Day - On the Wings of the Morning

Flight Commander Jeffery Day brings alive the feelings of freedom and delight felt by the young pilots flying well above the suffering of the soldiers in the trenches:

On the Wings of the Morning

[omitting verses 4-8]

A sudden roar, a mighty rushing sound,
    a jolt or two, a smoothly sliding rise,
a trembled blur of disappearing ground,
    and then all sense of motion slowly dies.
        Quiet and calm, and earth slips past below,
        as underneath a bridge still waters flow.

My turning wing inclines toward the ground;
    the ground itself glides up with graceful swing
and at the plane's far tip twirls slowly round,
    then drops from sight again beneath the wing

to slip away serenely as before,
a cubist-patterned carpet on the floor.

Hills gently sink and valleys gently fill.
The flattened fields grow ludicrously small;
slowly they pass beneath and slower still
until they hardly seem to move at all.
Then suddenly they disappear from sight,
hidden by fleeting wisps of faded white.

The engine stops: a pleasant silence reigns –
silence, not broken, but intensified
by the soft, sleepy wires' insistent strains,
that rise and fall, as with a sweeping glide
I slither down the well-oiled slides of space,
towards a lower, less enchanted place.

The clouds draw nearer, changing as they come.
Now like a flash, fog grips me by the throat.
Down goes the nose: at once the wires' low hum
begins to rise in volume and in note,
till, as I hurtle from the choking cloud
it swells into a scream, high-pitched, and loud.

The scattered hues and shades of green and brown
fashion themselves into the land I know,
turning and twisting, as I spiral down
towards the landing-ground; till, skimming low,
I glide with slackening speed across the ground,
and come to rest with lightly grating sound.

Life as a pilot in the war was not always such a peaceful idyll, as 'in 1917 the life expectancy of a new pilot on the Western Front was between eleven days and three weeks' (Brown, *IWM Book*, p.121). Flight Commander Day was himself killed in aerial combat on 27 February 1918. He was 21 years old.

Ewart Alan Mackintosh – In Memoriam R.M. Stalker
Another pilot to die was R.M. Stalker, formerly of the 5th Seaforths, who
had transferred to the Royal Flying Corps and was declared missing on
8 September 1916. He was a friend of Mackintosh, who wrote this moving
poem as a tribute to 'Stalk'. The third of 'the jolly three' was Lieutenant
William Reader, who had been mortally wounded on 30 July 1916, the
same day as Mackintosh himself had been wounded:

In Memoriam R.M. Stalker

As I go down the highway,
   And through the village street
I hear the pipers playing
   And the tramp of marching feet.
The men I worked and fought with
   Swing by me four on four,
And at the end you follow
   Whom I shall see no more.

Oh, Stalk, where are you lying?
   Somewhere and far away,
Enemy hands have buried
   Your quiet contemptuous clay.
There was no greeting given,
   No tear of friend for friend,
From us when you flew over
   Exultant to the end.

I couldn't see the paper,
   I couldn't think that you
Would never walk the highway
   The way you used to do.
I turn at every footfall,
   Half-hoping, half-afraid
To see you coming, later
   Than usual for parade.

The old Lairg clique is broken,
    I drove there yesterday,
And the car was full of ghosts that sat
    Beside me all the way.
Ghosts of old songs and laughter,
    Ghosts of the jolly three,
That went the road together
    And go no more with me.

Oh, Stalk, but I am lonely,
    For all the days we knew,
And the bed on the floor at Lesdos
    We slept in, I and you.
The joyful nights in billets
    We laughed and drank and swore –
But the candle's burnt out, Stalk,
    In the mess at Henancourt.

The candle's burnt out now, old man,
    And the dawn's come grey and cold,
And I sit by the fire here
    Alone and sad and old.
Though all the rest come back again,
    You lie in a foreign land,
And the strongest link of all the chain
    Is broken in my hand.

THE SINKING OF RMS *LUSITANIA*
(7 MAY 1915)

The threat from German U-boats was well known; on 3 September 1914 the British cruiser HMS *Pathfinder* had been sunk in the North Sea by a torpedo fired by a German U-boat, *U-21* (Gilbert, *First World War*, p.67).

German submarines had been attacking merchant ships for some time when, on 1 May 1915, the four-funnelled, 31,000-ton RMS *Lusitania* – built in 1906 for the Cunard Line by the John Brown shipyard on the Clyde and holder of the Blue Riband for the fastest Atlantic crossing – set sail from

New York to Liverpool. The German embassy had issued a formal warning a few days before the ship's departure that a state of war existed between Germany and Britain and that the safety of the ship could not be guaranteed, but few of the passengers were deterred, believing that the *Lusitania* could easily outrun any threat the German Navy could provide.

By 7 May the *Lusitania* had reached the west coast of Ireland where it was known that German U-boats were operating. The captain received a warning signal but decided to press on, increasing speed and extinguishing unnecessary lights and unaware that *U-20* was lurking off the Irish coast. It is possible that the commander of the U-boat thought that there were soldiers on board and not civilian passengers, as was the case. Whatever his understanding, the *Lusitania* provided too tempting a target to resist as she passed broadside on and the U-boat fired a torpedo which smashed into the great liner and holed her below the waterline. This was followed almost immediately by a further devastating explosion as the boiler – or possibly munitions – exploded. The ship began to list severely, with her bows buried deep into the sea and her stern standing high above the water. It was only possible to launch six of the lifeboats before, within minutes, the *Lusitania* had sunk, sliding to the bottom. One thousand, two hundred and two passengers and crew were drowned, including 128 Americans.

Germany received universal condemnation for sinking an unarmed passenger ship, although, in fairness, it later emerged that the liner had been carrying munitions amongst its cargo. Despite strong pressure, the American President Woodrow Wilson refused to declare war on Germany, but the outcome was that Germany did, for a time, rein in its attacks on the merchant ships of non-combatants (Brown, *IWM Book*, p.101).

AUBERS RIDGE AND THE BATTLE OF FESTUBERT (9 MAY AND 15–25 MAY 1915)

Ewart Alan Mackintosh - Cha Till MacCruimein
Mackintosh wrote his poem *Cha Till MacCruimein*, commemorating the departure of 4th Camerons, in 1915. His early optimism had gone and it is a sombre poem recognising both the mortality of war and also his personal mortality – the likelihood that he, too, would be killed:

Cha Till MacCruimein
(Departure of the 4th Camerons)

The pipes in the street were playing bravely,
    The marching lads went by,
With merry hearts and voices singing
    My friends marched out to die;
But I was hearing a lonely pibroch
    Out of an older war,
"Farewell, farewell, farewell, MacCrimmon,
    MacCrimmon comes no more"

And every lad in his heart was dreaming
    Of honour and wealth to come,
And honour and noble pride were calling
    To the tune of pipes and drum;
But I was hearing a woman singing
    On dark Dunvegan shore,
"In battle or peace, with wealth or honour,
    MacCrimmon comes no more"

And there in front of the men were marching,
    With feet that made no mark,
The grey old ghosts of the ancient fighters
    Come back again from the dark;
And in front of them all MacCrimmon piping
    A weary tune and sore,
"On the gathering day, for ever and ever,
    MacCrimmon comes no more"

(Bedford, 1915)

Vimy Ridge
The interminable fighting on the Western Front continued. France was determined not to be deterred by the consistent lack of tangible gains and launched an attack at Vimy Ridge. After a preliminary bombardment, French troops advanced across no man's land towards the German trenches to discover the wire was uncut. Troops struggled to cut the wire under intense

machine-gun fire before pressing on to the next line of wire. The Germans withdrew to a stronger defensive position and a few French troops reached their objective, the village of Vimy, where they had the reward of being shelled by their own artillery. Amongst the attacking troops were 3,000 men of the French Foreign Legion, of whom just under 1,900 were casualties, including their commanding officer, who was shot by a sniper.

Aubers Ridge

Not to be outdone in futility, Haig gave the order for a British assault on Aubers Ridge. Six Scottish battalions fought in the attack – 1st and 4th Battalions Seaforth Highlanders, 1st Battalion Cameron Highlanders and the 1st, 2nd and 4th Battalions Black Watch. Two thousand Scots were casualties, out of a total of 11,000 killed or wounded in just one day of fighting (Young, *Scottish Voices*, pp.118–22).

At 5 a.m. the British bombardment had begun with the objective of destroying the German trenches, disabling the barbed wire and demoralising the defenders. The bombardment continued for forty minutes before the first wave of attacking British troops went 'over the top' in an unbroken line of khaki. Yet again, the objectives of the artillery assault had not been achieved. Many of the artillery shells used had been shrapnel that had virtually no impact on the integrity of the German defences. Their trenches were still intact, the barbed wire was untouched and the German troops, far from being demoralised, fired machine guns at the advancing troops.

The attack was a disaster but this, self-evidently, could not have been a fault with the plan; it must have been a fault with the execution. Haig, therefore, ordered another assault at 2.40 p.m., having given the Germans ample time to bring in reinforcements. The assault was further delayed to 4 p.m. to allow the fresh troops to reach the line, and these forced their way through the communication trenches against the hordes of walking wounded returning from the earlier attack.

'Walking wounded' was a broad definition; it included, for example, men who had lost a leg but could 'walk' using their rifle as a crutch. It was the only way for them to reach medical help. There were no men to spare to act as stretcher bearers. Sergeant H.E. May of the Cameron Highlanders described the scene poignantly:

Down the track went a constant stream of battered humanity. Men minus an arm; those with huge dark stains on their uniforms to show where they had been hit – Highlander and Sassenach. Here a man badly burned by a petrol bomb; there a poor devil with his leg gone at the knee, who dragged a weary way backward, using his rifle as a crutch. On the faces of all a look of hopeless horror as they fled from the terror behind them. One must see something like that to realise the insane folly of war.   (Quoted in Young, *Scottish Voices*, p.225)

For his second attack Haig chose the pick of his fighting forces: the Highland regiments. He saw no need to change the plan. Again the attack was preceded by a forty-minute bombardment before the 1st Battalion Black Watch led the assault. After brave and fierce fighting they managed to secure a part of the German line. Reinforcements could not reach them, but retreat would have once again meant crossing the field of death under German machine-gun fire and so they stayed and fought until they died. It was glorious heroism but a tragic waste of life. Their bravery impressed the Germans. Young, in *Scottish Voices* (pp.121–2), quotes the *Frankfurter Zeitung*:

Then the British came into action with tremendous fierceness. They would break through, cost what it might. They attacked on three lines. The front regiment was mowed down by our fearful fire, and the following regiment, under a terrible hail from the guns, was unable to advance. Then the British sent one of their best Highland regiments to the front, the best they have anywhere. The Black Watch advanced. The gallant Scots came on, but even their really heroic bravery was in vain, for they were not able to turn the fate of the day.

Second Lieutenant Lionel Sotheby of the Argyll and Sutherland Highlanders, but attached to the 1st Battalion Black Watch, took part in the second attack. There was always a high rate of loss amongst the junior officers, who were expected to lead their men into the attack and who, in their distinctive uniforms, provided an obvious and tempting target to the German gunners. Sotheby was the only officer in his battalion not killed or wounded that day. He wrote:

[There were] awful losses on Sunday, which was to have been the great advance. The old fault, wire not cut. The 1st Black Watch, including myself, charged the German trenches 400 yards away. The whole 15 officers were killed, except 4. Of these 4, 3 were wounded and I survived. I tell you it is a miracle, and I felt quite changed as I lay out 15 yards from the German trenches for 4 hours before crawling back.

The attack stalled against the uncut wire. Some men got through but were seen to be disarmed and killed.

Those who penetrated into the rampart on our left held on for about ten minutes and were then stripped of their equipment by the Germans, shot and thrown over the parapet ... Here one battalion had in part succeeded when a whole lot had failed in the morning. The Colonel has been praised by all the other Colonels and Generals for what the battalion did. Not a man hung back, all charged as far as possible. A finer set of men than these ... could not be found anywhere.

We lost over 500 men.   (Quoted in Young, *Scottish Voices*, p.120)

It would have been, no doubt, a comfort to those 500 men killed, captured or wounded to know that the general was proud of them. The final tribute to the bravery of these troops, advancing to 'almost certain death' at the whim of a general safely positioned well behind the front line, is left to an officer in the 1st Battalion Scots Guards, who understandably remained anonymous:

Although it made one's blood run cold, it was a most heroic sight to see the Black Watch and the Cameron Highlanders filing up to the front trench. They were magnificent; cheerful and quite calm, going in an hour to almost certain death. The Black Watch advanced in line, with their officers five paces in front of their platoons, and their pipers playing in front. The Black Watch got into the German lines, but were unsupported, and our guns had to bombard for an extra half-hour to let them out again. Two companies disappeared and the remainder were sorely shattered. The whole affair was absolute carnage. The second attack was just murder, sending brave men to certain death, and, my God, they met it like men, too.   (Quoted in Young, *Scottish Voices*, p.121)

Festubert

Haig attributed the failure of the breakthrough at Aubers Ridge to the fact that a much longer and heavier bombardment was necessary to destroy the well-constructed German trench system. He planned a further attack to capture the German trenches at Festubert, but with a reduced ambition, not to seize a swathe of enemy territory by a dramatic push but just an attritional gain of 900yd. The plan was depressingly familiar, except that this time the attack would be preceded by a three-day bombardment to destroy the German defences.

The outcome was also depressingly familiar. The 4th Cameron Highlanders, a Territorial battalion comprised largely of men from Skye and the Outer Hebrides, distinguished themselves by their bravery in attack, but, although ground was won, none of the strategic objectives were achieved. British casualties totalled 16,000.

Lance Corporal William Angus, Highland Light Infantry

Angus had left school at the age of 14 to work in the mines. With the outbreak of war, he enlisted in the 8th Battalion Highland Light Infantry and was sent to France. He was on the front line on 11 June 1915 when Lieutenant James Martin, leading a bombing raid on the German lines, was spotted. The Germans detonated a mine and Martin was thought to have been killed by the explosion, but was then heard pleading with the Germans for water.

Angus volunteered to go into no man's land to rescue him. With a rope tied about his waist – to pull him back if he was shot – Angus crawled undetected to reach Martin. He then tied the rope around Martin's body and tried to carry him back, but as soon as he stood he was seen by the Germans who shot and wounded him. He lay on the ground, sheltering Martin with his body, before signalling back to the trench for them to pull Martin back, crawling at right angles to draw the Germans' fire. Although hit again, he managed to regain the trenches. He was awarded the VC 'for most conspicuous gallantry and devotion'. Both men survived the war and every subsequent year on the 11 June Martin sent a telegram to his saviour.

Robert Graves – Corporal Stare

Graves, in his account of his war experience, *Goodbye to All That*, gives a rather disturbing account of seeing a ghost while at Béthune. He writes that when Private Challoner, whom he had met while at Wrexham, had gone out with a draft to join the 1st Battalion Royal Welch Fusiliers, 'he shook my hand and said: "I'll meet you again in France, sir"'. Graves continues:

> In June he passed by our company billet, where we were just having a special dinner to celebrate our safe return from Cuinchy ... Private Challoner looked in at the window, saluted, and passed on. I could not mistake him, or the

cap-badge he wore; yet no Royal Welch battalion was billeted within miles
of Béthune at the time. I jumped up, looked out of the window, and saw
nothing except a fag-end smoking on the pavement. Challoner had been
killed at Festubert in May.   (*Goodbye to All That*, p.102)

Graves was obviously deeply affected by the experience, which he com-
memorated in his poem *Corporal Stare*. In this poem he eschews the
measured literary style of much of his poetry and instead matches the pace
and wit of Sassoon's poems:

Corporal Stare

Back from the Line one night in June
I gave a dinner at Béthune:
Seven courses, the most gorgeous meal
Money could buy or batman steal.
Five hungry lads welcomed the fish
With shouts that nearly cracked the dish;
Asparagus came with tender tops,
Strawberries in cream, and mutton chops.
Said Jenkins, as my hand he shook,
'They'll put this in the history book.'
We bawled Church anthems 'in choro'
Of Bethlehem and Hermon snow,
And drinking songs, a mighty sound
To help the good red Pommard round.
Stories and laughter interspersed,
We drowned a long La Bassée thirst –
Trenches in June make throats damned dry.
Then through the window suddenly,
Badge, stripes and medals all complete,
We saw him swagger up the street,
Just like a live man – Corporal Stare!
    Stare! Killed last month at Festubert,
Caught on patrol near the Boche wire,
Torn horribly by machine-gun fire!
He passed, saluted smartly, grinned,
Then passed away like a puff of wind,

Leaving us blank astonishment.
The song broke, up we stared, leant
Out of the window – nothing there,
Not the least shadow of Corporal Stare,
Only a quiver of smoke that showed,
A fag-end dropped on the silent road.

NO MAN'S LAND

Night patrols would take place in no man's land, the battle-scarred strip between the opposing lines of trenches, when a few selected soldiers would crawl their way towards enemy lines, past the water-filled shell holes and the rotting bodies of their former comrades. Occasionally there would be an informal truce to allow each side to send out stretcher bearers to bring back their dead and wounded, but this was frowned upon by the army top brass, as it was regarded as fraternising with the enemy.

Robert Graves, in his autobiography *Goodbye to All That* (pp.110–11), writes vividly of his first experience of a patrol in no man's land in the summer of 1915:

My first night, Captain Thomas asked whether I would like to go out on patrol. It was the regimental custom to test new officers in this way, and none dared excuse himself. During my whole service with the Welch I had never once been out in No Man's Land, even to inspect the barbed-wire.

He continues:

Sergeant Townsend and I went out from Red Lamp Corner at about ten o'clock; both carrying revolvers. We had pulled socks, with the toes cut off, over our bare knees, to prevent them showing up in the dark and to make crawling easier. We went ten yards at a time, slowly, not on all fours, but wriggling flat along the ground. After each movement we lay and watched for about ten minutes. We crawled through our own wire entanglements and along a dry ditch; ripping our clothes on more barbed-wire, glaring into the darkness until it began turning round and round. Once I snatched my fingers in horror from where I had planted them on the slimy body of an old corpse. We nudged each other with rapidly beating hearts at the slightest noise or suspicion: crawling, watching, crawling, shamming dead under the blinding light of enemy flares, and again crawling, watching, crawling ...

We found the gap in the German wire and at last came within five yards of the sap-head. We waited quite twenty minutes, listening for any signs of its occupation. Then I nudged Sergeant Townsend and, revolver in hand, we wriggled quickly forward and slid into it. It was about three feet deep and unoccupied. On the floor were a few empty cartridges, and a wicker basket containing something large and smooth and round, twice the size of a football. I groped and felt all around it in the dark. I was afraid that it might be some sort of infernal machine. Eventually I dared lift it out and carry it back, suspecting that it might be one of the German gas-cylinders we had heard so much about.

We got home after making a journey of perhaps two hundred yards in rather more than two hours. The sentries passed along the word that we were in again. Our prize proved to be a large glass container quarter-filled with some pale yellow liquid. This was sent down to battalion headquarters, and from there to the divisional intelligence officer. Everybody seemed greatly interested in it. The theory was that the vessel contained a chemical for re-damping gas-masks, although it may have been dregs of country wine mixed with rain water. I never heard the official report. The Colonel, however, told Captain Thomas ... 'Your new wart [officer] seems to have more guts than the others.'

Ewart Alan Mackintosh – In No Man's Land
Mackintosh had been appointed in 1915 to battalion bombing officer, responsible for leading raids at night into no man's land to destroy forward German listening posts. The men chosen for the mission would blacken their faces, remove from their pockets any item that might allow them to be identified if killed or captured and, armed with Mills bombs, would crawl out of the trenches through gaps that had been made in the barbed wire towards the enemy lines. Not only were they in danger from enemy fire, perhaps when exposed by the light of a flare, but even of being shot by their own side when they returned if the sentries mistook them for Germans.

Despite – or perhaps because of – the stress and tension in such missions, Mackintosh wrote a somewhat light-hearted poem about his reluctance to shoot a German soldier with a cold while operating in no man's land:

In No Man's Land

The hedge on the left, and the trench on the right,
And the whispering, rustling wood between,
And who knows where in the wood tonight,
Death or capture may lurk unseen,
The open field and the figures lying
Under the shade of the apple trees –
Is it the wind in the branches sighing
Or a German trying to stop a sneeze.

Louder the voices of night come thronging,
But over them all the sound is clear,
Taking me back to the place of my longing
And the cultured sneezes I used to hear,
Lecture-time and my tutor's 'handker'
Stopping his period's rounded close,
Like the frozen hand of a German ranker
Down in a ditch with a cold in his nose.

I'm cold too, and a stealthy snuffle
From the man with a pistol covering me,
And the Bosche moving off with a snap and a shuffle
Break the windows of memory –
I can't make sure till the moon gets lighter –
Anyway, shooting is over bold,
Oh, damn you, get back to your trench, you blighter,
I really can't shoot a man with a cold.

(Hammerhead Wood, Thiepval, 1915)

SUCH IS DEATH – A SONNET BY CHARLES HAMILTON SORLEY

For all who fought in Flanders, death was an inescapable presence – death from enemy fire in an attack, death through the targeted shot from an unseen sniper, random death from an exploding shell, or the deaths of one's friends and comrades – but death would be 'a slate rubbed clean'. Sorley expressively captured this in a sonnet, *Such is Death*, written poignantly just a few months before he was himself killed:

Such is Death

Such, such is Death: no triumph: no defeat:
Only an empty pail, a slate rubbed clean,
A merciful putting away of what has been.

And this we know: Death is not Life effete,
Life crushed, the broken pail. We who have seen
So marvellous thing, know well the end not yet.

Victor and vanquished are a-one in death:
Coward and brave: friend, foe. Ghosts do not say
'Come, what was your record when you drew breath?'
But a big blot has hid each yesterday
So poor, so manifestly incomplete.
And your bright Promise, withered long and sped,
Is touched, stirs, rises, opens and grows sweet
And blossoms and is you, when you are dead.

(12 June 1915)

THE POPPIES IN FLANDERS FIELDS

Nothing is more evocative than the poppies that have become the symbol of remembrance of those who died in the First World War – not just the poppies which tumble from the roof of the Albert Hall during the annual British Legion Festival of Remembrance, nor even the poppies sold in aid of the British Legion, but in November 2014, perhaps most memorably of all, the poppies which formed a carpet of blood in the moat of the Tower of London commemorating those who had died in the Great War.

The blood-red poppies flourished in the rich soil of Flanders, often growing amongst the barbed wire amid the detritus of war, providing a splash of vivid red amongst the horrors. Poppies became the symbol of the war in

Flanders following the publication in December 1915 of *In Flanders Fields* by John McCrae.

Lieutenant Colonel John McCrae was a Canadian serving with the Royal Canadian Medical Corps, but as his name suggests he was the son of a Scottish immigrant. He died of pneumonia in January 1918:

In Flanders Fields

In Flanders fields the poppies blow
Between the crosses, row on row
   That mark our place; and in the sky
   The larks, still bravely singing, fly
Scarce heard amid the guns below.

We are the Dead. Short days ago
We lived, felt dawn, saw sunset glow,
   Loved and were loved, and now we lie
      In Flanders fields

Take up our quarrel with the foe:
To you from failing hands we throw
   The torch; be yours to hold it high.
   If ye break faith with us who die
We shall not sleep, though poppies grow
      In Flanders fields.

THE BATTLE OF LOOS: THE 'SCOTTISH BATTLE' (5 SEPTEMBER–7 NOVEMBER 1915)

The true beginning of the martyrdom of the British army.

J. Terraine, *Douglas Haig: The Educated Soldier*, p.154. Quoted in MacDonald and McFarland, *Scotland*, p.7.

Ewart Alan Mackintosh - Miserere

Mackintosh wrote the poem *Miserere* while in the trenches at La Boisselle, just before the Battle of Loos. It contrasts the youthful confidence in personal immortality with the ever-present fear of dying, addressing a prayer to God to ease the suffering from a painful, lonely death and to grant that death, if it came, should be without shame:

Miserere

Gone is now the boast of power,
Strength to fight our foes again,
God of battles in this hour
Give us strength to suffer pain.
Lest the spirit's chains be rent,
Lest the coward flesh go free
Unto thee our prayer is sent,
        Miserere Domine.

Death unseen beneath our feet,
Death above us in the sky,
Now before Thy judgement-seat
Grant us honourably to die.
Lustful, sinful, careless all,
In the martyr's road are we.
Lest from that high path we fall,
        Miserere Domine.

Men that mocked thee to Thy face,
Fools who took Thy name in vain –
Grant that in this deadly place
Jests and blasphemy remain.
On the pallid face of death,
Gasping slow and painfully
Curses with its latest breath,
        Miserere Domine.

Where we see the men we know
Rags of broken flesh and bone,
And the thing that hurt them so
Seems to wait for us alone,
Where the silence of the grave,

Broods and threatens soundlessly,
On the souls we cannot save,
        Miserere Domine.

The men who fought at the Battle of Loos required all the support they could glean from a belief in God and in the justice of the fight. It would be slaughter.

The Rationale

General Joffre, commander of the French forces, wanted to stage a co-ordinated attack on the German lines using French forces to attack Lens while the British attacked on a front extending from Loos in the north to Vimy Ridge in the south. The British commanders were less than enthusiastic. Haig declared firmly that to launch an attack at Loos would be madness because the ground was bare and open, giving no possibility of cover to the advancing troops, and because no significant strategic advantage would be gained. French was indecisive but Kitchener allowed himself to be persuaded by Joffre and ordered the attack to go ahead. The reality was worse, far worse, than could have been imagined.

The Battle

The tactics remained unaltered: a heavy artillery barrage intended to demolish the German defences and destroy the barbed wire to be followed by a frontal assault. The shortcomings also remained unaltered: the critical shortage of high-explosive artillery shells; the failure to destroy the German defences; an attack spread across a wide front rather than concentrated on a narrower objective with a significant superiority of force; the inability to demolish the German barbed-wire entanglements and the lack of any element of surprise, as a result of the extensive artillery bombardment which preceded the attack.

Controversially, the British would use chlorine gas for the first time. The views of Captain Thomas on the morality and efficacy of using gas are recorded by Graves in his book *Goodbye to All That* (p.123):

It's damnable. It's not soldiering to use stuff like that, even though the Germans did start it. It's dirty, and it'll bring us bad luck. We're sure to bungle it. Take those new gas-companies – sorry, excuse me this once, I mean accessory companies [accessory was the term euphemistically used to refer to the gas] – their very look makes me tremble. Chemistry-dons from London University, a few lads straight from school, one or two N.C.O.s of the old-soldier type, trained together for three weeks, then given a job as responsible as this. Of course they'll bungle it. How could they do anything else?

Not only was there a shortage of high-explosive shells, there were few heavy artillery guns – just 110 heavy guns thinly spread along an extended line of advance. The barrage was ineffective and the German defences remained untouched. Even the gas moved randomly in the light and fickle breeze – it did not seem to have occurred to anyone that to use gas successfully it would be helpful to have a steady breeze blowing towards the German lines. And to cap it all, despite initial successes, there was again too great a delay before reserves were introduced into the battle, thus allowing the Germans to regroup. The second wave of the attack was greeted by heavy German artillery and machine-gun fire and much of the ground which had been so expensively gained was lost.

Haig again relied heavily on his Scottish troops. Forty-five Scottish battalions were in action at the Battle of Loos, accounting for half of all those who fought (Young, *Scottish Voices*, pp.133–4). When the command to attack was given, the 15th (Scottish) Division, with thirteen Scottish battalions, led the attack in the south, advancing in good order in line abreast across the bare, open ground, through swirling clouds of British gas.

The 7th Battalion of the King's Own Scottish Borderers hesitated to go over the top under the pressure of the heavy German artillery barrage and the British gas which was being blown back into the trenches. 'For God's sake, Laidlaw, pipe them together,' came the command. Piper Laidlaw scaled the parapet of the trenches and the eerie silence was broken by the skirl of the pipes as a lone Scottish piper of the King's Own Borderers marched towards the enemy lines playing the regimental march *Blue Bonnets Over the Border*, inspiring by example those hesitant to go 'over the top'. Sergeant Piper Daniel Logan Laidlaw was awarded the VC for this outstanding act of selfless bravery.

The gas swirled across the battlefield as the men advanced, some dying from exposure to the British gas, and then as the troops approached the German lines the silence was harshly broken by the sudden and insistent chatter of the German machine guns. The slaughter was horrific as body piled up upon body. There was nowhere to hide, nowhere safe from the death dealt by the murderous machine guns, but the Scots pushed on to capture the village of Loos. A watching staff officer noted with pride:

It was magnificent ... As the men reached our wire they made their way through it with perfect coolness and deliberation, in spite of the enemy's increasingly heavy rifle fire. Once in No Man's Land they took up their dressing and walked – yes coolly walked – across towards the enemy trenches. There was no running or shouting; here and there a man finding himself out of line would double for a pace or two, look to his right and left, take up his dressing and continue to advance at a steady walk. The effect of those seemingly unconcerned Highlanders advancing upon them must have had a considerable effect on the Germans. I saw one man whose kilt had got caught in our wire as he passed through a gap; he did not attempt to tear it off, but, carefully disentangling it, doubled up to his correct position in the line and went on.   (J. Stewart and John Buchan, *The Fifteenth (Scottish) Division 1914-19*, p.34)

The German view, given by a regimental diarist, was somewhat different:

They moved forward in ten columns 'each about a thousand men, all advancing as if carrying out a parade-ground drill'. The German defenders were astounded by the sight of an 'entire front covered with the enemy's infantry'. They stood up, some even on the parapet of the trench, and fired triumphantly into the mass of men advancing across the open grassland. The machine-gunners had opened fire at 1,500 yards range. 'Never had machine-guns had such straightforward work to do ... with barrels becoming hot and swimming in oil, they traversed to and fro along the enemy's ranks; one machine-gun alone fired 12,500 rounds that afternoon. The effect was devastating. The enemy could be seen falling literally in hundreds, but they continued their march in good order and without interruption' until they reached the unbroken wire of the Germans' second position. 'Confronted by this impenetrable obstacle the survivors turned and began to retire.'   (Keegan, *First World War*, p.218)

It all made a mockery of Haig's report to the British War Council just five months earlier that 'the machine gun is a much overrated weapon and two per battalion is more than sufficient' (quoted in Gilbert, *First World War*, p.199).

Graves was in the trenches waiting until dawn for the order to attack. In *Goodbye to All That* he gives a graphic description of the attack, which turned all too quickly into a slaughter (pp.126-31):

Half a mile of communication trench, known as 'Maison Rouge Alley', sepa-
rated us from the firing line. At half past five the gas would be discharged. We
were cold, tired, sick and not at all in the mood for battle, but tried to snatch an
hour or two of sleep squatting in the trench. It had been raining for some time.

He continues:

The events of the next few minutes are difficult for me now to sort out. I found
it more difficult still at the time. All we heard back there in the sidings was a
distant cheer, confused crackle of rifle fire, yells, heavy shelling on our front
line, more shouts and yells, and a continuous rattle of machine-guns. After a
few minutes, lightly wounded men of the Middlesex came stumbling down
Maison Rouge Alley to the dressing-station. I stood at the junction of the
siding and the Alley.

'What's happened? What's happened?' I asked.

'Bloody balls-up,' was the most detailed answer I could get.

Among the wounded were a number of men yellow-faced and choking,
their buttons tarnished green – gas cases. Then came the badly wounded.
Maison Rouge Alley being narrow, the stretchers had difficulty in getting
down. The Germans started shelling it with five-point-nines.

He later explains the shambolic gas attack:

It seems that at half past four an R.E. captain commanding the gas-com-
pany in the front line phoned through to divisional headquarters: 'Dead calm.
Impossible discharge accessory.' The answer he got was: 'Accessory to be
discharged at all costs.' Thomas had not over-estimated the gas-company's
efficiency. The spanners for unscrewing the cocks of the cylinders proved, with
two or three exceptions, to be misfits. The gas-men rushed about shouting
for the loan of an adjustable spanner. They managed to discharge one or
two cylinders; the gas went whistling out, formed a thick cloud a few yards
off in No Man's land, and then gradually spread back into our trenches.
The Germans, who had been expecting gas, immediately put on their gas-
helmets: semi-rigid ones, better than ours. Bundles of oily cotton-waste were
strewn along the German parapet and set alight as a barrier to the gas. Then
their batteries opened on our lines. The confusion in the front trench must have
been horrible; direct hits broke several of the gas-cylinders, the trench filled
with gas, the gas-company stampeded.

The 9th (Scottish) Division, comprising a further thirteen Scottish battalions, was sent in a second wave to attack the Hohenzollern Redoubt and succeeded in reaching the German second line despite heavy losses from British gas and German crossfire. The 6th Battalion King's Own Scottish Borderers and the 10th Battalion Highland Light Infantry both suffered heavy losses as they were trapped in no man's land (Young, *Scottish Voices*, pp.132-4).

Private Thomas Williamson of the Royal Scots Fusiliers was in the second attack:

> The great attack had begun, and our infantry had left the trenches and were at grips with the Bosch [*sic*]. Half an hour after the attack the Royal Scots Fusiliers moved forward in company formation ... I felt a queer sensation inside me, as I kept step with the boys, and then witnessed a magnificent spectacle. Coming across the open towards us were hundreds of our Tommies, who were all more or less seriously wounded. Men wounded in the face head and arms were assisting those who were wounded in legs or feet. It was an inspiring sight, comradeship at its very best, all striving to help each other. As they passed us on their way to the first field dressing station, I saw the grim determination on each face. I saw more than that; blood streaming from their wounds, their clothes rent and torn. Others were deathly pale, portraying the awful ordeal they had been through, but in their eyes shone the light of a battle. As they passed us by, those scarred and battered human beings gave us a shout of encouragement 'Up you go Jock and give them Hell.' (Quoted in Young, *Scottish Voices*, p.136)

Losses were heavy: the 15th (Scottish) Division lost 7,000 men, killed or captured, while the 9th (Scottish) Division lost 6,000 men (Young, *Scottish Voices*, pp.132-4). In a rare but touching gesture of humanity, the Germans were so appalled by the slaughter that after the first day's fighting they ceased firing to let the British recover the wounded. Men worked throughout the night and managed to recover most of the injured and the bodies of those who had died before dawn.

So, after such a slaughter what strategy would Haig adopt? The French and British commands had agreed that success would not come from the first wave of attack but by rapidly deploying a second wave to advance through the first wave to maintain the momentum of the attack. Crucially, however, command of the second wave had been given to Sir John French as supreme commander, rather than to the commanders on the front. As a result, the reserves did not reach the fighting until the next morning and any momentum was irretrievably lost. This did not deter Haig.

On the second day, 10,000 reserve troops were sent in, advancing deliberately, purposefully and in line abreast towards the German lines; within four hours, 8,000 men had been killed or wounded and it proved impossible to hold the ground taken.

At last the order to retreat was given. The tattered remnants of the brave advance – many wounded, some near death, but helped by their comrades – limped back towards the safety of the British line. The machine guns stayed strangely quiet, the German gunners sickened by the needless carnage. Sixteen thousand British soldiers had been killed and a further 25,000 wounded. German losses had been minimal (Keegan, *First World War*, p.218).

The Battle of Loos was one of the worst disasters in the war so far, but worse was to come.

Ronald Leighton, Vera Brittain's fiancé, fought at Loos and was enraged by the horror and the futility, contrasting the reality of war with the platitudinous sentiments expressed in the poems by Rupert Brooke which she had sent him. He wrote:

> Let him who thinks War is a glorious thing, who loves to roll forth stirring words of exhortation, invoking Honour and Praise and Valour and Love of Country ... let him but look at a little pile of sodden grey rags that cover half a skull and a shin bone and what might have been Its ribs, or at this skeleton lying on its side ... and let him realise how grand & glorious a thing it is to have distilled all Youth and Joy and Life into a foetid heap of hideous putrescence. Who is there who has known & seen who can say Victory is worth the death of even one of these?   (Letter to Vera Brittain, September 1915, quoted in Bostridge (ed.), *Because you Died: The Poetry and Prose of the First World War and After*, p.xxi)

To offset the horror there were instances of astonishing humanity and bravery. Graves recounts the story of Private Baxter, who was awarded the DCM for an act of considerable bravery:

> On the morning of the 27th a cry arose from No Man's Land. A wounded soldier of the Middlesex had recovered consciousness after two days. He lay

close to the German wire. Our men heard it and looked at each other. We had a tender-hearted lance-corporal named Baxter ... As soon as he heard the wounded Middlesex man, he ran along the trench calling for a volunteer to help fetch him in. Of course, no one would go; It was death to put one's head over the parapet. When he came running to ask me I excused myself as being the only officer in the company. I would come out with him at dusk, I said – not now. So he went alone. He jumped quickly over the parapet, then strolled across No Man's Land, waving a handkerchief; the Germans fired to frighten him, but since he persisted they let him come up close. Baxter continued towards them and, when he got to the Middlesex man, stopped and pointed to show the Germans what he was at. Then he dressed the man's wounds, gave him a drink of rum and some biscuit that he had with him, and promised to be back again at nightfall. He did come back, with a stretcher party, and the man eventually recovered. (*Goodbye to All That*, pp.137–8)

How Had the French Offensive Fared?

The French had fared no better, as they had failed to reach the German second line of defence – a line of trenches out of the range of the French artillery and hidden from view by a reverse slope. Their attacks at Vimy Ridge and in Champagne had failed with the French, losing, in all, 140,000 dead or wounded. Joffre survived as French commander-in-chief, claiming after the event that the rationale for the attack had been, 'We shall kill more of the enemy than he can kill of us' (quoted in Strachan, *First World War*, p.177). The argument was somewhat specious, as the French and British forces suffered far more casualties than the Germans.

As the year ended, the advantage lay with the Central Powers.

Douglas Haig

Sir John French was not so fortunate as his French counterpart, as Douglas Haig did not miss the opportunity to blame French for the delay in releasing the reserves and to use his influence with King George V to have himself installed as commander-in-chief in French's place.

Haig relished his role as commander-in-chief of the BEF, serving as a determined and effective leader. It could conversely be argued that he was tactically unimaginative, not particularly intelligent (he had failed his examination at staff college), stubborn and strategically inflexible. Despite repeated failures and heavy losses he would persist with the policy of frontal attacks on the German lines, achieving little territorial gain at a severe cost in casualties, and believing in a strategy of attrition – that one should wear down the size and morale of the enemy's forces by repeated attacks before finally defeating them on the battlefield.

Patrick MacGill – After Loos

Patrick MacGill was born in Ireland but had migrated to Scotland. In 1914 he enlisted in the London Irish Rifles and served as a stretcher bearer. He was wounded and gassed at the Battle of Loos and was invalided back to Britain where he worked in Intelligence at the War Office. His poem *After Loos* succinctly summarises the losses suffered by the British:

After Loos

Was it only yesterday
Lusty comrades marched away?
Now they're covered up with clay.

Seven glasses used to be
Called for six good mates and me –
Now we only call for three.

Little crosses neat and white,
Looking lonely every night,
Tell of comrades killed in fight.

Hearty fellows they have been,
And no more will they be seen
Drinking wine in Nouex les Mines.

Lithe and supple lads were they,
Marching merrily away –
Was it only yesterday?

(Café Pierre le Blanc, Nouex les Mines, Michaelmas Eve, 1915)

Edith Cavell: 12 October 1915

Edith Cavell was born near Norwich in December 1865. She trained as a nurse at the London Hospital and after working at a number of hospitals in England was recruited to the position of matron at the newly established Belgian Nursing School, L'École Belge d'Infirmieres Diplomées, in Brussels.

In November 1914, after the German invasion of Belgium, she began sheltering British and French soldiers and helping them to reach neutral Netherlands in contravention of German military law. On 3 August 1915 she was betrayed by a collaborator, arrested by the German military and charged with treason. She was held a prisoner for ten weeks and admitted that she had helped sixty British and fifteen French soldiers to escape from occupied Belgium, making no attempt to defend herself.

On 12 October she was executed by a German firing squad. Her words on the evening before her death, 'Patriotism is not enough. I must have no hatred or bitterness to anyone,' are engraved on her statue near Trafalgar Square in London. Her execution became a symbol of German cruelty.

WHEN YOU SEE MILLIONS OF THE MOUTHLESS DEAD – CHARLES HAMILTON SORLEY

On 13 October Sorley was shot in the head by a sniper at the Battle of Loos as he took command of his company. He was 20 years old. This moving poem, written in the expectation he might soon die, was found written in pencil in his kitbag:

When You See Millions of the Mouthless Dead

When you see millions of the mouthless dead
Across your dreams in pale battalions go,
Say not soft things as other men have said,
That you'll remember. For you need not so.
Give them not praise. For, deaf, how should they know
It is not curses heaped on each gashed head?
Nor tears. Their blind eyes see not your tears flow.
Nor honour. It is easy to be dead.
Say only this, 'They are dead.' Then add thereto,
'Yet many a better one had died before.'

Then, scanning all the o'ercrowded mass, should you
Perceive one face that you loved heretofore,
It is a spook. None wears the face you knew
Great death has made all his for evermore.

THE MEETING OF GRAVES AND SASSOON

It was after the Battle of Loos that Graves first met Sassoon, who had been posted to the 1st Battalion Royal Welch Fusiliers. Graves, a battle-hardened officer, saw a book in the mess which was 'neither a military text-book nor a rubbishy novel'. The name on the flysheet was Siegfried Sassoon. He introduced himself and they ate cream buns together, discussing poetry. Sassoon was new to the front and Graves criticised his literary efforts as being too naïve, saying that battle experience would soon change his style.

Unsurprisingly, they developed a friendship which would later save Sassoon from court martial (Graves, *Goodbye to All That*, p.146). Graves records their meeting and friendship in his poem *Two Fusiliers*:

Two Fusiliers

And have we done with War at last?
Well, we've been lucky devils both,
And there's no need of pledge or oath
To bind our lovely friendship fast,
By firmer stuff
Close bound enough.

By wire and wood and stake we're bound,
By Fricourt and by Festubert,
By whipping rain, by the sun's glare,
By all the misery and loud sound,
By a Spring day,
By Picard clay.

Show me the two so closely bound
As we, by the wet bond of blood,
By friendship blossoming from mud,

By Death: we faced him, and we found
Beauty in Death,
In dead men, breath.

CHRIST IN FLANDERS

The needless slaughter tested the faith of Christians. How could a just and loving God condone such horror? Church parades were compulsory and the reaction to sermons could be mixed. Generally, chaplains were more effective and popular if they suffered with the soldiers, many going to the front either to ease a soldier's last moments or to assist in medical care.

The Reverend Victor Tanner, chaplain to the 2nd Battalion Worcestershire Regiment, received the Victoria Cross for bravery during heavy fighting in the early part of the Battle of Passchendaele in September 1917. He stationed himself in a forward aid post in a captured German pillbox and provided support to the men under heavy German fire. He also helped carry the wounded in the absence of the RAMC stretcher bearers (Brown, IWM Book, p.66).

Father Bernard Marshal, Roman Catholic chaplain to the 62nd Infantry Brigade, 21st Division, would be awarded the Military Cross for 'giving help to men in a shelled area'. He used to visit the trenches in search of Catholics, and in September 1915 wrote in one of the school exercise books he used as a diary that in 'my first battle' (the Battle of Loos) he had taken cover with a group of British soldiers sheltering in what remained of a farm:

I made use of the time by finding out the Catholics amongst the men there, and heard a few confessions standing where we were amongst all the noise and din of battle - great aids to contrition.   (Quoted in Brown, IWM Book, p.249)

Ewart Alan Mackintosh - Christ in Flanders

Christ in Flanders

Oh, you that took our sin and pain
Upon your shoulders long ago,
Are you come back to earth again,

About the battle do you go?
By trenches where with bitter cries
Men's spirits leave their tortured clay,
Oh, wanderer with the mournful eyes,
Are you on Flanders soil today?

The battle fog is wreathed and curled
Before us, that we cannot see
The darkness of the newer world
As your eternal agony,
The gallant hearts, the bitter blood,
The pains of them that have not died,
A bright light in the eyes of God
A sharp spear-point in his side.

(Written in 1915 after a church parade)

Siegfried Sassoon - "They"
Siegfried Sassoon was characteristically mocking in his poem "They", written in London in October 1916:

"They"

The Bishop tells us: "When the boys come back
They will not be the same; for they'll have fought
In a just cause: they lead the last attack
On Anti-Christ; their comrades' blood has bought
New right to breed an honourable race,
They have challenged Death and dared him face to face."

"We're none of us the same!" the boys reply,
"For George lost both his legs; and Bill's stone blind;
Poor Jim's shot through the lungs and like to die;
And Bert's gone syphilitic: You'll not find
A chap who's served that hasn't found some change."
And the Bishop said: "The ways of God are strange."

THE CARE OF THE WOUNDED

Back to 'Blighty'

There was a well-organised path for medical care of the wounded. First aid at the front would be administered by the regimental aid post, manned by a medical officer and serviced by stretcher bearers. The stretcher bearers would then carry the wounded back to the collecting post, where horse-drawn or mechanised ambulances would take them to the advanced dressing station, which was under regimental control, and then to the main dressing station. From there, the more seriously wounded would be shipped to the casualty clearing station and then to the base hospital. Those fit enough returned to duty; those more seriously wounded were shipped back to 'Blighty'; those most seriously wounded were given what comfort could be provided before death freed them from further suffering (David Rorie, *A Medico's Luck in the War*, diagram facing p.5).

The Scottish Women's Hospital: Royaumont Abbey

Ce charmant hôpital Ecossais, que les poilus appellent 'Paradis'.

Private Breuilh (*le poilu*, the 'hairy one', was the slang term used for a private in the French Army). Quoted in Eileen Crofton, *The Women of Royaumont*, p.103.

Elsie Inglis, the founder of the Scottish Women's Hospitals, had realised at the outbreak of the war that there would be a role for a hospital staffed solely by women and had proposed setting up a unit in France. Unsurprisingly, this was too advanced for the War Office, who advised her, 'My good lady. Go home and sit still.' The French were more open-minded and the first Scottish Women's Hospital of 200 beds was established in the medieval abbey of Royaumont under the auspices of the French Red Cross.

The Scottish nurses left Edinburgh on 2 December and crossed the Channel in a fearsome gale. The abbey had been unoccupied for eight or nine years and was virtually derelict; it was spacious, but this was about its only virtue. There was no water supply, no lighting and only one stove, but above all it was encrusted with dirt accumulated over a number of years. 'The weather was icy, with snow on the ground, and the only facilities for washing were tap and sink situated in a vaulted chamber which had stood unwarmed for the better part of ten years' (Cicely Hamilton, a volunteer at Royaumont, quoted in Trevor Royle, *Isn't All This Bloody?*, p.105). They worked all hours to meet the required standards, even scrubbing floors by candlelight, and on 10 January 1915, after a detailed inspection, permission was given from the French Red Cross for the admission of patients. Now the work of the hospital could start.

The hospital at Royaumont was unique amongst the hospitals supporting the injured soldiers and airmen on the Western Front in that it was staffed exclusively by women. Women drivers collected the patients, often driving their ambulances into the firing line; women stretcher bearers lifted the patients to carry them into the hospital; women nurses cleaned their wounds; women surgeons operated on them; and women nurses and orderlies looked after them on the wards, nursing them back to health.

The majority of the patients were French, stretching the French-speaking abilities of the staff, but by the end of the war the hospital had treated British, Canadian and American soldiers, as well as a few local patients.

The French Army, in their wisdom, did not issue the wounded with replacement uniforms, so one of the tasks of the staff was to fumigate the uniforms, wash them thoroughly and mend them with whatever was available so that they could be worn again by the soldier on discharge. *Les poilus* received poor treatment from the army, receiving only 20 *sous* a day in pay (in old money, two pence), poor rations and enduring, appalling living conditions, sometimes spending weeks in the trenches before being relieved. Their only consolation was *le pinard* – a quart of rough, red wine per day – while their officers lived in comparative comfort.

In June 1916 the hospital was warned to be ready for a big influx of patients from the Great Push (the Battle of the Somme), increasing its capacity from 200 beds to 400. One of the radiographers, V.C.C. Callum, gave a vivid account of working in the hospital in early July 1916, bringing to life the dreadful statistics of the casualties incurred in the fighting:

> Their wounds were terrible ... Many of these men were wounded – dangerously – in two, three, four and five places. That great enemy of the surgeon who would conserve life and limb, gas gangrene,* was already at work in

* Gas gangrene was caused by soil-borne bacteria infecting an open wound and producing gas in the body tissues, which caused bubbles in the blood. The stench was overwhelming. Gas gangrene was usually fatal and the only treatment was immediate surgery to amputate the infected limb.

90% of cases. Hence the urgent need for immediate operation, often for immediate amputation. The surgeon did not stop to search for shrapnel and pieces of metal: their one aim was to open up and clean out the wounds, or to cut off the mortifying limb before the dread gangrene had tracked its way into the vital parts of the body. The stench was very bad. Most of the poor fellows were too far gone to say much.

She continues:

[Our hospital] had accommodation for 400. And for weeks we worked, once we were filled, with never a bed to spare. Our operating theatre was hardly ever left vacant long enough to be cleaned during the small hours and it became a problem how to air the x-ray rooms during the short hours of dawn that stretched between the ending of one day's work and the beginning of another's. We were fighting gas gangrene and time was the factor that counted most. We dared not stop work in the theatre until it became physically impossible to continue.

For us who worked, and for those patient suffering men, lying along the corridor outside the x-ray rooms and the theatre, on stretchers, awaiting their turn, it was a nightmare of glaring lights, of appalling stenches of ether and chloroform, and violent sparking of tired x-ray tubes, of scores of wet negatives that were seized upon by their respective surgeons and taken into the hot theatre before they even had time to be rinsed in the dark room.

Beneath and beyond the anxiety of saving men's lives, there was the undercurrent of anxiety of the theatre staff as to whether the boiling of instruments and gloves could be kept level with the rapidity with which the cases were carried in and put on the table, as to whether the gauze and wool and swabs would last!

She ended, proudly:

I do not think we lost a case from delay in locating the trouble and operating in all that first terrible week of July. The losses were due to delay in reaching the hospital.   (Quoted in Eileen Crofton, *The Women of Royaumont*, pp.72-3)

The staff would again come under intense pressure in May 1918 when the satellite hospital situated near the front line at Villers-Cotterêts was overwhelmed by the heavy casualties suffered by the French as the Germans relentlessly advanced in what became known as the Second Battle of the Marne. As the Germans came ever nearer, the staff were forced to evacuate, transporting the patients along the road back to Royaumont, joining the stream of refugees fleeing from the front line and meeting thousands of French soldiers marching towards the line as reinforcements. As the staff escaped, they ran the gauntlet of German shelling and bombing targeted on the French reinforcements.

The staff continued to work all hours until the Allied counter-attack in August when the front line moved way from Royaumont and the number of wounded arriving at the hospital began to decline.

Four weeks after the end of the war, on 12 December 1918, Miss Ivens, chief medical officer, and another twenty-two members of her staff were awarded the Croix de Guerre by a grateful French government. The official closure date for the Royaumont Hospital was 31 December 1918, and it closed completely in March 1919. During its time as a hospital, Royaumont had cared for an astonishing 10,861 patients. Of these, 8,752 were *blessés* – wounded soldiers – and of these, just 159 had died, a tribute to the skill, dedication and hard work of the medical staff (Crofton, *Women*, p.225).

Vera Brittain: 25 December 1915

Vera Brittain had won a scholarship to Somerville College, Oxford when war broke out. Her brother Edward and his friend Roland Leighton also had places at Oxford, but instead enlisted. Vera believed that she, too, should contribute to the war effort and after her first year at Oxford suspended her studies to enrol in 1915 as a nurse with the Voluntary Aid Detachment (VAD), commencing training at the 1st London General Hospital in Camberwell, the military extension of St Bartholomew's Hospital.

Her autobiography, *Testament of Youth*, is a very readable account of her experiences during the war, giving a vivid account of her nursing training and the effect of the war on a girl from a sheltered middle-class background. She recounts her developing relationship with Roland Leighton, with whom she became engaged after a chaste and intellectual courtship. In December 1915 she was granted special Christmas leave to meet her fiancé who was also coming home on leave. She tells of waiting in the lounge of the Grand Hotel in Brighton for the telephone call confirming he was home, but when she did not receive a call, she had gone to bed, tired but unworried. The next day she received the telephone call that every mother, wife, fiancée and girlfriend dreaded, the call that told her that he had died of his wounds in a casualty clearing station in France on 23 December (Vera Brittain, *Testament of Youth*, p.210).

Vera Brittain wrote the poem *Perhaps* to mark his loss. Perhaps life would continue, but a part of her was lost and gone forever:

Perhaps
(To R.A.L. Died of wounds in France, December 23rd 1915)

Perhaps some day the sun will shine again,
    And I shall see that still the skies are blue,
And feel once more I do not live in vain,
    Although bereft of You.

Perhaps the golden meadows at my feet
    Will make the sunny hours of Spring seem gay,
And I shall find the white May blossoms sweet,
    Though You have passed away.

Perhaps the summer woods will shimmer bright,
    And crimson roses once again be fair,
And autumn harvest fields a rich delight,
    Although You are not there.

Perhaps some day I shall not shrink in pain
    To see the passing of the dying year,
And listen to the Christmas songs again,
    Although You cannot hear.

But, though kind Time may many joys renew,
    There is one greatest joy I shall not know
Again, because my heart for loss of You
    Was broken, long ago.

(1st London General Hospital, February 1916)

In August 1917 she volunteered to go to France and was posted to the 24th General Hospital at Étaples, a base hospital located on the coast but adjacent to the main railway line. Here, she worked in a ward caring for injured German prisoners. The experience affected her deeply, as she realised that a dying German prisoner needed and deserved to be comforted just as much as a dying British soldier. She was particularly moved by the death of one of her patients, writing:

> Another badly wounded boy – A Prussian lieutenant who was being transferred to England – held out an emaciated hand to me as he lay on the stretcher waiting to go, and murmured: 'I thank you, Sister.' After barely a second's hesitation I took the pale fingers in mine, thinking how ridiculous it was that I should be holding this man's hand in friendship when perhaps, only a week or two earlier, Edward [her brother] up at Ypres had been doing his best to kill him. The world was mad and we were all victims; that was the only way to look at it. These shattered, dying boys and I were paying alike for a situation that none of us had desired or done anything to bring about.   (*Testament of Youth*, pp.342–3)

Vera Brittain suffered further loss. She had returned to England to care for her elderly parents when she learnt of the death of Edward in June 1918. She wrote:

> ... there came the sudden loud clattering at the front-door knocker that always meant a telegram ... I opened and read it in a tearing anguish of suspense. 'Regret to inform you Captain E. H. Brittain killed in action Italy June 15th.' 'No answer,' I told the boy mechanically, and handed the telegram to my father, who had followed me into the hall. As we went back into the dining-room I saw, as though I had never seen them before, the bowl of blue delphiniums on the table; their intense colour, vivid, ethereal, seemed too radiant for earthly flowers.   (*Testament of Youth*, p.401)

Eva Dobell – Night Duty

Another VAD who wrote movingly of her experience as a nurse in France was Eva Dobell. One of her most moving poems was *Night Duty*, which examined the shattered lives of the fit young men now lying maimed and injured in hospital beds:

Night Duty

The pain and laughter of the day are done,
So strangely hushed and still the long ward seems,
Only the Sister's candle softly beams.
Clear from the church nearby the clock strikes "one;"
And all are wrapt away in secret sleep and dreams.

They bandied talk and jest from bed to bed;
Now sleep has touched them with a subtle change.
They lie here deep withdrawn, remote and strange;
A dimly outlined shape, a tumbled head.
Through what far lands do now their wand'ring spirits range?

Here one cries sudden on a sobbing breath,
Gripped in the clutch of some incarnate fear:
What terror through the darkness draweth near
What memory of carnage and of death?
What vanished scenes of dread to his closed eyes appear?

And one laughs out with an exultant joy.
An athlete he – Maybe his young limbs strain
In some remembered game, and not in vain
To win his side the goal. Poor crippled boy,
Who in the waking world will never run again.

One murmurs soft and low a woman's name;
And here a vet'ran soldier, calm and still
As sculptured marble sleeps, and roams at will
Through eastern lands where sunbeams scorch like flame,
By rich bazaar and town, and wood-wrapt snow-crowned hill.

Through the wide open window one great star,
Swinging her lamp above the pear-tree high,
Looks in upon these dreaming forms that lie
So near in body, yet in souls as far
As these bright worlds thick strewn on that vast depth of sky.

Siegfried Sassoon - The Hero

It was the duty of officers to write letters of condolence to the relatives of those killed. These letters were often somewhat economical with the truth, disguising the extent of injuries suffered or downplaying the suffering caused by a lingering death, even embroidering the details of a less than heroic death, all to spare the feelings of those at home.

Sassoon wrote *The Hero* in August 1916 while recuperating from severe gastric fever in Somerville College, Oxford. Somerville had been requisitioned in 1916 as a hospital for officers and its lady students had been transferred to Oriel College where they were lodged in St Mary's Hall, safely isolated from the dangers of contact with the few male students remaining:

The Hero

"Jack fell as he'd have wished" the Mother said,
And folded up the letter she'd read.
"The Colonel writes so nicely." Something broke
In the tired voice that quavered to a choke.
She half looked up. "We mothers are so proud
Of our dead soldiers." Then her face was bowed.

Quietly the Brother Officer went out.
He'd told the poor old dear some gallant lies
That she would nourish all her days, no doubt.
For while he coughed and mumbled, her weak eyes
Had shone with gentle triumph, brimmed with joy,
Because he'd been so brave, her glorious boy.

He thought how "Jack" cold-footed, useless swine,
Had panicked down the trench that night the mine
Went up at Wicked Corner, how he'd tried
To get sent home, and how, at last, he died,
Blown to small bits. And no one seemed to care
Except the lonely woman with white hair.

THE DEFEAT OF SERBIA

Elsie Inglis in Serbia

In April 1915 Elsie Inglis, the founder of the Scottish Women's Hospitals, went to Serbia to take charge of one of the hospitals, which had been set up in January 1915 under the auspices of the Scottish Women's Hospitals, replacing the doctor in charge who had contracted diphtheria.

There were three hospitals in Serbia when Inglis arrived: a surgical unit to deal with battlefield injuries; a special unit to deal with typhus, which was rampant; and a general unit. In total they provided 570 beds. The staff worked in conditions of extreme difficulty with insufficient supplies of clean water and ineffective sanitation; in one hospital the raw sewage was drained through holes in the floor and thence by a ditch running beneath the floor of the ward to a cesspit (Andrew Ferguson, *Scots Who Enlightened the World*, pp. 171–7).

The War in Serbia

The railway link between Germany and the Ottoman Empire which, if opened, would allow free movement of men, munitions and armaments between the fronts, ran through Serbia. Despite this strategic importance, Serbia received no help from the Allies and in September 1915 was attacked by 400,000 German, Austrian and Bulgarian troops. The Serbian forces were overwhelmed, suffering 90,000 casualties and a further 170,000 captured or missing; the remnants of their army escaped through snow and blizzards over the mountains of Albania.

A combined British and French force landed at Salonika in October 1915 with the aim of supporting the Serbs, but with a total strength of just 30,000 men it was a case of too little, too late. British, French and Italian ships took the few survivors of the defeated Serbian Army to safety, accompanied by a horde of terrified civilian refugees. British soldier, Private William Knott, wrote about the refugees in his diary:

In the afternoon a long line of refugees passed under military escort. What a heart-rending sight it was, thin, half-clad, starved women and children dragging their weary way, many with sore bare feet ... [while their] husbands drove little skeletons of donkeys loaded with all their belongings, consisting of a few old tins and spare clothing; almost pushing some of them, in fact some lay down and died.

Rather charmingly, he continues:

> The night was bitter cold, so I got fifteen fellows to sacrifice their issue of cocoa
> and off we went up the hillside where we found some stragglers who, abso-
> lutely exhausted, had dropped helpless at the wayside. We first gave drink to
> women and children, then the men, all of whom were chattering away, prob-
> ably trying to thank us.   (Quoted in Brown, *IWM Book*, pp.173-4)

Elsie Inglis and the Remnants of the Scottish Women's Hospitals

In December 1915 most of the staff of the hospitals were repatriated, but
Inglis and a few others remained, taken prisoner by the Germans and only
freed through the intervention of the United States.

Inglis remained faithful to the Serbs and in August 1916 went to Russia
to found a field hospital for Serbs who were fighting with the Russians. The
Serbs, who had only 4,000 men left out of an initial force of 10,000,
were forced to retreat from the advancing German forces after fierce fight-
ing alongside the Russians. After the October Revolution, Inglis feared for
the safety of the remnants of the Serbian regiment and pleaded with the
British Foreign Office to allow the Serbs to come to Britain. In October 1917
her persistence was rewarded; she cabled, 'On our way home. Everything
satisfactory, and all well except me' (Eva Shaw McLaren, *The Woman with
the Torch*, p.81).

Inglis was somewhat economical with the truth. She was terminally ill with
cancer but survived long enough to reach Newcastle by ship in November
1917 after a bitterly cold voyage and fierce storms. Here, she summoned
up the strength to say farewell to her Serbian friends but, exhausted by her
illness, died three days later.

Churchill wrote that she and her nurses 'would shine in history' (quoted in
Ferguson, *Scots*, p.177).

Romania Intervenes - Briefly

Further Allied troops were landed at Salonika to resist a projected attack
by the Bulgarians but, in the event, the Bulgarians proved reluctant to fight.
The Allied forces stayed in Salonika, fearing the impact of a further defeat
after the disaster of Gallipoli and in the hope that Romania, with its exten-
sive oil fields, would join the Allied side.

Encouraged by Russian successes, Romania did eventually join the Allies
in August 1916, but although its army was large in number it was poorly

equipped and trained. They were outfought and outflanked by com-
bined German and Austrian forces under the command of General von
Falkenhayn, and Bucharest was captured on 6 December 1916. The only
consolation for the Allies was that Romania's oil reserves did not fall into
the hands of the Central Powers, as the day before the Germans entered
Bucharest a British aide serving in Romania had blown up 800,000 tons
of fuel in a spectacular explosion.

The Allied troops remained in Salonika for the majority of the war,
effectively isolated in what was appropriately described by a German as
'the greatest Allied internment camp' of the war (quoted in Brown, *IWM
Book*, p.171).

SNOW IN FRANCE

Ewart Alan Mackintosh wrote an evocative poem, *Snow in France*, while in
Bois d'Authuille in the winter of 1915, in which he contrasts the boyish delight
of playing in the snow (a memory shared by both German and British
troops) with the harsh realities of the present. Were the Germans so very
different, or did they share the same hopes, the same childhood memories
and the same fears as their British opponents?

Snow in France

The tattered grass of No Man's Land
    Is white with snow today,
And up and down the deadly slopes
    The ghosts of childhood play.

The sentries, peering from the line,
    See in the tumbled snow
Light forms that were their little selves
    A score of years ago.

We look and see the crumpled drifts
    Piled in a little glen,
And you are back in Saxony
    And children once again.

From joyous hand to laughing face
    We watch the snow-balls fly,
The way they used to ere we were men
    Waiting our turn to die.

To-night across the empty slopes
    The shells will scream once more,
And flares go up and bullets fly
    The way they did before;

But for a little space of peace
    We watch them come and go,
The children that were you and I
    At play among the snow.

Archduke Franz Ferdinand and his wife during their official visit to Sarajevo shortly before their assassination, 28 June 1914. (© IWM, Q 114772)

The seizure of Cabrinovich, one of the group of assassins who threw a bomb shortly before Gavrilo Princip shot and killed Archduke Franz Ferdinand and his wife. (© IWM, Q 91841)

'Women of Britain Say – Go': the use of women in the encouragement of men to volunteer. (© IWM, Q 46428)

'Your Country's Call': a kilted Scottish infantryman stands before rolling English hills and picturesque thatched cottages. This poster is a graphic illustration of the contradictions within British national identity. It is difficult to imagine the obverse of this image – an English soldier in the Scottish Highlands. (© IWM, Art.IWM PST 0320)

Zeppelin *L48* in flight. (© IWM, Q 58467)

Mr Ellis standing in front of his house, which was destroyed by the Zeppelin raid on Great Yarmouth, 19 January 1915. (© IWM, Q 53586)

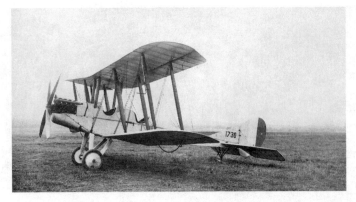

A British Aircraft Factory BE2c, of the type used to shoot down the first Zeppelin. (© IWM, Q 57576)

RMS *Lusitania*, sunk by German U-boat *U20* on 7 May 1915. (© IWM, Q 43227)

A German U-boat at full speed. (© IWM, Q 20222)

Wounded Australian soldiers heading for the Australian 3rd Battalion Dressing Station in Shrapnel Gully during the Gallipoli Campaign, 26 April 1915. (© IWM, Q 114177)

Scottish troops marching to the Battle of Loos, September–October 1915. (© Paul Maze)

The ruins of the village of Loos, 24 November 1915. Loos had been taken by the 15th (Scottish) Division on 25 September 1915. (© IWM, Q 58151)

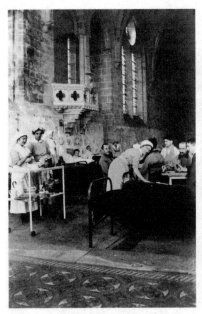

A ward in Royaumont Military Hospital in France c. 1915. (© IWM, Q 115371)

Royaumont Hospital. (© IWM, Q 115413)

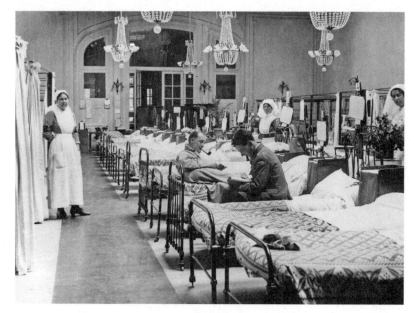

A hospital ward in France. (Reproduced with the permission of Historic Environment Scotland)

Serbian refugees fleeing through Macedonia. (© IWM, Q 52308)

An infantry attack at the Battle of the Somme. (© IWM, Q 65408)

The Battle of the Somme - bringing in the wounded, 2 July 1916. (© IWM, Q 101064)

The Battle of the Somme – serving coffee to the wounded, Hamel, November 1916. (© IWM, Q 4547)

The Battle of the Somme – an exhausted soldier asleep in a front-line trench, Thiepval, September 1916. (© IWM, Q 1071)

The Battle of the Somme - dressing the wounds of a German prisoner, 19 July 1916. (© IWM, Q 802)

Full-length portrait of T.E. Lawrence in Arab dress. (© The rightsholder IWM, Q 59314)

Guerilla operations. Demolitions at Ghadir el Haj on the Hejaz Railway, carried out by T.E. Lawrence's forces. (© IWM, Q 104083)

A tank production line. (Reproduced with the permission of Historic Environment Scotland)

British Mark IV Female tanks being loaded aboard flat-bed railway trucks for transportation to the forward area prior to the Battle of Cambrai. The fascine, or bundle of wood, carried on the roof was intended to be dropped into the enemy trench to allow the tank to cross. (© IWM, Q 46933)

Loading a 15in howitzer near the Menin Road in the Ypres Sector, October 1917. This is one of the many large howitzers that pounded the enemy's position and demolished concrete fortifications. (© IWM, E(AUS) 921)

A line of British troops blinded by gas at an advanced dressing station near Bethune during the German offensive. Each man has his hand on the shoulders of the man in front, 10 April 1918. (© IWM, Q 11586)

Female workers turning shell casings, North British Locomotive Company. (Reproduced with the permission of Historic Environment Scotland)

The assembly room at the munitions factory of Messrs C.A. Vandervelt where the women are assembling hand grenades c. 1917. (© IWM, Q 108429)

6 ACT THREE: HAIG TAKES COMMAND

THE BATTLE OF VERDUN
(21 FEBRUARY–18 DECEMBER 1916)

Germany reverted to its original belief that the way to win the war was first to defeat France, leaving the British isolated and enabling Germany to concentrate all her forces on Russia. The new plan was to mount a major attack on a key sector of the French lines requiring the French to commit all their forces and then force a way to Paris. Verdun, which had fallen in 1870 after a siege of six weeks, was chosen as the weak spot in the French line. The French had warning – the Germans could hardly hide the concentration of men and artillery – but, obsessed with their own plan to attack at the Somme, they did not bring in reinforcements or even strengthen the defences.

On 21 February the Germans, with 850 heavy artillery guns, began an immense bombardment of the French defences, firing over 1 million artillery shells on the first day alone and concentrating their attack on an 8-mile front. In just three days the French trench system degenerated into a tangled mess of mud, barbed wire and concrete. The German infantry advanced across the devastated ground using storm troopers to make the breakthrough, followed by reserve divisions to consolidate the gains.

The French suffered heavy casualties and a decisive German break-through looked imminent, but the Germans had advanced too far, too fast and were pounded by French artillery in a desperate defence of the town of Verdun, which was seen by the French as a test of their will and their ability to win the war, encapsulated in General Pétain's famous order, 'They shall not pass.'

In April the Germans widened their offensive over a 20-mile front but, in desperate fighting, were still unable to make the decisive breakthrough. Both armies, amounting together to as many as 1 million men, remained locked in combat throughout the summer, with German attacks being met by French counter-attacks until, in October, a decisive French counter-offensive regained much of the ground lost. The battle lasted, in all, for ten months and was effectively a draw, with 140,000 Germans and 160,000 French killed and another 200,000 Germans and 200,000 French wounded – all together the population of a sizeable town (Strachan, *First World War*, p.184).

René Arcos – The Dead

In this poignant French poem, René Arcos summarises the meaningless folly of the Battle of Verdun – all the fighting, all the battles, all the sadness, all the sorrow are, in the final reckoning, worthless because 'the dead are all on the same side':

The Dead

In the wind that blows
The veils of widows
All float on one side

And the mingled tears
Of a thousand sorrows
In one stream glide

Pressing each other close the dead
Who own no hatred and no flag,
Their hair veneered with clotted blood,
The dead are all on the same side.

In the one clay where endlessly
Beginnings blend with the world that dies
The brothered dead lain cheek to cheek
Today atone for the same defeat.

Divided sons, fight on, fight on,
You lacerate humanity
And tear the earth apart in vain,
The dead are all on the same side;

Under the earth no more than one,
One field, one single hope, abide,
As for the universe can be
One combat and one victory.

(Translated from French by Christopher Middleton)

IN MEMORIAM: PRIVATE D. SUTHERLAND

In May 1916 Mackintosh was selected with another officer to lead a retaliatory raid against the Germans for an attack on the 6th Seaforth Highlanders which had caused severe casualties. Mackintosh took his responsibility seriously, carrying out nightly reconnaissance for two weeks before carefully selecting the men for the raid and rehearsing the planned attack on the German trenches, a task made more difficult by their construction of 10ft-deep wooden sides, which would make the evacuation of casualties difficult.

The raid took place on the evening of 16 May with a team of fifty men selected from the 100 who had trained. The men, divided into two teams, positioned themselves in craters until the time of the attack, which would be preceded by an artillery bombardment. The team led by Mackintosh successfully captured the German trenches, clearing the remaining Germans from the trenches by throwing bombs and then successfully linking with the second team. It was then that things went awry. As a number of his men had been wounded by shelling, possibly British (the euphemism 'friendly fire' was not yet in use), Mackintosh gave the order to withdraw. There were three severely wounded men left in the German trench and Mackintosh returned to the trench with his sergeant to rescue them, believing that he owed it to his men, who had trusted in him, to provide for their safe return.

Mackintosh graphically described the raid in a letter to his sister (quoted in 'A Voice From the Front', the introduction to his book *War, the Liberator and Other Pieces*):

You will probably have noticed in the official report that a raid was made on the 16th on the trenches ... That, my dearest, was me and I don't want to do another. We killed seven Germans in the trench and about thirty or forty more in their dug-out. I should say they would have lost about thirty more by our artillery. Our losses were slight, but three of my men had their legs blown off in the Boches' trench and we had to pull them out and get them back. I and Charles Mackay [the other officer] and Sergeant Godstone were alone, and I can tell you it was no joke pulling a helpless man a yard, and then throwing a bomb to keep the Boches back – then pulling him another yard and throwing another bomb.

Charles was guarding our left while the Sergeant and I got our man up the parapet with both his legs pulped. Then I went back for the next. Poor devil! He screamed, 'Ma airm and ma leg's off' to me again and again. I was wasting no sympathy just then. Said I, 'Crawl on your other arm and leg then,' and lugged him up. Sergeant Morrison had got back to our own trench, but he returned to us and helped me get my man up into the open. We went back for the next man but he said, 'Leave me. I'm done.' Both his legs were off, so I said, 'None of that, my lad, you're coming with us.' He died on the Boche parapet and we had to leave him. We got the other two home.

Sergeant Morrison and Charles got wounded, but they both came back to us again until the men were in. I just gave myself up. The shrapnel was busting right in my face and the machine-guns – ugh! I wasn't touched except for a hole in my hose-top. I didn't stop swearing the whole time, except when I was praying – but I'd promised the men that I wouldn't leave the Boche trench while there was a man alive in it and I kept my word. One poor devil was a Catholic; he started confessing to me, thinking I was a priest – I meanwhile praying. 'O God, let us get these poor beggars in.' All the men I have brought in have died.

I believe I've been recommended for the Military Cross, but I'd rather have the boys' lives. If I get one, I'll get home on special leave soon. I've had my taste of a show. It's not romantic. It's hell.

For this action Mackintosh was awarded the Military Cross, the citation reading:

For conspicuous gallantry. He organised and led a successful raid on the enemy's trenches with great skill and courage. Several of the enemy were disposed of and a strong point destroyed. He also brought back two wounded men under fire.

The boy who he left on the parapet of the German trench was David Sutherland. The citation for the award of the Military Cross might have praised Mackintosh, but he was himself haunted by the knowledge that he had not brought the youngster back alive and by a feeling of guilt that he had betrayed the trust that his men had in him. He wrote one of his finest poems, *In Memoriam*, as a tribute to 'Private D. Sutherland. Killed in Action in the German Trench, May 16, 1916, and the Others who Died', in which he movingly compares the responsibility he felt for the men under his command with that of a father:

In Memoriam

So you were David's father,
And he was your only son,
And the new-cut peats are rotting
And the work is left undone,
Because of an old man weeping,
Just an old man in pain,
For David, his son David,
That will not come again.

Oh, the letters he wrote you,
And I can see them still,
Not a word of the fighting
But just the sheep on the hill
And how you should get the crops in
Ere the year got stormier,
And the Bosches have got his body,
And I was his officer.

You were only David's father,
But I had fifty sons
When we went up in the evening
Under the arch of the guns,
And we came back at twilight –
O God! I heard them call
To me for help and pity
That could not help at all.

Oh, never will I forget you,
My men that trusted me,
More my sons than your fathers'
For they could only see
The little helpless babies
And the young men in their pride.
They could not see you dying,
And hold you while you died.

Happy and young and gallant,
They saw their first-born go,
But not the strong limbs broken
And the beautiful men brought low,
The piteous writhing bodies,
The screamed, 'Don't leave me, Sir,'
For they were only your fathers
But I was your officer.

THE BATTLE OF JUTLAND
(31 MAY 1916)

This War is really the greatest insanity in which white races have ever been engaged.

Letter from Admiral von Tirpitz, Grand Admiral of the German Navy, written to his wife and dated 4 October 1914. Quoted in Gilbert, *First World War*, p.88.

The story of the First World War is dominated by the struggle on the Western Front between the armies of the Allies and those of the Central Powers who were locked in destructive combat on land. This was contrary to expectations, which had been of a major trial of strength at sea as the nascent German Navy flexed its muscles and tested the established control of the seas exercised by the British Royal Navy, which was better equipped than that of any other nation and had long been the cornerstone of British defensive policy, protecting Britain from attack and defending the trade routes to the empire. In the event, there would be just one major naval battle, the Battle of Jutland, which took place two years into the war.

When war broke out, the perceived strength of the Royal Navy contained the German fleet to the North Sea, enabling British warships to operate freely elsewhere, in particular safeguarding the transport of soldiers across the Channel to and from the BEF in France. Vice Admiral Sir David Beatty spelt out the strategic position succinctly to First Lord of the Admiralty Winston Churchill:

> The British Isles form a great breakwater across German waters thereby limiting the passage of vessels to the outer seas to two exits, the one on the South (the English Channel), narrow, easily blocked and contained, and the other on the North of such a width that with the forces at our disposal it could be easily commanded so as to preclude the possibility of the passing of any hostile force without our knowledge and without being brought to action by a superior force.   (B. McL. Ranft (ed.), *The Beatty Papers*, pp.36-7, quoted in Strachan, *First World War*, p.196)

Britain had invested heavily in the new Dreadnought-class battleships and by April 1916 had thirty-one Dreadnoughts and ten battlecruisers, compared with Germany's eighteen Dreadnoughts and just five battlecruisers (Keegan, *First World War*, p.290). Yet, paradoxically, the influence of these leviathans was itself compromised, as they were considered vulnerable to U-boat attacks. This vulnerability was highlighted early on in the war when, on 22 September 1914, three British armoured cruisers, HMS *Aboukir*, HMS *Hogue* and HMS *Cressy*, were torpedoed one after the other by the German U-boat *U9* as they rather foolishly persisted in patrolling 'up and down the North Sea practically on the same course and at the same speed' (letter from Lieutenant Ronald Trevor, quoted in Brown, *IWM Book*, p.94). This reverse dramatically affected Royal Navy thinking, encouraging a risk-averse mentality so that the two British fleets spent the majority of the war safely at anchor, the Grand Fleet at Scapa Flow and the Battlecruiser Fleet at Rosyth.

As a result, there had been little action at sea, apart from when a small fleet of German cruisers had rather cheekily sailed towards the British coast and shelled Hartlepool. This was an attempt to lure the British Fleet into a reckless pursuit into dangerous, newly sown minefields.

In the spring of 1916 this changed. Admiral Scheer, commander of the German High Seas Fleet, concocted a plan whereby the German Navy would challenge not the full might of the Royal Navy but just a part of it –

the Battlecruiser Fleet based at Rosyth – tempting them out to sea where the German fleet and deadly U-boats would be waiting. The battlecruisers were less well armoured than the Dreadnoughts and, therefore, more vulnerable to enemy shelling, but the reduction in weight meant they were faster, with a top speed of 30 knots, relying on their speed and ability to operate at long range for their safety.

The British Admiralty had the strategic advantage of knowing the enemy's plans. When the war was but four months old, two Imperial Russian Navy cruisers had opened fire on the German light cruiser SMS *Magdeburg* which had gone aground off the coast of Estonia. The Russians had secured a copy of the vital naval codes used by the German Navy in transmitting wireless messages which they had passed to the British. German radio signals were regularly intercepted by Admiralty intelligence and decoded using the captured code books (Freeman, 'Unsinkable', p.66). Accordingly, the German plan was revealed, enabling the British to trump it by bringing Admiral Jellicoe's Grand Fleet, based in Scapa Flow in the Orkneys, into the equation. It sailed south to link with the battlecruisers of Admiral Beatty.

The combined British Fleet had a total of twenty-eight Dreadnought-class battleships (compared with the German Navy's sixteen), nine battlecruisers, thirty-four cruisers, eighty destroyers and a supporting fleet of submarines. It was the greatest display of naval power ever seen.

The two navies met off the Danish coast at Jutland. Admiral Beatty was the first to engage the German fleet but, faced by the full firepower of the German Navy and with three of his battlecruisers destroyed when shells ignited their ammunition stores, withdrew and ran north, chased by the German fleet. Cleverly he lured them into the trap set by Admiral Jellicoe and into the teeth of the Grand Fleet which was heading south from Scapa Flow. When the Grand Fleet came within range the tables were turned. Three German ships were sunk after a brief but heavy onslaught and it became the turn of the German fleet to run back to port and safety.

The result of the battle was inconclusive. The Royal Navy had suffered slightly higher losses but remained too powerful for the German fleet, which did not venture out to sea again, leaving the Royal Navy in control of the North Sea. It was 'an assault on the gaoler followed by a return to gaol' (quoted in Keegan, *First World War*, p.296).

The U-Boat Threat

The neutralisation of its battle fleet was not the end of the German naval threat. At the outbreak of the war Britain had been importing as much as 60 per cent of its food. The Kaiser believed that if Germany could not defeat Britain on the battlefield, then the British should be starved into submission. He therefore authorised the use of its U-boat fleet to sink the merchant ships that were bringing essential food, armaments and other supplies to Britain – not just British merchant ships but, controversially, those of other countries.

By April 1917 one in four of the merchant ships supplying Britain with essential supplies was being attacked and sunk by German U-boats and in that month alone 500,000 tons of British merchant ships were lost, together with a further 300,000 tons of ships from other countries who were supplying Britain with vital food and armaments. During the war a total of 2,000 British naval and merchant ships were sunk by submarines, mines or in action, with the loss of 12,000 lives (Gilbert, *First World War*, p.279).

Food supplies were badly affected and the government urged the British people to grow more and to eat less. A quarter of a million women were recruited to work on Britain's farms and even the flower beds of Buckingham Palace were used to grow vegetables. By 1917 the situation was becoming serious and the British government was forced to bring in food rationing: first on sugar from 1 January, then in April 1917 meat was added, and in July, butter and tea. Strangely, rationing was popular as it was felt that all were sharing in the hardships rather than an exempt and privileged few being excluded.

German submarines continued to be a menace until Lloyd George overruled the navy and ordered the introduction of a convoy system to reduce the heavy losses. Royal Navy cruisers and destroyers were provided to protect the convoys of merchant ships and to hunt down the enemy submarines. Losses of merchant shipping fell dramatically.

The Death of Lord Kitchener and his Replacement by Lloyd George

Lord Kitchener was a notable victim of the German U-boats when, in June 1916, he sailed from Scrabster in the north of Scotland to Scapa Flow in the Orkneys to board HMS *Hampshire* on a mission to Britain's Russian allies. On 5 June, in a force-9 gale, HMS *Hampshire* struck a mine laid by a German U-boat and sank to the west of the Orkneys. Kitchener, his staff and all but twelve of the crew were drowned.

Lloyd George's first impact upon the war effort had been in 1915 when, in response to the repeated claims that the success of the BEF was being hampered by a lack of artillery shells, he was appointed Minister of Munitions and dramatically increased production. On the death of Kitchener he was made Secretary of State for War.

THE BATTLE OF THE SOMME
(1 JULY–18 NOVEMBER 1916)

Alan Seeger - I Have a Rendezvous with Death

Alan Seeger was an American born in New York on 22 June 1888. In 1912 he had gone to Paris and immersed himself in the life of the Latin Quarter. Although the United States would not enter the war for another two years, Seeger, along with forty or so other Americans, enlisted in the French Foreign Legion just weeks after the outbreak of war. He was realistic as to the prospect of death, writing to his mother:

> You must not be anxious about my not coming back ... But if I should not, you must be proud, like a Spartan mother ... Death is nothing terrible after all. It may mean something even more wonderful than life. It cannot possibly mean anything worse to the good soldier.   (Letter from Seeger to his mother dated 18 June 1915, quoted in Alan Seeger, *Poems*, Introduction, p.xxxv)

Seeger was killed at the Battle of the Somme on 4 July 1916, his death movingly foretold in his poem *I Have a Rendezvous with Death*:

I Have a Rendezvous with Death

I have a rendezvous with Death
At some disputed barricade,
When Spring comes back with rustling shade
And apple blossoms fill the air –
I have a rendezvous with Death
When Spring brings back blue days and fair.

It may be he shall take my hand
And lead me into his dark land

And close my eyes and quench my breath –
It may be I shall pass him still.
I have a rendezvous with Death
On some scarred slope of battered hill,
When Spring comes round again this year
And the first meadow-flowers appear.

   God knows 'twere better to be deep
Pillowed in silk and scented down,
Where Love throbs out in blissful sleep,
Pulse nigh to pulse, and breath to breath,
Where hushed awakenings are dear ...
But I've a rendezvous with Death
At midnight in some flaming town,
When Spring trips north again this year,
And I to my pledged word am true,
I shall not fail that rendezvous.

The Strategy Behind the Battle of the Somme

Haig planned a massive operation to provide a diversion to help the hard-pressed French at Verdun and to break decisively both the German line and their spirit. Haig believed that Verdun had provided the 'wearing out' stage of the battle and that the British attack on the Somme would provide the decisive breakthrough. General Rawlinson counselled caution, restricting the action to just ten divisions and with the reduced objective of capturing the German front-line trenches and then consolidating, but he was over-ruled by Haig who wanted to press on to seize the German second line of defences (Colin Campbell, *Engine of Destruction*, p.77).

   The British tactics were depressingly familiar. The operation commenced with a massive artillery bombardment lasting for five days, so loud that it could even be heard in London, but signalling to the Germans the imminence of an attack. The objective was the same: to degrade the German defences and destroy the German forces. What had not, however, been taken into account in the master plan were the improvements the Germans had made to their defensive trench network during the lull in the fighting. The trenches and dugouts had been deepened and a second line of trenches had been constructed behind the ridge, out of sight of the British forces and negating the planned British artillery barrage.

The attack would not be concentrated upon perceived weak spots in the line, as might have seemed tactically sound, but was to be spread along the 25-mile front. The reasoning behind this was to protect the advancing troops from flanking fire if they had advanced on a narrow front, but the inevitable consequence was that the artillery bombardment was insufficiently concentrated. Worse, many of the guns were obsolete, many of the shells fired failed to explode and those that did were either shrapnel, intended to destroy life but of little effect on either the trench system or the barbed wire, or were not powerful enough to penetrate the German dugouts or to destroy their gun emplacements.

Colour Quartermaster Sergeant Robert Scott Macfie of the 10th Battalion King's Liverpool Regiment (the 'Liverpool Scottish') summarised the perceived incompetence in a letter to his father:

> The want of preparation, the vague orders, the ignorance of the objective and geography, the absurd haste, and in general the horrid bungling were scandalous. After two years of war it seems that our higher commanders are still without common sense. In any well-regulated organization a divisional commander would be shot for incompetence – here another regiment is ordered to attempt the same task in the same muddling way.   (Letter dated 15 August 1916, quoted in Brown, *IWM Book*, p.61)

Father Bernard Marshall wrote in his diary of watching a British bombardment in 1916, giving a powerful description of the awful effect of the massive barrage which must have been hard to reconcile with his Christian principles:

> It was appalling. I could see the flashes from our guns from every side, far in the distance, behind me, every side of me. Every kind of gun was working its hardest and fastest – the great monsters behind sending their heavily roaring giant missiles, the smaller howitzers and the sixty-pounders belching forth their whirring shells, the busy eighteen-pounders with their sharp savage voice spitting out their swirling projectiles. And there before me was the awful view of the German line where all these thousands of explosives were bursting blood red, sending debris of the enemy trenches high into the air.   (Quoted in Brown, *IWM Book*, p.72)

Independent thinking was not allowed to deflect the British from their master plan, which was controlled by Haig from his command headquarters

50 miles behind the lines and surrounded by his staff officers – a situation lampooned by Sassoon in his poem *Base Details*:

Base Details

If I were fierce, and bald, and short of breath,
    I'd live with scarlet Majors at the Base,
And speed glum heroes up the line to death.
    You'd see me with my puffy petulant face,
Guzzling and gulping in the best hotel,
    Reading the Roll of Honour. "Poor young chap"
I'd say – "I used to know his father well;
    Yes, we've lost heavily in this last scrap"
And when the war is done and youth stone dead,
I'd toddle safely home and die – in bed.

(Rouen, 4 March 1917)

The Attack

The assault began at 7.30 a.m. on 1 July. One hundred and twenty thousand men were committed to the attack on the first day. At the first whistle the men scrambled up the ladders, out of the trenches, through the gaps which had been cut in the barbed wire and then lay down forming a line to right and left. At the sound of the second whistle the men, led by their officers, walked as instructed steadily forward shoulder to shoulder in lines 300ft apart.

Military procedure required junior officers to lead their men into battle walking five paces ahead, carrying a revolver instead of a rifle and wearing their officer's uniform with riding breeches and Sam Browne belt – so that the German snipers would have no difficulty in identifying them. Unsurprisingly, casualties amongst junior officers were very high – the life expectancy of a young officer arriving in the trenches was just six weeks. (Graves does point out one advantage that was granted to officers – they had the right to commission horses and ride into Amiens and thus avail themselves of the pleasures of the 'Blue Lamp' establishments reserved exclusively for the use of officers; the men were restricted to using establishments sporting a 'Red Lamp'. Graves records that he was not aware of any especial characteristics or talents required by the ladies working in the 'Blue Lamp' establishments which entitled them, or indeed the officers, to this privileged status. Graves, *Goodbye to All That*, p.151.)

Speed was essential to success but the British troops, weighed down by their equipment,* could only advance slowly towards the German lines through the morass of mud pitted by deep craters which had been created by the incessant bombardment. As they neared the German lines the British artillery barrage lifted and rolled forward, concentrating on the second defensive line of German trenches. The Germans now emerged from the dugouts where they had been sheltering during the artillery bombardment and with their machine guns raked the lines of the advancing British troops led by their young officers.

It was not war, but slaughter. On the first day alone the British lost 57,000 men, almost half of the total of those committed to the battle. Haig was characteristically understated in his diary entry for Sunday, 2 July when he wrote, 'The news ... was not altogether good' (Martin Marix Evans, *The Somme 1914–18*, p.111).

The Times, 3 July 1916

How was this disaster received at home? There was very tight censorship on reporting from the front line under the Defence of the Realm Act. Access was restricted on the grounds that sensitive information relating to military activities might reach the enemy, and reports were censored to avoid a negative impact on the populace. In effect, this meant being economical with the truth when reporting upon any defeat or setback. Solidly within these guidelines, *The Times* of 3 July had reported, 'Everything has gone well ... Our troops have successfully carried out their missions, all counter-attacks have been repulsed and large numbers of prisoners taken.'

---

* Martin Gilbert, in his excellent book *First World War* (p.259), details the equipment carried by a typical British soldier, which weighed 66lb (30kg) and comprised a rifle and bayonet, grenades, ammunition, waterproof cape, two gas helmets and a set of goggles, field dressing, rations, mess tin, full water bottle, four empty sandbags, a steel helmet and a pick or shovel.

Medical Care

Special provision had been made for treating casualties from the planned attack. A casualty clearing station had been provided, with tented wards to provide for 1,000 casualties, but in the first twenty-four hours this was completely overwhelmed with the arrival of more than 10,000 casualties.

The area surrounding the hospital became covered with stretchers, each containing an injured victim of the battle - 6 acres of badly injured or dying men all needing attention. The medical staff were hopelessly overwhelmed and they had to decide between those injured who had a chance of survival and those to be allowed to die, often in the most distressing circumstances. It was the most poignant indictment of the folly of the military leadership.

Father Bernard Marshall wrote movingly - albeit from a Catholic viewpoint - of visiting the 'moribund tents', areas set aside by the doctors for those deemed too near death to warrant a precious place on an ambulance:

> The moribund tent - sometimes there was more than one - was a tragic place. A bell tent with one, two or three men on stretchers on the ground at close quarters with death - and none with time to stay by them and help them and watch them. Now and again one of the doctors would look in to see developments - and the padres did their best to ease and spiritualize these deathbeds. But they mostly lay alone and died alone - for how could doctor or chaplain spend long hours by their side with the constant stream of war's victims arriving at the station?
>
> There were several Catholics who found their way to the moribund tent - and what a blessed thing the faith was there - such light in the gloom for the sufferer - such definite spiritual business for the priest. One boy who died there - he looked very young - was a Scotch lad in the Black Watch. His was a perforating wound in the abdomen and he suffered terrible agony. When I warned him to prepare for death his first thought was 'It will kill my poor mother.' I stayed as long and visited him as often as I could. I raised him in my arms from time to time because it eased the awful pain. He made his confession, received extreme unction and prayed with me as well as the torture would allow. It was an edifying [sic] death.   (Quoted in Brown, *IWM Book*, pp.250-1)

Siegfried Sassoon - Died of Wounds

Sassoon, in a characteristically pithy poem, highlights the transitory state of the patients being cared for - they recovered, were sent home to 'Blighty' or died, leaving an empty bed for the next patient. *Died of Wounds* refers to July 1916 when Sassoon was in hospital at Amiens and watched a young soldier as he raged in the bed opposite before dying of wounds incurred at High Wood:

Died of Wounds

His wet white face and miserable eyes
Brought nurses to him more than groans and sighs:
But hoarse and low and rapid rose and fell
His troubled voice: he did the business well.

The ward grew dark; but he was still complaining
And calling out for "Dickie". "Curse the Wood!
It's time to go. O Christ, and what's the good?
We'll never take it, and it's always raining."

I wondered where he'd been; then heard him shout,
"They snipe like hell! O Dickie, don't go out" ...
I fell asleep ... Next morning he was dead;
And some Slight Wound lay smiling on the bed.

'The Attack on High Wood' - An Extract from Memoirs of an Infantry Officer by Siegfried Sassoon

On 14 July an attack was launched at High Wood with the intention of straightening the line. The 51st (Highland) Division were a part of this attack and lost 3,500 men in two attacks on enemy positions. The aftermath of the attack is memorably described by Siegfried Sassoon in *Memoirs of an Infantry Officer* (pp.83–4). Sassoon was waiting for the return of the battalion from an attack on High Wood, preparing the camp with Dottrell, the quartermaster:

> An hour before dawn the road was still an empty picture of moonlight. The distant gun-fire had crashed and rumbled all night, muffled and terrific with immense flashes, like waves of some tumult of water rolling along the horizon. Now there came an interval of silence in which I heard a horse neigh, shrill and scared and lonely.
>
> Then the procession of returning troops began. The camp-fires were burning low when the grinding jolting column lumbered back. The field guns came first, with nodding men sitting stiffly on weary horses, followed by

wagons and limbers and field-kitchens. After this rumble of wheels came the infantry, shambling, limping, straggling and out of step. If anyone spoke it was only a muttered word, and the mounted officers rode as if asleep. The men carried their emergency water in petrol-cans, against which bayonets made a hollow clink; except for the shuffling of feet, this was the only sound. Thus, with an almost spectral appearance, the lurching brown figures flitted past with slung rifles and heads bent forward under basin-helmets. Moonlight and dawn began to mingle, and I could see the barley swaying indolently against the sky. A train groaned along the riverside, setting up a cloud of whitish fiery smoke against the gloom of the trees.

He continued:

I had seen something that night which overawed me. It was all in the day's work – an exhausted Division returning from the Somme offensive – but for me it was as if I had watched an army of ghosts. It was as though I had seen the War as it might be envisioned by the mind of some epic poet a hundred years hence.

It was during the Battle of the Somme that Sassoon performed one of his exploits of extraordinary bravery by:

taking, single-handed, a battalion frontage that the Royal Irish Regiment had failed to take the day before. He went over with bombs in daylight, under covering fire from a couple of rifles, and scared away the occupants. A pointless feat, since instead of signalling for reinforcements, he sat down in the German trench and began reading a book of poems which he had brought with him. When he finally went back he did not even report ... [The colonel in charge raged] 'I'd have got you a D.S.O., if you'd only shown more sense.'   (Graves, *Goodbye to All That*, p.174)

20 July 1916 – The 'Death' of Robert Graves
Graves was serving as captain with the Royal Welch Fusiliers and waiting in reserve for the attack on High Wood when he was hit by a fragment of shell. In *Goodbye to All That*, he wrote:

I heard the explosion and felt as though I had been punched rather hard between the shoulder-blades, but without any pain. I took the punch merely for the shock of the explosion; but blood trickled into my eye and, turning faint, I called 'I've been hit.' Then I fell.

A piece of shrapnel had passed through his thigh, near to the groin – as Graves writes, 'I must have been at the full length of my stride to escape emasculation' – and another went through his lung coming out 2in above his right nipple. He had his wounds dressed and was then put on a stretcher and taken to the dressing station where he remained unconscious for twenty-four hours. That night the colonel visited the dressing station and was told Graves was 'done for', and so on the 22 July he wrote a letter of sympathy to Graves' mother. Graves' obituary was duly published in *The Times*, generating, as Graves later commented, a number of enthusiastic letters of condolence from 'people with whom I had been on the worst terms'.

However, on the morning of 21 July when they came to clear the dead, Graves was found to be still breathing and so was carried, screaming with the pain, to a tented field hospital where he spent five days on a stretcher in a tent made 'insufferably hot' from the warm July weather, and watching 'the little bubbles of blood, like scarlet soap-bubbles, which my breath made in escaping from the opening of the wound'. He was then lifted on his stretcher onto a hospital train to hospital in Rouen and then by hospital ship back to England. He was taken to Queen Alexandria's Hospital at Highgate where 'the lung healed up easily' (Graves, *Goodbye to All That*, pp.181–7).

Ewart Alan Mackintosh – High Wood
Mackintosh captured the mood of despair in his poem *High Wood*, which he dedicated to the 51st Highland Division:

High Wood

Oh gay were we in spirit
In the hours of the night
When we lay in rest in Albert
And waited for the fight;
Gay and gallant were we
On the day that we set forth,
But broken, broken, broken
Is the valour of the North.

The wild warpipes were calling,
Our hearts were blithe and free
When we went up the valley
To the death we could not see.
Clear lay the wood before us
In the clear summer weather,
But broken, broken, broken
Are the sons of the heather.

In the cold of the morning,
In the burning of the day,
The thin lines stumbled forward,
The dead and dying lay.
By the unseen death that caught us
By the bullets' raging hail
Broken, broken, broken
Is the pride of the Gael.

(July–August 1916)

The First Use of the Tank

There was one innovation in September with the first use in action of a revolutionary new British weapon. It was a motorised 'landship' with caterpillar tracks, heavy armour plating, a mounted gun and a crew of eight – a fire-belching monster which is better known as the tank.

This was Britain's secret weapon, designed to break the stalemate of trench warfare. The initial concept of 'landships' – they were referred to as 'tanks' in order to protect the idea from enemy intelligence – owes much to Winston Churchill. Early in 1915, concerned at the heavy losses of men, he had written to Asquith:

> It would be quite easy in a short time to fit up a number of steam tractors with small armoured shelters, in which men and machine guns could be placed, which would be bulletproof. Used at night, they would not be affected by artillery fire to any extent. The caterpillar system would enable trenches to be crossed quite easily, and the weight of the machine would destroy all barbed-wire entanglements.   (Quoted in Gilbert, *First World War*, p.124)

During his time as First Lord of the Admiralty he had organised experiments to determine the best form of mechanised vehicle to deal with the barbed wire and trenches of the Western Front, settling on the concept of a tracked vehicle. After the Gallipoli fiasco and his 'exile' from office, Churchill commanded the 6th Battalion Royal Scots Fusiliers. He spent his time in the trenches at 'Plugstreet', as Ploegsteert Wood was known to the British soldier, and realised the futility of trench warfare, reinforcing his belief in the use of metal rather than men to force a breakthrough.

Churchill believed that the tank should not be used in action until it had proven reliability and could be used in overwhelming numbers but the top brass decided otherwise. Haig had only forty-nine tanks when they were first deployed in the Battle of the Somme; of these, seventeen failed even to reach the front line. The majority of the remainder became bogged down in the unforgiving mud of no man's land, pitted as it was by the craters of exploded artillery shells, while others became fiery infernos incinerating their crews who were trapped inside. There were two models of the Mark 1 tank: the 'male', which was fitted with two six-pounder naval guns in pods fitted on either side, and the 'female', which had twin Vickers machine guns (Evans, *Somme*, p.135).

Gordon Hassell, a second lieutenant in the 8th Battalion Tank Corps, wrote expressively of what it was like to serve in one of these new mechanical monsters:

> Terribly noisy, oily, hot, airless and bumpy! Without any sort of cushion, as we had no springs and had thirty tons' weight, any slight bump and crash was magnified and many a burn was caused by a jerk throwing the crew about. Instinctively one caught at a handhold, and got a burn on the hot engine. The crew had very little knowledge of where they were going, only by peeping through slits and weapon apertures could they see anything. In action if the tank was hit slivers of hot steel began to fly – bullets hitting the armoured plates caused melting and the splash, as in steel factories, was dangerous to the eyes. For protection we used to wear a small face mask.   (Quoted in Brown, *IWM Book*, p.86)

In the same attack on 15 September, Raymond Asquith was shot in the chest. To avoid affecting the morale of his men he lay calmly smoking a cigarette but he was mortally wounded. His father, the prime minister, never recovered from the loss. Harold Macmillan, a future British prime minister, was also wounded that day, lying in a shell hole under artillery fire while reading *Prometheus* by Aeschylus, in the original Greek, before he was rescued (Gilbert, *First World War*, p.286).

Four More Months of Fighting

Haig was not one to allow failure to change his plans, although with flexible logic he did change his rationale for the battle. It was now no longer an attempt to make the decisive breakthrough but had become a stage in a prolonged war of attrition in which the resources and morale of the enemy would be ultimately ground down.

Whatever the rationale, it was a tragic fiasco. Haig was obdurate, and although the initial attempt at a breakthrough had comprehensively failed, he opted for the long haul. A bolder, more imaginative man than Haig might have called a halt to this futile slaughter, but Haig had promised victory and victory he would deliver. Attack after attack battered the German lines only to be repulsed with heavy losses.

The fighting continued for four and a half months. Lieutenant Crerar of the Royal Scots Fusiliers wrote of being wounded in an attack in broad daylight on 12 October:

> Shortly before 2 we all lined up, the men with fixed bayonets, I with walking stick, revolver and a useful looking heavy knobkerrie with a round metal head with metal studs dangling from my belt. I don't know where I got that, it certainly wasn't a standard issue.
>
> Anyway at 2.08 I blew my whistle loud and clear and we clambered over the parapet into the open facing the German lines about 3-400 yards in front. Immediately there was an appalling din and we advanced under a hail of thousands of bullets whizzing through the air from rifles and machine guns, and with high explosive shells exploding and throwing up earth and metal, just Hell let loose. After covering about 120 yards with men falling left and right, there seemed to be very few of us still advancing, as the murderous machine gun fire had taken a heavy toll, and a few minutes later, having advanced with a handful of men about another 100 yards, I felt a sledge hammer blow on my left thigh, and fortunately for me tumbled headlong into a shallow shell hole where I lay partially stunned and feeling rather like a shot rabbit in the mouth of its burrow wondering what had happened. I listened to the din of battle overhead and wondered how long it would be before I got picked up by

stretcher bearers. [He would lie for two nights in his shell hole before he managed to crawl back to the British lines.]   (Quoted in Young, *Scottish Voices*, p.147)

Beaumont-Hamel

Haig ordered a final push to capture Beaumont-Hamel, which had been one of the objects of the first day's fighting. The attack was preceded by a fierce artillery bombardment, with twice the concentration of artillery fire as in July. The attack had to be postponed again and again because of atrocious weather, but on 13 November, after three weeks of artillery bombardment, two brigades of the 51st (Highland) Division advanced behind a creeping barrage of artillery fire against Beaumont-Hamel Ridge, which was secured after hard fighting by the 51st, who had earned a reputation with the Germans as one of the most feared infantry forces in the British Army. They suffered 2,000 casualties.

It is often forgotten that the fighting was not the end; the casualties had to be retrieved from the battlefield and taken for treatment. David Rorie had been born in Edinburgh of Aberdeenshire parents and at the outbreak of the war was working as a general practitioner on Lower Deeside. Although by then 47 years old, he enlisted with a reserve commission in the Royal Army Medical Corps and served in France with the 1st/2nd Highland Field Ambulance. He writes amusingly of his experiences, once quoting a two-page memorandum he was asked to write to justify the use of safety pins, which was considered excessive by a an overzealous staff officer – a memo that, he felt, changed the course of the war.

After the attack on Beaumont-Hamel he was charged with collecting, treating and evacuating the casualties, both British and German. He wrote movingly of his experiences:

And now came the inevitable stage of clearing up the battlefield and searching all possible places where wounded, either British or Boche, who had not been picked up in the actual battle, might have sought shelter.

He describes the operation, in which he was accompanied for protection by 'two Jocks with rifles':

It was drizzling wet and vilely cold, the trenches in places thigh deep in clay and an awful mess of smashed barbed wire, mud, disintegrated German dead and debris of all sorts. In one trench our occupation for half an hour was hauling each other out of the tenacious and bloodstained mud; and during our mutual salvage operations we had evidently made ourselves too visible, as the enemy started shelling. There was nothing for it but to take to the open road and make for another trench, which we promptly did: doing a hundred yards in rather good time.

He tells of exploring a captured German dugout:

This dug-out was typical of the many with which Beaumont Hamel was honeycombed. On descending about forty steps one was in a large floored and timbered chamber some fifty feet long; and at the further end a second set of steps led to a similar chamber, one side of each being lined with a double layer of bunks filled with dead and wounded Germans, the majority of whom had become casualties on the morning of the 13th.

The place was, of course, in utter darkness; and, when we flashed our lights on and the wounded saw our escort with rifles ready, there was an outbreak of 'Kammerad!' while a big bevy of rats squeaked and scuttled away from their feast on the dead bodies on the floor. The stench was indescribably abominable: for many of the cases were gas-gangrenous. Any food or drink they had possessed was used up, and our water bottles were soon emptied amongst them. After we had gone over the upper chamber and separated the living from the dead, we went to the lower one where the gas curtain was let down and fastened. Tearing it aside and going through with a light, I got a momentary jump when I caught a glimpse in the upper bunk of a man, naked to the waist, and with his right hand raised above his head. But the poor beggar was far past mischief - stark and stiff with a smashed pelvis. Some twenty other Germans lay about, at the disposal of the rat hordes. The romance of war had worn somewhat thin here.   (Rorie, *A Medico's Luck*, pp.112-13)

Had Haig's Objectives been Achieved in the Battle of the Somme?

Nothing could justify the horror and needless slaughter. It was a military disaster. In just one section of the front, 23,000 Australian and New Zealand troops were lost in order to gain 1 mile of territory - a mile of mud-covered, shell-pocked wasteland. The verdict of the ANZACS on the British generals was harsh but understandable - incompetent, self-opinionated, callous and deluded were some of the politer comments.

In five months of bitter fighting the British had gained just a few miles of Godforsaken land and facing them now were the new and stronger defences that had been built by the Germans. And the cost? One hundred and forty-six thousand British, French and Empire soldiers were recorded as killed or missing in battle. Total Allied casualties were 614,000, of whom 420,000 were British (Strachan, *First World War*, p.191).

Ten divisions of the New Army had taken part in the fighting on the Somme and there were three Scottish Divisions taking part: the 9th (Scottish) Division, the 15th (Scottish) division and the 51st (Highland) Division, in addition to Scottish battalions serving with other divisions. The 9th (Scottish) Division alone lost over 300 officers and 7,200 men (Royle, *Flowers*, p,110).

The confidence of the troops in ultimate victory remained but the early promise that the German forces could be swept aside by a determined attack had been revealed as a costly illusion. The commanders paid a price, but a small price in comparison with the suffering of their men. The French sacked Joffre as commander-in-chief and replaced him with General Robert Nivelle, who had earned his reputation at Verdun, while Lloyd George, who had become disillusioned with Haig's management of the war, placed the BEF under the overall authority of Nivelle, much to Haig's chagrin.

It was no better for the Germans. They had also suffered huge losses – more than half a million men killed, missing or captured – and a new commander was introduced. Paul von Hindenburg, the architect of the defeat of the Russians at the Battle of Tannenberg, was appointed over-all commander, supported by the cautious Erich Ludendorff. Hindenburg adopted a strategy of resolute defence, constructing a virtually impregna-ble line of trenches that effectively secured Germany's western front and which was known as the Hindenburg Line. He also demanded a dou-bling of Germany's production of munitions and a trebling of artillery and machine-gun production by spring 1917; 700,000 Belgians were forcibly deported to work in the German armaments factories in an attempt to meet these ambitious targets.

Violet Jacob – To A.H.J.

A mother whose son was killed in the battle should be given the final words.
Violet Kennedy-Erskine was born in 1863 in Montrose; her family had lived
in Angus since the fifteenth century. On her marriage in 1894 to Major
Arthur Jacob she lived in India for five years before returning to Britain.
She never forgot her roots in Angus and wrote a number of poems in the
vernacular. Her most moving war poem was dedicated to A.H.J., her only
son Harry, who was killed in the Battle of the Somme. He was 21.

To A.H.J.

Past life, past tears, far past the grave,
    The tryst is set for me,
Since, for our all, your all you gave
    On the slopes of Picardy.

On Angus, in the autumn nights,
    The ice-green light shall lie,
Beyond the trees the Northern Lights
    Slant on the belts of the sky.

But miles on miles from Scottish soil
    You sleep, past war and scaith,
Your country's freedman, loosed from toil,
    In honour and in faith.

For Angus held you in her spell,
    Her Grampians, faint and blue,
Her ways, the speech you knew so well,
    Were half the world to you.

Yet rest, my son: our souls are those
    Nor time nor death can part,
And lie you proudly, folded close
    To France's deathless heart.

THE BALEFUL BARD – EWART ALAN MACKINTOSH

Mackintosh was gassed and wounded by shrapnel at High Wood on 30 July. He was evacuated to England and after recovery was posted to Cambridge where, for eight months, he taught the skills of bombing to new recruits. Mackintosh wrote a number of comic poems and songs which he would declaim at informal concerts. He shows this side of his character in his humorous poem *The Baleful Bard*:

The Baleful Bard
(or The Muse Munition-Making)

Time was when squatting in a noisome ditch,
I used to while away monotonous days
By writing many doggerel lyrics, which
Were set to various untuneful lays,
And the rude soldiery who heard them sung
In billets, when we rested from the fight,
Picked up the words from me, and then gave tongue
Waking with discord all the quiet night,
And sung them, thinking it tremendous fun,
Unto the musical and writhing Hun.

And I've been told, and can believe it true,
That once, as they intoned these songs of mine,
The Germans heard and trembled, for they knew
What men were these who came into the line,
And sent a message to our Colonel,
Saying the thing was worse than what the Tanks were;
He answered, begging them to go to Hell.
And thus we took that village on the Ancre
(This line is bad, but I have not the time
Or dictionary to find a proper rhyme.)

And now sequestered in this quiet nook,
I struggle to instruct the wise Cadet
In bombing (not according to the book)
Patrols and how most surely to revet

The crumbling trenches on the local hill,
And oft to the jocund piano's strain,
I mount upon the platform with a will
To sing these ancient songs of mine again,
And place, obedient to my country's call,
A deadlier strafe in their hands than all.

For these young officers shall find the pote
A weapon to avenge the nation's wrongs,
And they with many a discordant note
Shall chant in many a trench my poignant songs;
And the pale enemy (to whom I fear
For the rhyme's sake I must refer to as "Hunes")
Shall tremble in their deep dug-outs to hear
Across the night these wild untuneful tunes,
And shall beseech their officers and cry,
"Let us retire at once, or else we die."

But lo, there comes a yet more dreadful day,
When with his pleasant months of Blighty o'er,
The bard shall lift his pack and hie away
To land again upon the Gallic shore,
And set his ribald muse to work anew,
And fresh atrocities shall vex the Huns,
And men shall sing them as they used to do
The while from Bosche to Bosche the whisper runs
Down the whole line from Belgium to Champagne,
"The man who wrote these songs is out again."

(Undated, probably 1917)

THE ARAB REVOLT
(5 JUNE 1916)

The War in the Middle East

Mesopotamia 1915-1918: The Siege of Kut

The countries of the Middle East, in particular Iraq and Syria, are currently under threat from the militant 'self-styled' Islamist State but have existed for less than 100 years, created after the First World War by lines drawn arbitrarily on a map with little reference to the underlying tribal realities.

In 1914 the Middle East was divided between Iran, known then as Persia, and Arabia, which formed, nominally at least, a part of the Ottoman Empire. In symmetry with the Austro-Hungarian Empire, the Ottoman Empire was a multi-national conglomerate beset by nascent nationalism. Also in symmetry, it was losing its authority, having been driven out of much of its extensive territory in North Africa and, through the Balkan Wars, losing much of its grip over the Balkan states.

The Ottoman Empire had declared war on Britain in November 1914 and despite its waning powers it still posed a powerful threat to British interests. Britain obtained its oil from Persia and needed to protect its source from Turkish attack. Accordingly, a force of British and Indian soldiers was landed at the head of the Persian Gulf on the shores of what is now Iraq. The British force advanced up the Shatt al Arab waterway capturing Basra and Kut-al-Amara, with the British cavalry scattering the Turkish troops. Encouraged by this success and fired with the desire for a victory against the despised Turkish Army to compensate for the disaster in Gallipoli, the British commander-in-chief in Mesopotamia, Sir John Nixon, ordered an advance on Baghdad against the advice of the local commander, Major General Sir Charles Townshend, who was concerned both as to the quality of his Indian troops and the length of his supply lines.

In November 1915, while still 30 miles short of Baghdad, he was confronted and defeated by the Turkish forces and withdrew to Kut where his army of 11,000 men – 3,000 British and 8,000 Indian troops – was surrounded by substantial Turkish forces. He had supplies for two months, but the siege would last for five. Four attempts were made to relieve Townshend but, despite the brave efforts of a force of Indian troops supported by the 2nd Battalion Black Watch and 1st Battalion Seaforth Highlanders, the Scottish and Indian troops were beaten back by the besieging Turkish troops. The relief operations resulted in 23,000 casualties amongst the British and Indian troops – more than twice the number of those holed up in Kut. The siege remained unbroken.

Townshend was forced to surrender on 29 April. The defeated British forces were compelled to undergo a two-week death march over 1,200 miles to concentration camps in Anatolia. Four thousand British and Indian soldiers died on the march. General Townshend, on the other hand, was very properly treated as an officer should be and taken in comfort to Constantinople.

The Arab Revolt

The British decided to strengthen their hand against the Ottoman Empire by fermenting a revolt amongst the Arabs against their Turkish overlords. As early as September 1914 Lord Kitchener had made contact with the Arab leader, Sherif Hussein, and offered religious leadership of Arabia; but in October 1915 the British High Commissioner in Egypt, Sir Henry McMahon, went the whole way and promised the Arabs that if they fought with the British they would be given independence by the creation of an Arab state carved out of the relics of the Ottoman Empire.

Unfortunately, this promise would prove to be in direct conflict with the Sykes–Picot Agreement, which was secretly negotiated in December 1915 between the British diplomat Sir Mark Sykes and Francois Georges-Picot of France. This stated that in the event of the defeat of the Ottoman Empire Arabia would be divided into two spheres of influence, one under British control and the other French. There was no provision for an independent Arab state (Strachan, *First World War*, p.277).

The Arab revolt did not start too well. On 5 June 1916, 50,000 Arabs attacked the Turks near Medina but were heavily defeated. Later, with support from British troops, the Arab forces captured both Jeddah and the holy city of Mecca (Gilbert, *First World War*, p.255). The British forces were brought back to fighting strength and with the addition of the 1st Highland Light Infantry, the new British commander, Major General Maude, began an offensive on 12 December 1916 to take Baghdad, which was finally captured in March 1917.

This prompted a response from the Germans, who sent a combined force of 18,000 German and Austrian troops under German command. Falkenhayn, who was also given command over the Turkish forces, was charged with the dual objectives of recapturing Baghdad and of resisting the advance from Egypt of British troops who were threatening Palestine.

Palestine 1917-18

The imperative for the British was to defeat the Turkish forces in Palestine. In June 1917 General Allenby, who had earlier commanded the British 3rd Army in the Battle of Arras, was appointed to the command of the British forces. Lloyd George tasked him with taking Jerusalem by Christmas, while at the same time disrupting any planned Turkish attempt to recapture Baghdad by engaging the Turkish forces which were being massed in Syria.

Allenby commanded a substantial force comprising two infantry divisions, including the 52nd (Lowland) Division, and desert mounted cavalry to give speed and mobility in attack. The plan was to invade Palestine through first capturing Beersheba and, as a feint, orders were 'inadvertently lost' to the Turkish forces indicating that Gaza and not Beersheba was the main target. Allenby adopted the innovative tactic of a combined operation using French and Royal Navy ships to shell the Turkish at Gaza and British aircraft to carry out bombing raids.

The attack began on 27 October with heavy artillery shelling Gaza, but then Allenby switched the attack using the cavalry to make a surprise attack on Beersheba, which was taken on 31 October, thereby bringing pressure on Gaza, which was captured on 7 November (Gilbert, *First World War*, pp.370-1). The Turkish Army was forced to retreat north and on 11 December Allenby entered Jerusalem, fulfilling his objective.

Allenby was making imaginative and effective use of his military resources, but he realised that his task of driving back the Turkish Army would be made much easier if accompanied by a guerrilla operation to destroy Turkish morale. The logical partners would be the Arabs. What was needed was someone to inspire this revolt ...

Lawrence of Arabia and the Arab Revolt

T.E. Lawrence was born in 1888, the illegitimate son of Sir Thomas Chapman who had scandalously abandoned his wife in Ireland and eloped with the children's governess. Her role obviously developed beyond that of governess, as she bore Chapman five sons, of whom Lawrence was the second. The errant couple moved extensively, living in Wales, Scotland, Brittany and Jersey before finally settling in Oxford under the assumed names of Mr and Mrs Lawrence.

Lawrence was very intelligent and overcame his 'unorthodox' background to read history at Oxford University, during which time he spent three months on a walking tour examining the Crusader castles in what is now Syria. After university he worked as an archaeologist in Syria, and using the cover given by this role he was co-opted by the British Army in 1914 to carry out a clandestine survey of the Negev Desert, which provided a barrier to any Ottoman Army attempting to attack Egypt, then under British 'protection'.

Following the outbreak of war, Lawrence enlisted in October 1914 and was attached to British Military Intelligence in Cairo. With his knowledge of Arabic and his extensive travelling within the region he was a natural choice to work with the Hashemite forces to co-ordinate their activities against the Ottoman Empire with those of the British Army. Lawrence worked alongside Faisal, one of the sons of Sherif Hussain, and they formed a close bond. They targeted the Hejaz Railway, which provided the Turkish forces with vital supplies, blasting the steam engines off the track and then killing the Turkish soldiers isolated in the carriages. With the destruction of the railway, the Turkish troops were tied down in their garrisons.

Lawrence was promoted to major by General Allenby and given full authority for the conduct of operations in conjunction with the Arab forces. Lawrence feared, with some justification, that the British would renege on the promise of an Arabian state and to pre-empt any such betrayal he, together with Faisal, carried out a ruthless advance over the desert to capture Damascus. Lawrence helped set up a provisional Arab government under Faisal, but the dream of an Arab state was soon to be shattered when the French entered Damascus and took control.

Lawrence was disillusioned when the promises which had been made to the Arabs were brutally broken and the Middle East was arbitrarily divided between the British and the French under the Sykes-Picot Agreement to create the countries now forming the Middle East (including the provision of a homeland for the Jews, in accordance with the Balfour Declaration of November 1917).

Lawrence wrote of his experiences in his classic *The Seven Pillars of Wisdom*. He wrote three versions of the manuscript; one was a rewrite because he had lost the original while changing trains at Reading Station. Lawrence was unable to live with the collapse of his Arabian dream and in 1922 enlisted in the RAF under the name T.E. Ross. Unmasked in 1923, he joined the Tank Corps using the name T.E. Shaw. He was killed at the age of 46 in a motorcycle accident, riding his beloved Brough Superior.

7 ACT FOUR: THE WAR IN 1917

THE WINTER OF 1916–1917

Lloyd George Becomes Prime Minister: 7 December 1916

Asquith had been a successful barrister and had led his government through difficult constitutional issues as a peacetime prime minister, but he became indecisive and remote as a wartime prime minister, seemingly more concerned with his bridge, his brandies and his beloved Venetia than with the conduct of the war.

In 1916 Asquith created a small war committee, which he chaired, but it soon increased in size from five to an unmanageable eleven members as Asquith tried to 'buy off' opposition. He was distraught at the death of his son Raymond in the Battle of the Somme, a loss from which he never recovered and which affected his resolve, but despite his inadequacies he rejected Lloyd George's demand to chair a small and effective war council. His weakness as a war leader was being increasingly exposed and in December 1916 he was forced out of office, resigning as prime minister. Lloyd George was appointed prime minister of the coalition government and proved an energetic and decisive war leader, playing a pivotal role in securing Britain's eventual victory.

The Winter Cold

It was the coldest winter in France in living memory. Men serving in the trenches endured intense cold, suffering from frostbite, pneumonia and bronchitis, and could only serve for up to forty-eight hours in the exposed trenches before being relieved. Young men were being crippled by rheumatism as if they were old men four times their age.

Wilfred Owen poignantly described the conditions in a letter to his mother dated 4 February 1917. The horror he portrays is not the horror of war but the horror of living in conditions so cold and desolate that it becomes a struggle just to survive. Owen writes that his platoon had no dugouts:

> but had to lie in the snow under the deadly wind. By day it was impossible to stand up or even crawl about because we were behind only a little ridge screening us from the Bosche's periscope.
>
> We had 5 Tommy's cookers between the platoon, but they did not suffice to melt the ice in the water-cans. So we suffered cruelly from thirst.
>
> The marvel is that we did not all die of cold. As a matter of fact, only one of my party actually froze to death before he could be got back, but I am not able to tell how many have ended up in hospital. I had no real casualties from shelling, though for 10 minutes every hour whizz-bangs fell a few yards short of us. Showers of soil rained on us, but no fragments of shell could find us.

He was shocked by the desolation and revolted by the horror of unburied bodies:

> Hideous landscapes ... everything unnatural, broken, blasted; the distortion of the dead, whose unburiable bodies sit outside the dug-outs all day, all night, the most execrable sights on earth. In poetry we call them most glorious. But we sit with them all day, all night ... and a week later to come back and find them still sitting there, in motionless groups, THAT is what saps the 'soldierly spirit ...'   (Quoted in Jon Stallworthy, *Wilfred Owen*, pp.158-9)

Siegfried Sassoon - Lamentations

Sassoon wrote of bereavement in his bitterly ironic poem, *Lamentations*, after an incident at Rouen in February 1917:

Lamentations

I found him in the guard-room at the Base.
From the blind darkness I had heard his crying
And blundered in. With puzzled, patient face
A sergeant watched him; it was no good trying
To stop it; for he howled and beat his chest.
And, all because his brother had gone west,
Raved at the bleeding war; his rampant grief
Moaned, shouted, sobbed, and choked, while he was kneeling

Half-naked on the floor. In my belief
Such men have lost all patriotic feeling.

(Written in the Summer of 1917)

THE TSAR ABDICATES
(15 MARCH 1917)

The autocratic powers of the tsarist regime had provoked democratic unrest in Russia for some time. After the 1905 revolution the tsar had authorised the setting up of the Duma (effectively a parliament which was elected on a broadly democratic basis and was liberal in outlook) in the hope that this grudging move towards democracy would dampen the discontent, as would the economic growth achieved in the early years of the twentieth century.

With the outbreak of war it became apparent that the Duma had little real power and no influence on foreign policy or upon the conduct of the war, as the tsar had assumed absolute command of the army – although his ability to make the right strategic decisions was unhampered by any relevant military experience. Basing himself in the army headquarters, he soon became dangerously isolated both from the troops at the front and just as dangerously from political opinion in Moscow.

Military failures, the lack of sufficient food to feed the people and the rapidly rising cost of living fermented rebellion, which erupted in early 1917 in a series of strikes. Tsar Nicholas hesitated and then compromised, grudgingly yielding power bit by bit until he was forced to abdicate on 15 March 1917.

The Effect on Russia's War Effort
At first the new Socialist government under Kerensky supported the war and Brusilov was appointed supreme commander of the Russian Army. On 18 June Russian troops attacked the Austrian forces; after an artillery bombardment, thirty-one Russian divisions forced their way through the Austrian defences, advancing 50 miles and capturing Lemberg. The success was short lived; Czechs serving within the Russian Army were in touch with Czechs in the Austrian Army and laid down their weapons. The die was cast. The festering infection of mutiny and defeat would soon spread throughout the Russian forces.

A month later the Germans counter-attacked and routed the fleeing Russian armies. Soldiers threw away their weapons and fled; any Russian officer protesting was murdered by the men he was supposed to be commanding. The Germans advanced steadily, encountering little opposition, and by the end of July had recaptured Ukraine and the other captured territory which had been lost to the Russians. The Russians surrendered in their thousands.

On 15 September Russia was declared a republic, but the collapse of the armed forces continued, with Russian troops on the Baltic joining the mutiny. Lenin had been in exile in Switzerland but, with the abdication of the tsar, the German authorities in April had guaranteed him safe passage to Russia in the hope his extreme views might help to bring down the Russian state. They were right.

On 8 November (26 October under the old Russian calendar, which is why it is called the October Revolution) Lenin and the Bolsheviks seized power. Lenin read out his Decree of Peace, but when, to the Bolsheviks' surprise, their offer of universal peace was not instantly adopted and worldwide revolution did not ensue, they offered a bilateral three-month armistice to Germany. The Germans responded, but after negotiations had dragged on decided enough was enough and told the Russians that the ceasefire would be terminated forthwith unless their proposals were agreed in full. Receiving no response the Germans advanced deep into Russian territory on 17 February, meeting no resistance. In panic the Soviet leadership ordered their delegation to sign the treaty immediately, ceding not only the territory lost to Germany in the war but also all that won by the tsarist forces over the last 200 years, including most of Russia's coal mines, the agricultural grain store of Ukraine and the Baltic Fleet.

It was a humiliating defeat for Russia, but the implication for the war on the Western Front would be equally dramatic, as, freed from any danger on its eastern front, Germany could move its armies to the Western Front for one last great push.

THE UNITED STATES DECLARES WAR ON GERMANY (6 APRIL 1917)

The United States had distanced itself from the war from the outset, appalled that so-called civilised nations could embark upon such widespread slaughter and carnage, and there was popular approval for the position of neutrality taken by President Woodrow Wilson.

Sentiment had changed when, as described earlier, a German U-boat had sunk the British Cunard liner *Lusitania*, leading Wilson to warn Germany that if she continued to attack American ships the United States would enter the war on the side of the Allied powers. Officially the United States continued to preserve its neutral stance, but in practice it supplied – or, more correctly, sold – vast amounts of food and equipment to the Allies, particularly Britain, financed by loans which a post-war Britain would struggle to repay.

The uneasy stand-off between the United States and Germany ended with the Zimmermann Telegram, one of the greatest diplomatic blunders of all time and one that, as A.J.P. Taylor wrote, could only have been hatched up in the rarefied atmosphere of a foreign office, in this case the German Foreign Office. German Foreign Secretary Arthur Zimmermann thought it would be a good idea to put pressure on the United States by encouraging Mexico to 'recover' the territories of Texas, New Mexico and Arizona, a fairly far-fetched idea given the disparity in military and financial resources between Mexico and the United States, but understandably inflammatory to the Americans.

Zimmermann sent the telegram to the German minister in Mexico on 19 January 1917. Unfortunately for Zimmermann – and for Germany – it was intercepted by Admiralty intelligence and deciphered and passed on to President Wilson. This forced Wilson's hand and on 6 April 1917 the United States declared war on Germany.

A number of Americans, such as the poet Alan Seeger, had been serving in the French Foreign Legion, enlisted in the British or Canadian armies, or served in the Red Cross or American-sponsored aid organisations, and American pilots had served with the French Air Force, all of which had helped to influence American opinion. Until now, America had stood aside from the war in Europe, but with its entry the balance of power dramatically changed. America possessed a powerful navy and although its army was small (numbering just 100,000 men), with no experience of large-scale combat and no significant weaponry, it did have immense potential resources of manpower and an industrial capacity which could be harnessed to the war effort. President Wilson immediately introduced conscription, but it would be some time before raw new recruits could be trained and transformed into an effective fighting force and America's huge industrial resources could be switched to the manufacture of weapons and munitions. There was still a lot of fighting to be done before the Americans arrived.

THE BATTLE OF ARRAS
(9 APRIL–16 MAY 1917)

The Germans had consolidated their position and on 16 March began a phased withdrawal to the formidable defences of the Hindenburg Line, laying waste to the land as they withdrew. Nivelle, the French commander, proposed a joint assault on the German lines: British troops would target Arras and the Canadians Vimy Ridge in the north, while the French would attack the German lines in the south.

The Battle of Arras

The Battle of Arras started with a barrage of artillery from nearly 3,000 guns, which continued for five days before the British and Canadian forces, under the overall command of General Allenby, launched simultaneous attacks on 9 April. Scottish troops were well represented in the fighting. The 9th (Scottish), 15th (Scottish) and 51st (Highland) Divisions all took part, with altogether forty-four Scottish battalions involved; many of the Canadian regiments also had Scottish origins (Royle, *Flowers*, pp.113–14).

The attack had been carefully planned with the infantry advancing behind a creeping artillery barrage stunning the German defences. On the first day, the British overran the German front-line trenches, penetrating the feared Hindenburg Line and taking more than 5,000 German prisoners. The Canadians were similarly successful, advancing 4,000yd – an almost unheard of distance when gains of territory were measured in tens of yards – capturing the strategically important Vimy Ridge and taking another 4,000 prisoners in three days.

The advancing troops spent the first night unprotected in bitterly cold weather before the attack was resumed, but on the third day, as so often happened, the attack petered out as the Germans brought up reinforcements (Gilbert, *First World War*, pp.320–5). By 15 April losses totalled 20,000 and Haig ordered an end to the offensive (Keegan, *First World War*, p.352).

The Nivelle Offensive

On 16 April, the French attacked the Germans on the Aisne, also in appalling weather conditions, in what was known as the Nivelle Offensive. Again the strength of the German defences was in the reserves deployed on the reverse slope and outside the range of the French artillery. The advancing French forces encountered murderous German machine-gun fire and in the first five days of the fighting lost over 100,000 casualties (the expectation had been for just 15,000) while advancing just 600yd and capturing just one ridge. The French troops, demoralised by the heavy losses, refused to continue fighting and the discredited French commander, Robert Nivelle, was replaced by Philippe Pétain (Gilbert, *First World War*, p.323).

A Resumption of the Fighting at Arras

On 23 April Haig was urged to resume the offensive to take the pressure off the French, but the Germans were now prepared and the British troops suffered from crushing German artillery fire. On 1 May General Allenby, commanding the British forces at Arras, implored Haig to call off the fighting because of the heavy losses but Haig continued the attack. On 7 May Allenby repeated his request, warning that the troops he was sending into battle were but 'semi-trained' (quoted in Gilbert, *First World War*, p.325). Haig eventually complied, but a few weeks later Allenby was despatched to Cairo and given command of the Egyptian Expeditionary Force. Haig encouraged free expression of opinion by his officers – provided they agreed with him.

By the end of the battle the British had gained little ground beyond that won the first day and had suffered more than 150,000 casualties; 130,000 of these from when fighting had been resumed. Scottish regiments had suffered heavily, as they had comprised as much as a third of the attacking forces, and the Royal Flying Corps lost 131 aircraft, a third of its strength (Gilbert, *First World War*, p.322). The Canadians suffered 10,500 casualties, of whom 3,500 were killed.

Edward Thomas – No One Cares Less than I

The war poet Edward Thomas was amongst those killed at Arras. He was born in 1878, educated at St Paul's School and Lincoln College, Oxford, and pursued a precarious and impecunious career as a writer and poet. Thomas was a tortured man, tortured both by his ability to hurt his wife and children and by his inability to successfully provide for them. His wife, Helen, in her autobiography *World without End*, wrote of his days of silence and despair, of days when he would just disappear and times when he was suicidal. He had the power to hurt his wife and children with his life, how much more hurt could he cause by his death?

He volunteered in July 1915 at the age of 37. He was not posted to France until the end of January 1917 and was killed just ten weeks later on 9 April 1917. It was an unusual death, perhaps in keeping with the man. It was the first day of the battle and the Germans had been in retreat. The shelling had stopped and Thomas stepped out of the dugout and lit his clay pipe. The Germans fired one last shell; Thomas was not hit, but the shell burst so close to him that the shock from the blast stopped his heart. He died with no signs of an injury – even his clay pipe was unbroken. His poem *No One Cares Less than I* was written in May 1916:

No One Cares Less than I

'No one cares less than I,
Nobody knows but God,
Whether I am destined to lie
Under a foreign clod,'
Were the words I made to the bugle call in the morning.

But laughing, storming, scorning,
Only the bugles know
What the bugles say in the morning
And they do not care, when they blow
The call that I heard and made words to early this morning.

Siegfried Sassoon - The General

Siegfried Sassoon writes of his experiences in the battle. He was in the battalion when in it advanced in a snowstorm to relieve soldiers occupying a part of the Hindenburg trench, for so long the unassailable defence of the German line, which had been captured in the first assault. He records seeing the bodies littered on the ground between the outpost trench and the main trench (now the British front line). The outpost trench had been devastated by the British bombardment; the ground was pitted by shell holes and everywhere there were the distorted remains of the dead. He writes, in *Memoirs of an Infantry Officer* (p.157), of seeing:

a pair of hands (nationality unknown) which protruded from the soaked ashen soil like the roots of a tree turned upside down; one hand seemed to be pointing at the sky with an accusing gesture. Each time I passed that place the protest of those fingers became more expressive of an appeal to God in defiance of those who made the War. Who made the War? I laughed hysterically as the thought passed through my mud-stained mind. But I only laughed mentally, for my box of Stokes gun ammunition left me no breath to spare for an angry guffaw. And the dead were the dead; this was no time to be pitying them or asking silly questions about their outraged lives. Such sights must be taken for granted, I thought as I gasped and slithered and stumbled with my disconsolate crew. Floating on the surface of the flooded trench was the mask of a human face which had detached itself from the skull.

His doubts as to the morality of the war were surfacing, as was his despair at the seeming incompetence of the British command, safely encamped some distance behind the front line and seemingly oblivious to the carnage from recurrent unsuccessful attacks on well-protected German defences – a situation Sassoon lampooned in his poem *The General*:

The General

"Good-morning, good morning!" the General said
When we met him last week on our way to the line.
Now the soldiers he smiled at are most of 'em dead,
And we're cursing his staff for incompetent swine.
"He's a cheery old card" grunted Harry to Jack
As they slogged up to Arras with rifle and pack.

But he did for them both by his plan of attack.

(Written while in Denmark Hill Hospital, April 1917)

'A SOLDIER'S DECLARATION'

After the action at the Battle of Arras, Sassoon was detailed to lead a team armed with Mills bombs, with the objective of clearing any residue of German troops from the newly captured Hindenburg trench.

The Germans were equipped with hand grenades from the start of the war, but the British had virtually none, until the introduction of the Mills bomb in 1915 when it became a weapon of choice. More than 75 million Mills bombs would eventually be produced. The use of Mills bombs was not without risk, and Private Thomas Williamson, Royal Scots Fusiliers, wrote of his experience:

> My first taste of death shook my whole nervous system: one of our bombers had been in the act of throwing his bomb when, for some unknown reason, it exploded blowing his head off. I had to step over the headless body. I cannot say just how I felt, the horror of it, the terrible sight revealed so suddenly before me. I felt sick.   (Quoted in Young, *Scottish Voices*, p.102)

Sassoon's platoon had gone to the support of the Cameronians, who had been driven out of the trenches they had captured. Sassoon, angered by the sight of a young, wounded Cameronian, regained the position with a bombing party consisting of himself and a corporal, but then foolishly decided to 'take a peep':

> No sooner had I popped my silly head out of the sap than I felt a stupendous blow in the back between my shoulders. My first notion was that a bomb had hit me from behind, but what had really happened was that I had been sniped from in front.   (Sassoon, *Memoirs of an Infantry Officer*, p.167)

He was repatriated to England for treatment.

In England, his disillusionment with war was intensified by the artificiality of civilian life, the lack of appreciation of the sufferings felt by those at the front and by the profiteers, politicians and generals who bemoaned the progress of the war while they lunched at the Savoy. He set out his views in a statement entitled, 'Finished with the War: A Soldier's Declaration.' He delivered a copy of the statement to his colonel and also arranged for it to be read in the House of Commons by a sympathetic Member of Parliament. His statement was published in *The Times* on 31 July 1917:

A Soldier's Declaration

I am making this statement as an act of wilful defiance of military authority, because I believe that the War is being deliberately prolonged by those who have the power to end it. I am a soldier, convinced that I am acting on behalf of soldiers. I believe that this War, upon which I entered as a war of defence and liberation, has now become a war of aggression and conquest. I believe that the purposes for which I and my fellow soldiers entered upon this War should have been so clearly stated as to have made it impossible to change them, and that, had this been done, the objects which actuated us would now be attainable by negotiation. I have seen and endured the sufferings of the troops, and I can no longer be party to prolong these sufferings for ends which I believe to be evil and unjust. I am not protesting against the conduct of the War but against the political errors and insincerities for which the fighting men are being sacrificed. On behalf of those who are suffering now I make this protest against the deception which is being practised on them; also I believe that I may help to destroy the callous complacency with which the majority of those at home regard the continuance of agonies which they do not share, and which they have not sufficient imagination to realize.   (Quoted in Sassoon, *Memoirs of an Infantry Officer*, p.218)

As a further gesture, Sassoon threw his Military Cross into the River Mersey; he was disappointed it was not heavier and had not sunk, but instead watched as 'the poor little thing fell weakly on the water and floated away as though aware of its futility' (Sassoon, *Memoirs of an Infantry Officer*, p.231). He awaited the inevitable court martial.

Graves had also been invalided out of France. In his case this had not been through injury but with bronchitis, and he had been sent first to hospital in Oxford and then to Osborne House on the Isle of Wight to convalesce. In July 1917 Graves received a letter from Sassoon, enclosing a newspaper cutting from the *Bradford Pioneer* of 27 July, featuring Sassoon's 'A Soldier's Declaration', made, he wrote, as 'an act of wilful defiance of military authority, because I believe the war is being deliberately prolonged by those who have the power to end it' (Graves, *Goodbye to All That*, p.213). Graves was concerned that Sassoon was in no fit physical or mental state to stand the inevitable court martial and imprisonment. He immediately got himself passed fit for service and met Sassoon in Liverpool.

Graves told Sassoon, without authority, that there would be no court martial, no publicity and no martyrdom; instead, he would be shut up in a lunatic asylum until the war was over. The alternative offered was for him to accept that he was suffering from shell shock. Sassoon reluctantly agreed to go before a medical board, but writes that he was at the time unaware that he had probably been saved from being sent to prison by being told a very successful lie – 'No doubt I should have done the same for him if our positions had been reversed' (Sassoon, *Memoirs of an Infantry Officer*, p.235).

Graves was due to escort Sassoon to Edinburgh but missed the train, so Sassoon reported alone to 'Dottyville', as he called the neuropathic hospital in Edinburgh, known to the authorities more conventionally as Craiglockhart Hospital, where he came under the care of Professor W.H. Rivers. Sassoon asked Rivers whether he thought he was suffering from shell shock. 'Certainly not,' was the reply.

'What have I got, then?' asked Sassoon.

'Well, you appear to be suffering from an anti-war complex,' replied Rivers, laughing (Siegfried Sassoon, *The Complete Memoirs of George Sherston*, p.632).

'DOTTYVILLE': CRAIGLOCKHART HOSPITAL

Craiglockhart Hydropathic Hospital was founded in Edinburgh in 1880 but had fallen into disuse until it was requisitioned in 1916 by the War Office as a hospital specifically to treat officers with psychological disorders, primarily 'shell shock' (a state of panic and fear, causing an inability to function properly, brought on as a reaction to the intensity of the bombardment and of the fighting). It has been estimated that as many as 80,000 men suffered from shell shock, due to the trauma of serving in the trenches. Officers were particularly susceptible to shell shock and to neurasthenia (the exhaustion of the central nervous system, causing excessive fatigue and anxiety); the ratio of officers to men in the front line was roughly one to thirty, but for every thirty men treated for shell shock there would be five officers. It may, of course, be that the authorities were more sympathetic to the distress of officers with symptoms of shell shock, which, in their men, was treated as cowardice (Munro, *Scotland's First World War*, p.79). The objective of the hospital was not to cure shell-shock victims, but to get them well enough to return to front-line duty.

Siegfried Sassoon – Survivors
Sassoon satirised the accepted view of shell-shock victims in his bitter poem *Survivors*:

Survivors

No doubt they'll soon get well; the shock and strain
    Have caused their stammering, disconnected talk.
Of course they're "longing to go out again," –
    These boys with old, scared faces, learning to walk.
They'll soon forget their haunted nights; their cowed
    Subjection to the ghosts of friends who died, –
Their dreams that drip with murder; and they'll be proud
    Of glorious war that shatter'd all their pride ...
Men who went out to battle, grim and glad;
Children, with eyes that hate you, broken and mad.

(Written at Craiglockhart Hospital, October 1917)

Wilfred Owen

Wilfred Owen was another war poet treated at Craiglockhart. On 17 March 1917 Owen had been concussed and fallen into a deep cellar; not surprisingly, this experience had affected his nerves. He stayed briefly in a makeshift hospital near the line, but shortly after his return to the front line he was in action at Saint Quentin where he spent four days and nights in the snow without sleep. Owen wrote to his mother, 'Not an hour passed without a shell amongst us ... We lay in wet snow. I kept alive on brandy, and the fear of death, and the glorious prospect of the cathedral Town just below us, glittering in the morning' (quoted in Stallworthy, *Wilfred Owen*, p.179). A week later, Owen returned to action, going 'over the top' twice in one day. He wrote:

The sensations of going over the top are about as exhilarating as those dreams of falling over a precipice, when you see the rocks at the bottom surging up towards you. I woke up without being squashed. Some didn't. There was an extraordinary exultation in the act of slowly walking forward, showing ourselves openly.

    There was no bugle and no drum for which I was very sorry. I kept up a kind of chanting sing-song:
    'Keep the Line straight!
    Not so fast on the left!
    Steady on the Left!
    Not so fast!'

He continued:

> Then we were caught up in a Tornado of Shells. The various 'waves' were all broken up and we carried on like a crowd moving off a cricket field. When I looked back and saw the ground all crawling and wormy with wounded bodies, I felt no horror at all but only an immense exultation at having got through the Barrage.

He continued:

> The Colonel sent round this message the next day: 'I was filled with admiration at the conduct of the battalion under heavy shellfire ... The leadership of the officers was excellent, and the conduct of the men was beyond praise.' The reward we got for all this was to remain in the Line 12 days. For twelve days I did not wash my face, nor take off my boots, nor sleep a deep sleep. For twelve days we lay in holes, where at any moment a shell might put us out. I think the worst incident was one wet night when we lay up against a railway embankment. A big shell lit on top of the bank, just 2 yards from my head. Before I awoke, I was blown in the air right away from the bank! I passed most of the following days in a railway Cutting in a hole just big enough to lie in, and covered with corrugated iron. My brother officer of B Coy, 2/Lt Gaukroger lay opposite in a similar hole. But he was covered with earth, and no relief will ever relieve him.   (Collected Letters, p.452, quoted in Stallworthy, Wilfred Owen, pp.181-2)

After four days spent with a corpse, 'who lay not only nearby, but in various places around and about', it is perhaps not surprising that on 1 May his commanding officer noted that Owen was trembling uncontrollably and that his speech was confused. He was invalided back to Britain and arrived at Craiglockhart Hospital on 26 June where he was diagnosed as suffering from neurasthenia. He became editor of The Hydra, the journal of Craiglockhart Hospital.

In August he writes to his mother of a new arrival, 'I have just been reading Siegfried Sassoon, and am feeling at a high pitch of emotion. Nothing like his trench life sketches has ever been written or ever will be written' (quoted in Stallworthy, Wilfred Owen, p.204).

Shortly after Sassoon's arrival, Owen knocked somewhat timorously at the door of the great poet. Owen had been writing poetry since a boy but none of his works had been published. At Craiglockhart he had been encouraged to deal with the devils in his dreams by transforming them into poetry and he showed his drafts tentatively to Sassoon, who criticised them as containing too much 'sweetness of sentiment' and recommended he adopt a more down-to-earth style. Sassoon contributed significantly to Owen's development as a poet, encouraging him to use his personal experiences of war to evoke the horror and anger he felt, just as Sassoon did in his own poems, often expressing his ideas in a bitter, satirical form. To this brew, Owen added the further ingredient of compassion.

Wilfred Owen - Mental Cases

In this poem, written in 1918, Wilfred Owen vividly portrays the sad existence of those suffering from shell shock:

Mental Cases

Who are these? Why sit they here in twilight?
Wherefore rock they, purgatorial shadows,
Drooping tongues from jaws that slob their relish,
Baring teeth that leer like skulls' teeth wicked?
Stroke on stroke of pain, - but what slow panic,
Gouged these chasms round their fretted sockets?
Ever from their hair and through their hands' palms
Misery swelters. Surely we have perished
Sleeping, and walk hell; but who these hellish?

-These are men whose minds the Dead have ravished.
Memory fingers in their hair of murders,
Multitudinous murders they once witnessed.
Wading sloughs of flesh these helpless wander,
Treading blood from lungs that had loved laughter.
Always they must see these things and hear them,
Batter of guns and shatter of flying muscles,
Carnage incomprehensible, and human squander
Rucked too thick for these men's extrication.

Therefore still their eyeballs shrink tormented
Back into their brains, because on their sense

Sunlight seems a bloodsmear; night becomes blood-black;
Dawn breaks open like a wound that bleeds afresh.
-Thus their heads wear this hilarious, hideous,
Awful falseness of set-smiling corpses.
-Thus their hands are plucking at each other;
Picking at the rope-knouts of their scourging;
Snatching after us who smote them, brother,
Pawing us who dealt them war and madness.

(Written at Ripon, May 1918; revised Scarborough, July 1918)

There were two principal doctors at Craiglockhart Hospital - Arthur Brock and the well-respected and empathetic William Rivers, who believed in curing his patients by getting them to tell of their experiences rather than repressing them. Rivers had observed the reluctance of both patients and their visitors to talk of the war and its impact and wrote in a paper to the Royal Society of Medicine in 1917:

> It is natural to thrust aside painful memories just as it is natural to avoid dangerous or horrible scenes in actuality, and this natural tendency to banish the distressing or the horrible is especially pronounced in those whose powers of resistance have been lowered by the long-continued strains of trench-life, the shock of shell-explosion, or other catastrophe of war.   (Munro, *Scotland's First World War*, pp.79-80)

Siegfried Sassoon - Repression of War Experience
Sassoon wrote this intensely disturbing poem in July 1917 after listening to a lecture given by William Rivers, which gives an insight into Sassoon's own troubled mind:

Repression of War Experience

Now light the candles; one, two; there's a moth;
What silly beggars they are to blunder in
And scorch their wings with glory, liquid flame -
No, no, not that, - it's bad to think of war,
When thoughts you've gagged all day come back to scare you;
And it's been proved that soldiers don't go mad

Unless they lose control of ugly thoughts
That drive them out to jabber among the trees.

Now light your pipe; look, what a steady hand.
Draw a deep breath; stop thinking; count fifteen,
And you're as right as rain ...
                              Why won't it rain? ...
I wish there'd be a thunder-storm tonight,
With bucketfuls of water to sluice the dark,
And make the roses hang their dripping heads.

Books; what a jolly company they are,
Standing so quiet and patient on their shelves,
Dressed in dim brown, and black, and white, and green,
And every kind of colour. Which will you read?
Come on; O do read something; They're so wise.
I tell you all the wisdom of the world
Is waiting for you on those shelves; and yet
You sit and gnaw your nails, and let your pipe out,
And listen to the silence: on the ceiling
There's one big, dizzy moth that bumps and flutters;
And in the breathless air outside the house
The garden waits for something that delays.
There must be crowds of ghosts among the trees -
Not people killed in battle - they're in France -
But horrible shapes in shrouds - old men who died
Slow, natural deaths - old men with ugly souls,
Who wore their bodies out with nasty sins.

You're quiet and peaceful, summering safe at home;
You'd never think there was a bloody war on! ...
O yes, you would ... Why, can't you hear the guns?
Hark! Thud, thud, thud - quite soft ... they never cease -
Those whispering guns - O Christ, I want to go out
And screech at them to stop - I'm going crazy;
I'm going stark, staring mad because of the guns.

Sassoon wrote of his stay that, during the daytime, the doctors could counteract the gloom of the surroundings:

> The War Office had wasted no money on interior decoration; consequently the place had the melancholy atmosphere of a decayed hydro, redeemed only by its healthy situation and pleasant view of the Pentland Hills' and the 'wrecked faces [who] were outnumbered by those who were emerging from their nervous disorders' so that Craiglockhart, so to speak, 'made cheerful conversation'.
>
> But by night they lost control and the hospital became sepulchral and oppressive with saturations of war experience. One lay awake and listened to feet padding along passages which smelt of stale cigarette-smoke; for the nurses couldn't prevent insomnia-ridden officers from smoking half the night in their bedrooms, though the locks had been removed from all doors.
>
> One became conscious that the place was full of men whose slumbers were morbid and terrifying – men muttering uneasily or suddenly crying out in their sleep ... In the daytime, sitting in a sunny room, a man could discuss his psycho-neurotic symptoms with his doctor, who could diagnose phobias and conflicts and formulate them into scientific terminology. Significant dreams could be noted down, and Rivers could try to remove repressions.
>
> But by night each man was back in his doomed sector of horror-stricken Front Line, where the panic and stampede of some ghastly experience was re-enacted among the livid faces of the dead. No doctor could save him then, when he became the lonely victim of his dream disasters and delusions. (*The Complete Memoirs of George Sherston*, p.680)

Sassoon began to experience feelings of guilt that he was comfortably ensconced in Dottyville while his former comrades were still facing the horrors of war. He wrote a haunting poem, *Sick Leave*, about the ghosts of soldiers reproaching him for his absence:

Sick Leave

When I'm asleep, dreaming and lulled and warm,
They come, the homeless ones, the noiseless dead.
While the dim charging breakers of the storm
Bellow and drone and rumble overhead,
Out of the gloom they gather about my bed.
 They whisper to my heart; their thoughts are mine.

"Why are you here with all your watches ended?
    From Ypres to Frise we sought you in the Line."
In bitter safety I awake, unfriended;
And while the dawn begins with slashing rain
I think of the Battalion in the mud.
"When are you going out to them again?
Are they not still your brothers through our blood?"

(Written while an inmate of Craiglockhart Hospital, 1917)

Sassoon was passed fit for front-line service in November 1917 and left the hospital to go first to Ireland, where he hunted, then to Palestine and back to France. On 13 July 1918, on his return from a foray with a corporal into no man's land with the task of taking out a German machine-gun post, he was accidentally shot in the head by one of his own men, the bullet grazing rather than entering his head. He was again invalided home to England where, this time, he remained on sick leave until the end of the war.

Wilfred Owen - Dulce et Decorum Est
The development of Owen as a poet, tempered by his experiences in Flanders and the encouragement of Siegfried Sassoon, is illustrated by his poem *Dulce et Decorum Est*, one of the finest poems of the First World War, written initially at Craiglockhart but finalised early in 1918. ('*Dulce et Decorum Est Pro Patria Mori*' is a quote from the Latin poet Horace, and translates as 'It is sweet and decorous to die for your country'. These words had first been used by Owen in an ephemeral poem *The Ballad of Purchase Money*, which he had written in 1914.) The poem began with an allusion to Horace:

O meet it is and passing sweet
To live in peace with others,
But sweeter still and far more meet
To die in war for brothers.

The Brooke-like sentiments of this poem, written before Owen had first-hand experience of the horrors of war, contrast with the hard edge of *Dulce et Decorum Est*:

Dulce et Decorum Est

Bent double, like old beggars under sacks,
Knock-kneed, coughing like hags, we cursed through sludge,
Till on the haunting flares we turned our backs
And towards our distant rest began to trudge.
Men marched asleep. Many had lost their boots
But limped on, blood-shod. All went lame; all blind;
Drunk with fatigue; deaf even to the hoots
Of tired, outstripped Five-Nines that dropped behind.

Gas! GAS! Quick, boys ! - An ecstasy of fumbling,
Fitting the clumsy helmets just in time;
But someone still was yelling out and stumbling,
And flound'ring like a man in fire or lime ...
Dim, through the misty panes and thick green light,
As under a green sea, I saw him drowning.
In all my dreams, before my helpless sight,
He plunges at me, guttering, choking, drowning.

If in some smothering dreams you too could pace
Behind the wagon that we flung him in,
And watch the white eyes writhing in his face,
His hanging face, like a devil's sick of sin;
If you could hear, at every jolt, the blood
Come gargling from the froth-corrupted lungs,
Obscene as cancer, bitter as the cud
Of vile, incurable sores on innocent tongues, -
My friend, you would not tell with such high zest
To children ardent for some desperate glory,
The old Lie: *Dulce et decorum est*
Pro patria mori.

Owen would write some of his best poems at Craiglockhart and in the brief
remaining months of his life, which would not be published until after his
death. Owen had written a moving preface:

This book is not about heroes. English poetry is not yet fit to speak of them.

Nor is it about deeds, or lands, nor anything about glory, honour, might, majesty, dominion, or power, except War.

Above all I am not concerned with Poetry.

My Subject is War, and the pity of War.

The Poetry is in the pity.

(Quoted in Stallworthy, *Wilfred Owen*, p.266)

While at Craiglockhart Hospital, Owen prepared the draft of a poem (which was revised in May 1918) dealing with the plight of those who could just not cope with the pressures of life in the trenches, or with the ever-present danger of death or injury from sniper or artillery shell, or who lacked the blind courage to go 'over the top' to very probable death. Self-inflicted wounds to get a pass back to Blighty were not uncommon. Owen's poem *S.I.W.* (army shorthand for Self-Inflicted Wound) shows the influence of Sassoon's poem *The Hero*:

S.I.W.

I The Prologue:

Patting goodbye, doubtless they told the lad
He'd always show the Hun a brave man's face;
Father would sooner see him dead than in disgrace, –
Was proud to see him going, aye, and glad.
Perhaps his mother whimpered how she'd fret
Until he got a nice safe wound to nurse.
Sisters would wish girls too could shoot, charge, curse ...
Brothers – would send his favourite cigarette.
Each week, month after month, they wrote the same,
Thinking him sheltered in some Y.M. Hut,
Because he said so, writing on his butt
Where once an hour a bullet missed its aim.
And misses teased the hunger of his brain.
His eyes grew old with wincing, and his hand
Reckless with ague. Courage leaked, as sand
From the best sandbags after years of rain.

But never leave, wound, fever, trench-foot, shock,
Untrapped the wretch. And death seemed still withheld
For torture of lying machinally shelled,
At the pleasure of this world's Powers who'd run amok.

He'd seen men shoot their hands, on night patrol.
Their people never knew. Yet they were vile.
'Death sooner than dishonour, that's the style!'
So Father said.

II The Action:

One dawn, our wire patrol
Carried him. This time Death had not missed.
We could do nothing but wipe his bleeding cough.
Could it be accident? Rifles go off ...
Not sniped? No. (Later they found the English ball.)

III The Poem:

It was the reasoned crisis of his soul
Against more days of inescapable thrall,
Against infrangibly wired and blind trench wall
Curtained with fire, roofed in with creeping fire,
Slow grazing fire, that would not burn him whole
But kept him for death's promises and scoff,
And life's half-promising, and both their riling.

IV The Epilogue:

With him they buried the muzzle his teeth had kissed,
And truthfully wrote the mother, 'Tim died smiling.'

['Y.M. Hut' - Young Men's Christian Association Hostel. 'Creeping fire' - a creeping artillery barrage.]

Owen Returns to the Front

Owen shared the feelings of guilt that he was safe in hospital while his comrades were fighting at the front, a feeling known as 'survivors' guilt'. He presented himself to the medical board and in October 1917 was pronounced fit for light duties and in August 1918 returned to France. Owen was very aware that Sassoon and Graves had both been awarded the Military Cross; had he the same courage? He would soon know the answer.

On 1-2 October the Manchesters broke through the German lines and had to repel repeated counter-attacks. Owen fought with conspicuous bravery and was awarded the Military Cross. The citation reads:

> For conspicuous gallantry and devotion to duty in the attack on the Fonsomme Line on 1st/2nd October 1918. On the Company Commander becoming a casualty, he assumed command and showed fine leadership and resisted a heavy counter-attack. He personally manipulated a captured enemy machine gun in an isolated position and inflicted considerable losses on the enemy. Throughout he behaved most gallantly. (Stallworthy, *Wilfred Owen*, p.279)

Owen need never doubt his courage again.

He was killed on 4 November 1918 in the crossing of the Sambre-Oise Canal, just one week before the ending of hostilities, encouraging his men as they tried to make a crossing under intense enemy fire. Owen is now recognised as one of the greatest of the war poets. His poem *Anthem for Doomed Youth* is one of his finest:

Anthem for Doomed Youth

What passing-bells for these who die as cattle?
  – Only the monstrous anger of the guns.
  Only the stuttering rifles' rapid rattle
Can patter out their hasty orisons.
No mockeries now for them; no prayers nor bells;
  Nor any voice of mourning save the choirs,
The shrill, demented choirs of wailing shells;
  And bugles calling for them from sad shires.

What candles may be held to speed them all?
    Not in the hands of boys but in their eyes
Shall shine the holy glimmers of goodbyes.
    The pallor of girls' brows shall be their pall;
Their flowers the tenderness of patient minds,
And each slow dusk a drawing-down of blinds.

(Written at Craiglockhart Hospital, September–October 1917)

THE THIRD BATTLE OF YPRES: THE BATTLE OF PASSCHENDAELE (31 JULY–10 NOVEMBER 1917)

The greatest martyrdom of the World War.

General von Kuhl, Chief of Staff on the Flanders front, quoted in Gilbert, *First World War*, p.365.

The British had failed to break through at Arras; the French had failed to break through on the Aisne. The Russians had collapsed so that the German divisions which had been fighting Russia were now free to move to the Western Front, presenting an impending threat of a German assault using fresh troops. Furthermore, British supplies of food were being threatened with the sinking of merchant ships by the German U-boat fleet. The war was not going well; a new initiative was needed.

Messines

Messines was the beginning. The plan was to tunnel under the enemy lines and then to blow away the German defences through the detonation of mines. Over the course of six months, British, Canadian and Australian tunnellers had dug a network of tunnels extending to around 4½ miles in total under the German lines, and nineteen mines had been filled with 500 tons of explosives. At 3.10 a.m. on 7 June 1917 these mines were detonated. The explosion could be heard as far away as London; reportedly, the prime minister arranged to be woken so that he could hear the biggest man-made explosion then known.

There had been no preliminary bombardment and the surprise was total. The shock to the defending German soldiers was such that British troops captured the ridge in just three hours, successfully exploiting the gap that had been created in the enemy defences and taking 7,000 German prisoners. It was estimated that a further 10,000 had been killed in the explosion or buried alive (Gilbert, *First World War*, p.336).

Ewart Alan Mackintosh - Mines

Mining was another technique used in an attempt to break the deadlock of the trenches. Specialist teams, usually composed of men who had been miners in civilian life, would dig tunnels under no man's land and under the enemy trenches. These tunnels were then packed with explosives and detonated with the hope that the resultant explosion would create a crater that would destroy the integrity of the enemy trench system - and, of course, also kill a significant number of the enemy. Mining became competitive, with tunnels dug underneath the enemy's tunnel system, and miners would listen intently for any sound of enemy tunnelling activity.

When enemy mining was taking place, the number of men in the vulnerable forward trenches was reduced, but sentries were still posted there to keep watch on enemy activity. In his poem *Mines*, Mackintosh writes of the impact of the threat of enemy mining upon these sentries, all too aware that at any moment they could be blown to infinity:

Mines

What are you doing, Sentry,
Fresh-faced and brown?
Waiting for the mines, Sir,
Sitting on the mines, Sir,
Just to keep them down.
Mines going up, and no one to tell for us
Where it will be, and maybe it's as well for us,
Mines going up. Oh! God, but it's hell for us,
Here with the bloody mines.

What are you doing, Sentry,
Cold and drawn and grey?

Listening to them tap, Sir,
Same old tap, tap, tap, Sir,
And praying for the day.
Mines going up, and no one can say for us
When it will be; but they are waiting some day for us.
Mines going up - oh! Folk at home, pray for us
Here with the bloody mines.

Where are you lying, Sentry?
Wasn't this your place?
Down below your feet, Sir,
Below your heavy feet, Sir,
With earth upon my face.
Mines gone up, and the earth and the clod on us -
Fighting for breath - and our own comrades trod on us.
Mines gone up - Have pity, oh God! On us,
Down in the bloody mines.

(Sent from France, November 1917)

The Battle of Passchendaele

Haig believed that Messines had been a turning point and that the stale-mate had at last been broken. Now was the time to make the conclusive attack which would defeat the Germans and win the war. The Battle of the Somme had been the wrong battle at the wrong time in the wrong place. The time was now right and the place was right - yet again Ypres - where success would enable British forces to threaten the German U-boat bases.

Haig put his ideas to the London War Committee in June, confident that Ypres could provide the decisive breakthrough that the Battle of the Somme had conspicuously failed to achieve. Lloyd George expressed, rightly as it proved, scepticism as to whether a breakthrough would be achieved and concern as to the probable loss of life; he also had doubts whether it would advance the end of the war, even if successful. As a civilian, however, he did not consider himself qualified 'to impose my strategical views on my military advisers' (quoted in Keegan, *The First World War*, p.384). And so approval was given. Lloyd George was not impressed with the quality of his military commanders, writing in his war memoirs:

> Some of the assaults on impossible positions ordered by our generals would never have been decreed if they had seen beforehand with their own eyes the hopeless slaughter to which their orders doomed their men.   (Quoted in Gilbert, *First World War*, p.537)

In this, he was possibly being charitable, as the same mistakes were repeated again and again.

The target was the village of Passchendaele, 4½ miles away. The strategy had not changed. The main attack took place on 31 July, preceded, as at the Somme, by an intense, continuous bombardment – 3,000 guns firing more than 4 million shells over ten days. The choice of battleground was not ideal; the German front line was based on the higher ground of the Passchendaele Ridge, which dominated the low-lying plain across which the British would have to advance. Three years of shelling had cleared any cover from the land and it was repeatedly flooded after the destruction of the ancient system of field drainage.

To compound the challenge, the Germans had constructed in-depth defences and had built a network of concrete bunkers, often concealed within ruined buildings. The German barbed wire, far from being destroyed by the shelling, had been congealed into an impenetrable tangle which would prove impervious to the efforts of the army standard-issue wire cutters.

Despite this, the initial attack with infantry supported by tanks was successful. Nine British and six French divisions attacked on a 15-mile front, advancing in 'good order' in line abreast through the mud until they reached the slopes of the Passchendaele Ridge. It was then that the Germans opened fire with devastating effect, launching a counter-attack using the reserves stationed in their second line of defences and unleashing a furious artillery barrage upon the British troops while torrential rain turned the battlefield into a morass of mud. It was the persistent rain that persuaded Haig to call a temporary halt to the fighting on 4 August.

The Capture of Passchendaele Village

Casualties had been 'relatively light', with just 8,000 killed or missing, and the initial failure would not deter Haig from persisting, despite the prospective number of casualties or the state of the battlefield. In September he ordered the offensive to be resumed. Fighting continued for a further three months, with repeated British assaults and German counter-attacks in the rain and mud until the British troops had fought themselves to a standstill.

It had become a charade, with British forces using a massive artillery bombardment to support the capture of the lightly defended German front-line trenches, only for the Germans to launch their own artillery barrage and recapture the ground lost.

By October, Haig had exhausted his reserves of British troops and committed first ANZAC and then Canadian troops in further meaningless assaults until 6 November when the village of Passchendaele, or what little remained of it, was eventually captured. Seventy thousand of Haig's troops had been killed and another 170,000 wounded (Keegan, *First World War*, p.394). The territory gained was less than 5 miles.

A Diary of the Battle

David Ferguson, Machine Gun Corps, wrote in his diary of going up a communication trench to the line for an attack in the last few days of the battle:

Friday 9th November 4.00 p.m.
After being fully loaded up like pack mules we started for the line. All went well altho' heavy shelling was going on. We got onto a duckboard track and wended our way slowly in the dark knowing only that it was not a picnic we were on. ... Things were getting very angry and each one and all expected death every minute but we had to just plod along. Just then I can remember hearing a terrible swishing noise and then screams and I with others were knocked head over heels. We lost a sergeant killed and one man killed and six men slightly wounded leaving only three (machine gun) teams now. We left our wounded and dead there as our orders were to go forward but we reported at the next dressing station up the line and they went down and attended to whoever survived. We got a rest at this dressing station as we were all badly shaken and fed up but knew there was worse to come ...

We started on the last lap about 10.30 p.m. dark and raining and a miserable night. We could see we were now on the worst part as the track was getting broken and spasmodic with men in Argylls lying dead on each side. I may mention the enemy had hundreds of guns trained on this track as he knew all our men used this one and only way and every half hour or so he would shell constantly for about 20 minutes and if you were caught in a shell it was death of the worst kind.

He continued:

About 2.00 a.m. in pitch darkness and heavy rain we got guides to take us to our kicking off point for morning. At this time we had 3 guns and gun teams but very little ammunition as most of it was dumped. We had to cross a strip of ground just a mass of water and mud and I shall never forget that journey. The first two or three in front soon left the remainder of us to struggle in utter blindness. Men stepped into shell holes and were drowned not under water but with mud. I became stuck in this mud and altho' only up to the knees I could not free myself altho' I used my rifle to such an extent that I had to leave it where it was. It was no use asking anybody for help as no one had any attention to you, being too busy getting along themselves. However one chap did give me a little help and my knowing my fate gave me increased energy and I managed to get a better footing and keep moving.

The attack was due to take place at 6.15 a.m. on 10 November:

At a ... quarter to six a.m. every British manned weapon down to machine guns commenced a hideous din. Shells of every calibre whistled and yelled in thousands. Of course this was the prelude to our advance which was to follow in about half an hour. I may say that it was simply pouring with rain and altho' it was just dawn it was darker with the black clouds hovering above ...

The attack was a failure and they had to make their way back down the duckboard track:

... what a mess on this duckboard track. Chaps were lying dead in all positions, some recognisable others blown to pieces. Stretcher bearers with wounded men blown to bits leaving just bundles of blood-soaked rags of blood.

We arrived at this dressing station where all sorts of chaps from different regiments [sic]. Wounded prisoners lay everywhere as our own chaps were served first. This place was crowded with chaps moaning and yelling. We stayed there about an hour and then we were led down a track, it was pitch dark now, to another pill-box called Albatross farm. This was somebody's headquarters and on the road down to it we passed the spot where one of our gun teams got blown up while we were wending our way up the line. On the other side of this track were masses of what was once men but now just bits of dirty flesh and rags here and there. A part of this track was under water and we had to wade through it up to our middles. If he had started shelling now we would have got it in the neck.

An officer selected three men to go for rations:

> I unfortunately clicked for one and we with our major leading (he was a gentleman in the line) made for that perilous duck board again. Altho' they (the enemy guns) were quiet the walking was dreadful and by the time we reached the washed away part the water had risen like a high tide. We had to make a chain and clasp one another's hands and went right through this small river. ... We waited in this place where a crowd were gathered, wounded, ration parties, wire parties, etc. He now started to shell the approaching tracks and we were astonished to see a party coming down and seemingly walking into death. It was very dark but you could see the outline of them. They were just about 30 yards when down came a shell and then screaming and a rush. It was pitiful to hear the cries of the wounded.

On Sunday, 11 November they made for the position where they were due to be relieved:

> We saw our position. ... We ran across the open as fast as we could and took up different positions in shell holes. This place was simply covered with dead. They appeared to me to have been mown down as they were advancing in line. I was in a hole along with my officer and three others; the rest were scattered about. We tried to dig deeper but we came across more dead and gave up. Fortunately they did not smell which was a blessing.

Ferguson spent the whole of the next day in the shell hole waiting for the relief before the officer took the only course of action, which was to return to the line. Ferguson eventually made it back to his company where 'after a stiff tot of rum ... we felt a lot better' (quoted in Young, *Scottish Voices*, pp.155–63).

Mustard Gas

In the fighting the Germans had used shells filled with mustard gas. The horrific effects of mustard gas were described by Vera Brittain in a letter written to her mother:

> I wish those people who write so glibly about this being a holy War, and the orators who talk so much about going on no matter how long the War lasts and what it may mean, could see a case – to say nothing of 10 cases – of

mustard gas in its early stages – could see the poor things burnt and blistered
all over with great mustard-coloured suppurating blisters, with blind eyes –
sometimes temporally [*sic*], sometimes permanently – all sticky and stuck
together, and always fighting for breath, with voices a mere whisper, saying
that their throats are closing and they know they will choke. The only thing
one can say is that such severe cases don't last long, either they die soon or
they improve – usually the former.   (*A Testament of Youth*, p.360) ·

THE BATTLE OF CAMBRAI
(20 NOVEMBER–7 DECEMBER 1917)

Tanks came of age in the Battle of Cambrai when, for the first time,
they were deployed in quantity and used as the breakthrough weapon.
Although tanks had been used earlier by both the British and the French,
their effectiveness had previously been outweighed by their unreliability and
by the mud of Flanders. The reliability of tanks had, by now, been improved
and the decision was made to use them on the more suitable dry, chalky
ground near Cambrai where they would lead the attack, destroying the
enemy's barbed-wire entanglements and clearing the way for the advanc-
ing infantry.

Siegfried Sassoon – Attack
Siegfried Sassoon wrote of the use of tanks in his poem *Attack*:

Attack

At dawn the ridge emerges massed and dun
In wild purple of the glow'ring sun,
Smouldering through spouts of drifting smoke that shroud
The menacing scarred slope; and, one by one,
Tanks creep and topple forward to the wire.
The barrage roars and lifts. Then, clumsily bowed
With bombs and guns and shovels and battle-gear,
Men jostle and climb to meet the bristling fire.
Lines of grey, muttering faces, masked with fear,
They leave their trenches, going over the top,
While time ticks blank and busy on their wrists,

And hope, with furtive eyes and grappling fists,
Flounders in mud. O Jesus make it stop!

(Written at Craiglockhart in 1917. Based on Sassoon's diary note while observing
the attack on the Hindenburg Line)

There was a change in tactics – the element of surprise. 'Secrecy being essential, all troops, guns, tanks and transport had to come up by night. The general idea was to conceal as large a force as could be rapidly and successfully hidden, and hurl the lot at the unsuspecting Boche' (Rorie, *A Medico's Luck*, p.159).

The attack commenced at 6.20 a.m. First there was a short barrage from 1,000 guns and then nine tank battalions with over 300 tanks advanced across a narrow 6-mile front towards the German positions, followed closely by the infantry. The absence of a prolonged preliminary bombardment meant that the Germans had not reinforced their positions, which were held by just two divisions. The tanks were able to crash through the heavy entanglement of barbed wire protecting the line and could cross the trenches by dropping bundles of brushwood to act as bridges. The job of the infantry was to follow behind the tanks to consolidate the ground captured and to take prisoners.

Lessons had at last been learnt: the key to a successful breakthrough was to have surprise, a targeted attack and an overwhelming superiority of force. Sadly, these come under the heading of the 'bleeding obvious', but military thinking was not receptive to new ideas. The one missing element would be the rapid deployment of a second wave to reinforce the initial gains.

On the first day the British forces, with the 51st Highland Division in the centre, advanced 5 miles and penetrated the legendary Hindenburg Line, while suffering relatively light casualties (just 4,000). Yet, predictably, there were insufficient British reserves to replace the exhausted men who had spearheaded the attack and to consolidate the ground gained. The Germans, on the other hand, brought in fresh reserves and recovered the territory lost in a determined counter-attack on 30 November using storm-trooper tactics, attacking in powerful groups rather than in waves.

Of the tanks, 179 became non-operational after the first day – seventy-one through mechanical failure, forty-three were ditched and sixty-five had been destroyed by enemy action. There was still work to be done!

British and Canadian casualties totalled 44,000, the Germans, 53,000 (Gilbert, *First World War*, p.383). Although the gains were insufficiently consolidated and the net result another draw, the benefits from the use of tanks in breaking the stalemate and from the changed tactics were absorbed by the British command, even though they would not be put into use for another year.

EWART ALAN MACKINTOSH

Ewart Alan Mackintosh had been invalided home after being injured at High Wood in August 1916 and was posted to train cadets. He was another who felt the guilt of being 'safe at home'. In September 1917 he had returned to France, probably less than fully fit:

From Home

Here there is peace and easy living,
And a warm fire when the rain is driving,
There is no sound of strong men striving,
Here where the quiet waters flow,
But I am hearing the bullets ringing,
Hearing the great shells onward winging,
The dead men's voices are singing, singing,
    And I must rise and go.

Here there is ease and comfort for me,
A warm soft bed and a good roof o'er me.
Here may be there is fame before me,
Honour and fame for all I know,
But I am seeing the thick rain falling,
Seeing the tired patrols out crawling,
The dead men's voices are calling, calling,
    And I must rise and go.

Back to the trench that I see so clearly,
Back to the fight I can see so nearly,
Back to the friends that I love so dearly,

The dead men lying amid the dew,
The droning sound of the great shells flying,
Filth and honour, and pain, and dying –
Dead friends of mine, oh, cease your crying,
　　For I come back to you.

(Cambridge, 1917)

While in England he had become engaged to Sylvia Marsh and they planned to set up home together in New Zealand after the war. Shortly after his return to France he wrote a poem to Sylvia, who was a Quaker and a pacifist, in which he tried to explain the reason for his decision to return to the front line:

To Sylvia

Two months ago the skies were blue,
The fields were fresh and green,
And green the willow tree stood up,
With the lazy stream between.

Two months ago we sat and watched
The river dribbling by –
And now – you're back at your work again
And here in a ditch I lie.

God knows – my dear – I did not want
To rise and leave you so,
But the dead men's hands were beckoning
And I knew that I must go.

The dead men's eyes were watching, lass,
Their lips were asking too,
We faced it out and paid the price –
Are we betrayed by you?

The days are long between, dear lass,
Before we meet again,

Long days of mud and work for me,
For you long care and pain.

But you'll forgive me yet, my dear,
Because of what you know,
I can look my dead friends in the face
As I couldn't two months ago.

(France, October 1917)

Mackintosh had by now become increasingly aware of death and that his own death may well be imminent, evidenced in his disturbing poem *The Dead Men*:

The Dead Men

It was yesterday I heard again
The dead men talk with living men,
And watched the thread of converse go
Among the speakers to and fro,
Woven with merriment and wit
And beauty to embroider it;
And in the middle now and then,
The laughter clear of happy men –
Only to me a charnel scent
Drifted across the argument,
Only to me his fair young head
Was lifeless and untenanted,
And in his quiet and even tones,
I heard the sound of naked bones,
And in his empty eyes could see
The man who talked was dead, like me.

Then in the conversation's swim,
I leaned across and spoke to him,
And in his dim and dreary eyes
Read suddenly a strange surprise,
And in the touch of his dank hand,

Knew that he too could understand;
So we too talked, and as we heard
Our friends' applause of each dull word
We felt the slow and mournful winds
Blow through the corpse house of our minds,
And the cool dark of underground.
And all the while they sat around
Weighing each listless thing we said,
And did not know that we were dead.

Mackintosh, in one of his last poems, foretells his own death and expresses the hope that should his spirit finally be broken by a lingering death it should be unobserved:

Death

Because I have made light of death
And mocked at wounds and pain,
The doom is laid on me to die –
Like the humble men in days gone by –
That angered me to hear them cry
For pity to me in vain.

I shall not go out suddenly
As many a man has done.
But I shall lie as those men lay –
Longing for death the whole long day –
Praying, as I heard those men pray,
And none shall heed me, none.

The fierce waves will go surging on
Before they tend to me.
Oh, God of battles I pray you send
No word of pity – no help, no friend,
That if my spirit break at the end
None may be there to see.

(France, November 1917)

Mackintosh addressed the last poem he wrote, *War, the Liberator*, to the 'Authoress of Non-Combatant'. In it he writes of war as a rite of passage, of an opportunity to experience the full range of emotions from the warmth of comradeship and the elation of victory to the horror of battle, an opportunity denied to those who do not fight:

War, the Liberator

Surely War is vile to you, you who can but know of it,
Broken men and broken hearts, and boys too young to die,
You that never knew its joy, never felt the glow of it,
Valour and the pride of men, soaring to the sky.
Death's a fearful thing to you, terrible in suddenness,
Lips that will not laugh again, tongues that will not sing,
You that have not seen their sudden life of happiness,
The moment they looked on death, a cowed and beaten thing.

Say what life would theirs have been, that it should make you weep for them,
A small grey world imprisoning the wings of their desire?
Happier than they could tell who knew not life would keep for them
Fragments of the high Romance, the old Heroic fire.
All they dreamed of childishly, bravery and fame for them,
Charges at the cannon's mouth, enemies they slew,
Bright across the waking world their romances came for them,
Is not life a little price when our dreams come true?

All the terrors of the night, doubts and thoughts tormenting us,
These are gone for ever now, truth is come contenting us,
Night with all its tricks is gone and our eyes are clear.
Now in all the time to come, memory will cover us,
Trenches that we did not lose, charges that we made,
Since a voice, when first we heard shells go shrilling over us,
Said within us, 'This is Death - and I am not afraid!'

Since we felt our spirits tower, smiling and contemptuous,
O'er the little frightened things, running to and fro,
Looked on Death and saw a slave blustering and presumptuous,
Daring vainly still to bring Man his master low.

Though we knew that at the last, he would have his lust of us,
Carelessly we braved his might, felt and knew not why
Something stronger than ourselves, moving in the dust of us,
Something in the Soul of Man still too great to die.

Mackintosh was killed on 21 November 1917 in the Battle of Cambrai.

8 THE LAST ACT

THE MICHAEL OFFENSIVE
(21 MARCH 1918)

Yvan Goll - Excerpt from Requiem for the Dead of Europe
In this German poem, Yvan Goll remembers not the soldier off to the Western
Front to fight but the effect his departure has on those left at home, a sad
and often tragic outcome of the war often ignored in the war poems, which
deal more often with the horror of battle and of life in the trenches:

Requiem for the Dead of Europe
Recitative (1)

Let me lament the exodus of so many men from their time;
Let me lament the women whose warbling hearts now scream;
Every lament let me note and add to the list,
When young widows sit by lamplight mourning for husbands lost;
I hear the blonde-voiced children crying for God their father at bedtime;
On every mantelpiece stand photographs wreathed with ivy, smiling, true to the past;
At every window stand lonely girls whose burning eyes are bright with tears;
In every garden lilies are growing, as though there's a grave to prepare;
In every street the cars are moving slowly, as though to a funeral;
In every city of the land you can hear the passing-bell;
In every heart there's a single plaint,
I hear it more clearly every day.

(Translated from German by Patrick Bridgwater)

The impact of the war on those left behind was undoubtedly tragic, but one last
effort by the Germans could win them the war before the arrival of American
troops, dramatically and finally, would swing the pendulum towards the Allies.

The Background

Germany was starving. Britain had enforced a blockade of German supplies as a tool of war and was preventing food from reaching the country, a situation exacerbated by the decline in agricultural production as the men and horses who worked the German fields were taken away to join the war effort, either to serve in the forces or to work in the munitions factories. The position was worsened by the failed harvest of 1916, so that emaciated mothers were queueing with their starving children in food lines to receive their allocation of bread. People were surviving on a diet of ersatz bread and turnips while the privileged still feasted – it is estimated that up to a third of all milk, meat, cheese and fruit 'disappeared', only to surface again in the restaurants and on the dining tables of the wealthy. This unfairness helped spread unrest against the war; by January 1918 morale was at breaking point and in Berlin 400,000 marched to protest. In 1917 more than a quarter of a million German civilians died from starvation. Even the armed forces suffered, and seamen mutinied in protest at the minimal rations they received while their officers still dined in comfort.

Yvan Goll – 'Recitative (VIII)' from **Requiem for the Dead of Europe**
In this poem, Yvan Goll expresses the despair beginning to affect the German forces and ironically hails the 'heroes' who did not realise the enemy were also but men:

Requiem for the Dead of Europe
Recitative (VIII)

Like a grey wall around Europe
The never-ending battle, the bogged-down battle, the softening-up battle,
The battle that never was the final battle.
Oh, the monotony of trench-warfare!
Oh, trench-grave!
Oh, sleep of starvation!
The bridges built of corpses;
The roads surfaced with corpses;
The walls cemented with corpses.
For months on end the horizon stared mysteriously and glassily like a dead man's eye.
For years on end the distance rang like the same old passing-bell.

The days were as alike as a pair of graves.

Oh, you heroes!

Crawling out on wet nights, mewling in the bitter cold, you from your all-electric cities!

The sentry swapped ten nights' sleep for one cigarette;

Whole regiments gambled away eternity for ten yards of wasteland.

Full-blooded curses spat into the scarlet mire.

Damp cellars littered with tinny booty captured from the enemy.

Oh, you Greek dancers, dwarfed in lousy caverns!

Popping up like Indians in fancy-dress when the drums sounded the attack:

Before sticking your bayonet into his groin,

Did not one of you see the Christ-like look of his opponent?

Did not one of you notice that the man over there had a kingly heart full of love?

Did not one of you still believe in his own and mankind's conscience?

You brothers, fellow-men! Oh, you heroes!

(Translated from German by Patrick Bridgwater)

German's iron and steel industries had been powerful at the outbreak of war, exceeding the combined capacities of the French and British industries; but Germany was crucially dependent upon imports of the raw materials to feed her industry and the British blockade meant it was difficult to secure these vital supplies. Germany could not continue to fight much longer, and desperate action was required.

Strategically, there were two important developments. On the positive side, the Russians had capitulated, allowing Germany to transfer fifty battle-hardened divisions from the Eastern Front to join the forces fighting the Allies in Flanders. On the negative side, the Americans had declared war on Germany, but, importantly, there would be breathing space before America's huge resources of men and equipment could be brought to bear upon the war.

General Ludendorff realised he had one last chance to win the war before the Americans arrived and the odds shifted decisively in favour of the Allied powers. He now had 192 divisions under his command, while the Allies had 178 (Keegan, *First World War*, p.421). He had the men – but did he have the time? Concentration of effort and mobility of force were the keys to his plan.

He planned to attack on three fronts. The first attack would be against the British in the belief that the Battle of Passchendaele had left the British forces under-strength and demoralised. On 21 March 1918 the German offensive began with a surprise artillery bombardment by 6,000 guns firing gas and explosive shells, not just on the trenches in the front line but also on the communication trenches behind the lines to eliminate the possibility of a counter-attack. After a fierce five-hour bombardment, sixty-three first-class divisions of German troops advanced towards the severely outnumbered and under-strength British 5th Army, comprising just eleven divisions, under the cover of fog, a fog made denser by the use of gas (Campbell, *Engine*, p.207). The speed of the advance rocked the British forces before they had time to react and the Germans penetrated deep into the British lines. More than 7,000 British soldiers were killed in the first day of fighting, many more were wounded and over 20,000 taken prisoner, making it one of the worst days in the history of the British Army (Keegan, *First World War*, p.430). The defeat became a rout and in a week British forces had retreated 20 miles as the Germans recaptured the battlefields of the Somme, threatening to drive a wedge between the British and French armies.

A concerted response was required. On 26 March at an emergency meeting of French and British ministers, Marshal Foch was appointed the supreme commander of the Allied forces. He co-ordinated the defence, bringing in twenty French divisions to support the hard-pressed British, but only just in time, as by 5 April the Germans had reached within 5 miles of Amiens.

Vera Brittain vividly portrays the impact of the attack in her autobiography *Testament of Youth*. She was working at the 24th General Hospital Étaples and writes of walking with Hope Milroy (the name given by Brittain to Faith Moulson, the eccentric sister who she mildly worshipped and with whom she became close friends) and watching a vivid sunset:

[reminiscent] ... of the lurid suns that had set over England in the July before the War, and the belief of the superstitious that they had seen blood upon the sun and moon. Once again everything seemed waiting, waiting. 'Doesn't it all look ominous!' said Hope at last. Almost without speaking, we walked back to the camp. There we learned that the rumours of the morning were confirmed, and the great German offensive had begun.

She continues:

I shall never forget the crushing tension of those extreme days. Nothing had ever quite equalled them before – not the Somme, nor Arras, not Passchendaele – for into our minds had crept for the first time the secret, incredible fear that we might lose the War. Each convoy of men that we took in – to be dispatched, a few hours later, to England after a hasty wash and change of dressing, or to the cemetery after a laying-out too hurried to be reverent – gave way to a discouragement that none of us had met with in a great battle before.

On 27 March Albert was taken and even Paris was shelled by a long-range gun (Germany's Big Bertha) from 75 miles away. On 4 April:

after a fortnight of fourteen-hour days, with the operating theatres going day and night, the 'Fall-In' sounding continuously, and the day staff taking it in turns to be called up with the night convoys, we limped wearily into the Mess for supper to hear a new and yet more hair-raising rumour.

'The Germans are in the suburbs of Amiens!' it ran round the tables.

We looked at each other, speechless, with blanched faces; I was probably as pale as the rest, for I felt as though cold fingers were exploring my viscera. We were already becoming a Casualty Clearing Station, with only the advance units at Abbeville between ourselves and the line; how much longer should we be able to remain where we were? How long before we too fled before the grey uniforms advancing down the road from Camiers? This horror ... monstrous, undreamed of, incredible ... This was defeat.   (*Testament of Youth*, pp.373–6)

The Battle of the Lys

On 9 April the Germans followed up their attack with a second offensive to the north in Flanders, with the objective of driving the British back to the Channel ports. Portuguese soldiers defending this sector fell back under the determined German attack, forcing the outnumbered British forces to also withdraw, and creating a real possibility that the Germans would break through.

Haig, secure in his headquarters located in a château well behind the lines, recognised that for the men fighting these were indeed 'the most trying circumstances' and defeat was a definite possibility, thereby issuing his famous 'Backs to the Wall' order of the day:

Order of the Day – 12th April 1918

Three weeks ago to-day the enemy began his terrific attacks against us on a fifty-mile front. His objects are to separate us from the French, to take the Channel Ports, and to destroy the British Army.

In spite of throwing already 106 divisions into the battle, and enduring the most reckless sacrifice of human life, he has, as yet made little progress towards his goals. We owe this to the determined fighting and self-sacrifice of our troops. Words fail me to express the admiration which I feel for the splendid resistance offered by all ranks of our Army under the most trying circumstances.

Many amongst us now are tired. To those I would say that victory will belong to the side that holds out longest. The French Army is moving rapidly and in great force to our support.

There is no other course open to us but to fight it out. Every position must be held to the last man; there must be no retirement. With our backs to the wall and believing in the justice of our cause, each one of us must fight to the end. The safety of our homes and the Freedom of mankind alike depend upon the conduct of each one of us at this critical moment.'

Ludendorff now directed his forces south of Ypres and recaptured Passchendaele, which the British had taken at such cost the previous year, but determined British resistance and heavy German losses of their elite troops destroyed the momentum of the advance.

The Third Battle of the Aisne

The advance in the north having stalled, on 27 May Ludendorff directed the next push against the French with a heavy bombardment followed by the advance of fifteen divisions, with another twenty-five in reserve, against sixteen Allied divisions (of which three were British). Crossing the bridges which the French had failed to blow up, they drove deep into Allied lines, reaching the Marne on 30 May (Keegan, *First World War*, p.436). The French, threatened with the possible fall of Paris and defeat, defended fiercely.

The Americans Arrive

And now the Americans started to arrive. By March, 318,000 American troops had arrived in France and more were coming at the rate of 250,000 men a month. The advantage dramatically swung back to the Allies.

To the despair of the French, General Pershing would only allow a part of his forces to fight with the Allies, retaining the majority until he could form an American Army, but the Americans who did fight brought new hope to the exhausted French troops. At an early stage a detachment of marines, the pick of the American Army, were met by retreating French forces who advised the marines to do the same. Famously, Captain Lloyd Williams of the marines said, 'Retreat? Hell, we just got here' (quoted in Keegan, *First World War*, p.437). Foch ordered counter-attacks using fresh American troops and the German advance was stemmed.

By 1 June the Germans were again threatening Paris. Two days later they crossed the Marne and on 9 June launched a further attack, preceded by an artillery bombardment of more than three quarters of a million shells containing mustard gas and phosgene. Despite being forewarned, the French troops suffered from the gas attack and were forced to retreat.

The Germans reached to within 45 miles of Paris and victory seemed within their grasp, but the speed of the advance had outrun their ability to provide supplies and reserves of men, and an Allied counter-attack of French and American troops drove them back. A last attack by the Germans on 15 July was again beaten back by a desperate defence by French and American troops, who then counter-attacked with the British using tanks and aircraft to support the infantry. The Germans had gambled all and had nearly won, but they were exhausted and unable to replenish the losses of men in battle. Defeat was now inevitable.

This was the first time the American troops had been in action, but by the end of the war there would be 2 million American soldiers in France, comparable in numbers with the British Army, which then numbered 1.8 million, and the French, which had fallen to 1.7 million. The American troops were physically magnificent compared with the exhausted, battle-worn and nerve-shot men of the Entente armies. However, they were untried and untested by battle and were commanded by largely inexperienced officers and, as a result, suffered heavy casualties before they became battle-wise.

Roderick Watson Kerr – The Corpse

Roderick Watson Kerr fought as a lieutenant in the 2nd Royal Tank Corps. He was wounded during the bitter resistance to the German offensive and was awarded the Military Cross. He wrote a number of poems, including his chilling poem *The Corpse*:

The Corpse

It lay on the hill,
A sack on its face,
Collarless,
Stiff and still,
Its two feet bare
And very white;
Its tunic tossed in sight
And not a button there –
Small trace
Of clothes upon its back –
Thank God! It had a sack
Upon its face!

Gavrilo Princip

On 28 April, Gavrilo Princip, who, by assassinating the Archduke Franz Ferdinand, had arguably lit the match that ignited the world in a war causing four years of unimaginable suffering and inconceivable losses, died of tuberculosis in a prison hospital in Austria.

THE BATTLE OF AMIENS: THE ALLIES ADVANCE (8 AUGUST 1918)

The Allied leaders agreed that now was the time for a major advance to crush the German Army once and for all. The Allies had geared up their industrial output and had achieved a vast superiority in both tanks and aircraft and the Americans were bringing badly needed reinforcements. Foch recognised that the Americans were not battle-hardened and that the British and French forces had been badly battered by the spring German offensive and therefore rejected the suggestion of an all-out attack, instead orchestrating a succession of attacks along a 100-mile front – the beginning of the Hundred Day Advance, which finally broke the morale of the German Army.

Fresh Canadian and Australian troops were used as infantry support for an immense armoured force of 600 tanks – 530 British and 70 French (Keegan, *First World War*, p. 440) – in a push to break through the

German lines on the Somme. Lessons had at last been learnt. Details of the attack were kept secret until just a week before the attack and British planes were used to scare away German reconnaissance aircraft to preserve the element of surprise, while a rumour was spread that the attack would take place in Belgium.

At last the British used their powerful new weapon, the tank, to proper advantage. The failure of Germany to develop a tank force ranks as one of the outstanding misjudgements of the war. By 1918 Germany had just a handful of cumbersome tanks, together with a few captured from the French, whereas the Allies had many thousands which had been developed through experience to become game-changers in the conduct of the war.

Surprise was maintained – there was no opening bombardment, which had so often been the signal to the Germans of an impending attack. Instead, the British tanks rolled implacably towards the German lines, supported by a creeping artillery barrage (it had at last been realised that the accuracy of artillery fire was more important than sheer weight of shells), followed closely by Canadian and Australian infantry who, within four days, had reached the tangled wire and battered trenches of the Somme and pushed the German Army back to the Hindenburg Line. The day was later described by Ludendorff as 'the blackest day for the German Army in the history of this war'.

THE FINAL ASSAULT
(26 SEPTEMBER 1918)

On 26 September French and American troops, supported by 700 tanks, launched a further offensive along the Meuse, breaking through the German defences. On 27 September British forces attacked the Hindenburg Line near Cambrai, supported by more than 1,000 aircraft, and two days later, using boats, ladders and lifebelts, crossed the Saint Quentin Canal and breached the German defences. On 28 September Haig attacked the German salient at Ypres in the Fourth Battle of Ypres, where again British forces advanced rapidly using tanks and infantry against a demoralised and defeated enemy. By 4 October Allied forces were advancing on all sectors and the Hindenburg Line had been breached.

The Kaiser Resigns Power

With the German lines broken by the advancing Allied forces, Ludendorff realised that, for Germany, defeat had become inevitable and the only option to mitigate the extent of that defeat was to withdraw his forces to the German borders in a desperate attempt to protect the integrity of the country. To have any hope of negotiating a settlement to the conflict which preserved this integrity Germany needed to be led by a civilian (the Kaiser was, nominally at least, the head of the German armed forces) and so, on 2 October, the Kaiser was 'persuaded' to stand down and his second cousin, Prince Maximilian von Baden, was appointed Chancellor.

Two days after becoming Chancellor, Maximilian approached the American president with the offer of an unconditional ceasefire. Wilson rejected this out of hand. There would be no peace until all German soldiers had been withdrawn from French and Belgian soil and Serbia was free of German and Austrian troops.

The Fighting Goes On

Foch and Haig agreed that the advance should not be allowed to peter out and the war be allowed to revert to defensive immobility. Using the British on the left, the French in the centre and the Americans on the right, Foch planned a huge pincer movement to make the decisive breakthrough that would lead to victory.

The Americans, supported by tanks and planes, advanced rapidly in the south; almost too rapidly, as they began to outrun their supplies until halted by a spirited German defence. The Americans reorganised and attacked again but, in their inexperience, suffered heavy losses from German machine-gun fire until they finally resumed the advance.

The Germans fought on, falling back to the supposedly impregnable Hindenburg Line of defensive fortifications, but new artillery tactics and the use of aircraft and tanks had rendered the Hindenburg Line obsolete. Allied forces continued to advance across the whole of the front line and fresh new American troops were arriving in large numbers. Defiantly, Ludendorff ordered a fight to the finish, but this order was counter-manded by Maximilian, who realised the German people could take no more. On 27 October Ludendorff resigned, and conveniently would not be part of the now inevitable surrender. On 28 October the German admirals decided on one final grand gesture and ordered the fleet to sail. However, five times the men refused, the stokers extinguishing the fires in the boilers, and on 30 October a German division on the Western Front refused an order to attack. Discipline in the armed forces and morale amongst civilians had collapsed.

The Allied forces continued their remorseless advance. In the 100 days since the Allies had launched their attack, the British had taken 186,000 prisoners, the French 120,000 and the Americans 43,000; even the Belgians had taken 14,000. Together, these represented one-quarter of Germany's army in the field. The German military machine was broken (Gilbert, *First World War*, p.499).

The war was not going well for the Central Powers on the Western Front. It was not going any better elsewhere.

Joseph Lee - German Prisoners

Joseph Lee was born in Dundee in 1876 and educated in Scotland. He travelled the world working as a stoker on the steamships before returning to Dundee where he became a journalist. He enlisted in 1914 as a private in the Black Watch and in 1917 received a commission in the King's Royal Rifle Corps. He was captured in 1917, but after the war returned to Scotland and a career in journalism. As a prisoner himself he empathised with the plight of German prisoners, recognising that, despite being enemies, German and British soldiers were ultimately all brothers of the human race:

German Prisoners

When first I saw you in the curious street,
Like some platoon of soldier ghosts in grey,
My mad impulse was all to smite and slay,
To spit upon you – tread you 'neath my feet.
But when I saw how each sad soul did greet
My gaze with no signs of defiant frown,
How from tired eyes looked spirits broken down,
How each face showed the pale flag of defeat,
And doubt, despair, and disillusionment,
And how were grievous wounds on many a head,
And on your garb red-faced was other red;
And how you stooped as men whose strength was spent,
I knew that we had suffered each as other,
And could have grasped your hand and cried, 'My brother!'

Serbia Reopens the Southern Front
(14 September 1918)

The war in Salonika had been a stalemate for most of 1916 and 1917, but the few British troops involved had not suffered many casualties (far greater losses had been incurred through the prevalence of malaria). The stalemate ended with the abdication in 1917 of King Constantine, who had favoured the Germans. Greece now entered the war on the Allied side, strengthening the position of the British and French forces stationed in Greece.

The newly appointed French commander, General Franchet d'Espèrey, seized the opportunity and on 15 September 1918 launched an attack on Bulgaria, beginning with a six-hour bombardment. The Bulgarians had become disillusioned with the war, were short of food and equipment, and proved no match for a determined assault by Allied troops. King Ferdinand of Bulgaria demanded of his generals that they fight to the last man, but they respectfully declined his suggestion and abandoned the struggle, laying down their arms. On 29 September Bulgaria signed an armistice with the Allied powers and King Ferdinand abdicated.

By 1 November, d'Espèrey had reached the Danube and the Serbs had entered Belgrade. Serbia, joined by Slovenians, Croats and Bosnians all seeking a new and independent Slav state, was now positioned to attack Austria-Hungary on the vulnerable southern front of the Central Powers.

The Middle East - The Taking of Damascus

In the Middle East it was the same story, as another former ally of Germany was forced to sue for peace. General Allenby's British and Indian forces, with the support of the Arab irregulars under the leadership of Faisal and Lawrence, entered Damascus on 1 October 1918 and swept on towards Aleppo, bringing about the defeat - and collapse - of the Ottoman Empire, which surrendered on 30 October.

Austria Surrenders to Italy
(4 November 1918)

Austria was the next to collapse. Austria had had enough and was ready for peace. Food was exorbitantly expensive and in short supply. It was becoming tired of its overbearing ally; Germany had fought alone on the Western Front but on other fronts had treated its ostensible allies more like mercenaries - and not very trusted mercenaries at that. Austria had no quarrel with France or Britain and an end to the war was looking more and more attractive.

Italy and Austria had been locked in combat for three years until the Italian Army had been driven back to the River Piave by a determined attack from German and Austrian forces in June 1918. Under their new general, Armando Diaz, the Italians, now fighting for the survival of their country, held this line. In October 1918, Diaz realised that the Central Powers were crumbling and on 29 October counter-attacked, forcing a wedge between the Austrian forces in the mountains and those on the plain; 500,000 Austrians were killed, captured or wounded and on 3 November Austria surrendered. The Austro-Hungarian Empire was no more.

Ceasefire Negotiations

In January 1918 President Wilson of the United States had presented Fourteen Points as a programme for world peace, including proposals for the freedom of the seas, an agreed reduction in military spending and the formation of a League of Nations. More controversially, he proposed that all nations should have the right of self-determination. This last proposal had received a mixed reception from France and Britain; on the one hand, it would mean the dismemberment of the Austro-Hungarian Empire, but on the other hand it could lead to independence for the French colonies and for the countries of the British Empire – surely a step too far!

With the surrender of the Ottoman Empire and of the Austro-Hungarian Empire, Germany was isolated but unrealistically still hoped for a negotiated peace that would enable it to maintain its pride and the territory it now occupied. On 7 November a signal was sent to Marshal Foch requesting a meeting. The German delegation would all too soon be disabused of their illusions.

On 9 November the Kaiser abdicated and Germany became a republic.

THE ARMISTICE IS SIGNED
(11 NOVEMBER 1918)

Three days earlier, two trains had arrived at Rethondes, 40 miles north of Paris. One was the train used as headquarters by Marshal Foch, commander-in-chief of the Allied forces. The other contained German civilian politicians and an assortment of senior, but obscure, military officers, enabling Hitler to later claim that Germany 'had been stabbed in the back' and betrayed by its politicians. Ludendorff, following his timely resignation, was conspicuously absent.

The Germans made their way to Foch's carriage where Foch enquired, 'Ask what these gentlemen want?' The German delegation replied that they had come to hear the proposals for peace, but when Foch replied, 'I have no proposals to make,' the Germans knew that it would not be an honourable, negotiated peace but a humiliating defeat. Germany was ordered to hand over all its artillery and machine guns, its fleet comprising six battlecruisers, ten battleships, eight light cruisers, fifty destroyers and its submarines, and its air force of 1,700 aeroplanes. It would withdraw to its original frontiers.

The Armistice was signed at 5.12 a.m. on 11 November but, for tidiness, it was agreed the ceasefire would take place at 11 a.m. on the 11th day of the 11th month. (In an extraordinary coincidence, the number plate of the car in which the Archduke Franz Ferdinand was travelling when he was assassinated was A 111 118.) It is estimated that in those last six hours of fighting a further 2,738 men were needlessly killed. The last to die, a Canadian soldier, was shot by a German sniper just two minutes before the bugles sounded the end of the fighting.

But it was not the end of war. Peace was but an interlude before the outbreak of the Second World War. In an action redolent with symbolism, Hitler would, on 22 June 1940, accept the surrender of France in that same railway carriage. In the meantime, in Britain, there was universal relief and celebration, as portrayed in Sassoon's poem *Everyone Sang*, written in April 1919:

Siegfried Sassoon - Everyone Sang

Everyone Sang

Everyone suddenly burst out singing;
And I was filled with such delight
As prisoned birds must find in freedom
Winging wildly across the white
Orchards and dark green fields; On; on; and out of sight.

Everyone's voice was suddenly lifted,
And beauty came like the setting sun.
My heart was shaken with tears and horror
Drifted away ... O but Everyone
Was a bird; and the song was wordless;
The singing will never be done.

Robert Graves - November 11th
Graves had a more jaundiced view of the celebrations and reflected upon all those who had died:

November 11th

Why are they cheering and shouting
    What's all the scurry of feet
With little boys banging on kettle and can
    Wild laughter of girls in the street?

O those are the froth of the city
    The thoughtless and ignorant scum
Who hang out the bunting when war is let loose
    And for victory bang on a drum

But the boys who were killed in the battle
    Who fought with no rage and no rant
Are peacefully sleeping on pallets of mud
    Low down with the worm and the ant.

(Draft of a poem contained in a letter to Edward Marsh, November 1918)

9 THE CURTAIN FALLS

THE TREATY OF VERSAILLES

The Allied leaders met to draft the treaty that would finally end the Great War. America had joined the war late, but industrially and commercially it had reaped huge benefits, while the European Allies were militarily exhausted and economically challenged by the huge debts they had incurred in financing the war. President Wilson was therefore able to dictate the terms of the peace, although he was joined by France, Britain, Italy and Japan in the council that drew up the terms.

The leaders had different, often mutually exclusive, objectives. Wilson believed in the creation of a League of Nations to prevent future wars; Georges Clémenceau, the French prime minister, believed that Germany should be so weakened that it would never again pose a threat to France or to peace in Europe and wanted Germany to pay heavy reparations; Lloyd George perceptively believed that if Germany were treated too harshly and stripped of her colonies, made to pay excessive reparations and reduced to a third-rate military power, 'she will find means of extracting retribution from her conquerors' (Lloyd George, *The Truth About the Peace Treaties*, quoted in Roberts, *Minds at War*, p.348). Neither Lloyd George nor Clémenceau were particularly enamoured by the suggestion of President Wilson that nations should be given the right of self-determination – what dangerous radicalism!

The German military machine was dismantled. The army would, in future, be limited to 100,000 men. The navy had already been neutralised. On 21 November 1918 the German fleet had met with the British 1st Battlecruiser Squadron under Admiral Sir David Beatty and been escorted to Scapa Flow in the Orkneys. Here they remained at anchor under the watchful eye of the Grand Fleet. However, when Rear Admiral von Reuter learnt that the treaty would shortly be signed, stipulating that the German fleet be handed over to the British, he ordered that the German fleet be scuttled on 21 June 1919. The British could only watch as the ships slowly sank.

On 28 June the treaty was signed at Versailles, but its terms were harsh. The eminent British economist John Maynard Keynes, who had been appointed as financial representative for the British Treasury at the peace negotiations, believed strongly that the compensation payments required of Germany should not be pitched so high that it would penalise the German citizen and limit Germany's ability to buy foreign goods, thus damaging world trade. However, his views were largely ignored and the reparations demanded were in the end set so high that the seeds of discontent which would fuel the Second World War had been sown. Keynes resigned from the Treasury in protest.

Robert Graves expressed a similarly sceptical opinion in *Goodbye to All That* (p.236):

> The Treaty of Versailles shocked me; it seemed destined to cause another war someday, yet nobody cared. While the most critical decisions were being taken in Paris, public interest concentrated entirely on three home-news items: Hawker's Atlantic flight and rescue; the marriage of England's reigning beauty, Lady Diana Manners; and a marvellous horse called The Panther, the Derby favourite, which came in nowhere.

It was not only Germany that would be affected. The genie in the bottle of national self-determination had been uncorked and would dominate Europe over the next twenty years. The Austro-Hungarian Empire and the Ottoman Empires had been dismantled. The tsar and his family had been assassinated by the Bolsheviks on 16 July 1918. Even the victorious British Empire had reached a peak from which it would steadily decline. For all of this, 10 million soldiers had died and a further 20 million had been maimed or incapacitated.

BRITAIN AFTER THE WAR

Rudyard Kipling - Corrmmon Form

If they question why we died,
Tell them, because our fathers lied.

Kipling had been a strong supporter of the war and had written a number of pamphlets and poems glorifying it and condemning those men who shirked their patriotic duty. In this spirit, he actively supported the efforts of his son John to enlist. John initially applied to the Royal Navy, but was turned down because of poor eyesight. He was then turned down twice by the army, but his father 'pulled strings' and John was enrolled with a commission in the Irish Guards.

John was just 18 years old when he was killed at the Battle of Loos, last seen as he stumbled blindly through the mud with half his face ripped away by an exploding shell. His body was never found. Kipling wrote these words after the death of his son, perhaps in expiation for the guilt he felt for procuring a commission for him and thus bringing about his death.

A 'Country Fit for Heroes'

In Britain, Lloyd George called an immediate general election and vowed to create a 'country fit for heroes'. The reality was very different.

On a positive note, the franchise for men, previously restricted to property owners, was made universal and even reluctantly extended to women who – provided they were 30 years of age – were given the vote. Full voting equality with men was not introduced until 1928. Vera Brittain bitterly records:

> The reason universally given for limiting the vote to women over thirty was that the complete enfranchisement of adult women would have meant a preponderant feminine vote ... because, unlike men, they had inconsiderately failed to die in large numbers. (*Testament of Youth*, p.529)

But, a generation of women had lost their husbands, their lovers or their brothers. Men who had lost a limb, men who had had their faces so cruelly disfigured that they hid from society, or men whose lungs had been irreversibly damaged by gas, had to live their lives out in a society that wanted to move on. This was bitterly captured in Wilfred Owen's poem *Disabled*, drafted at Craiglockhart Hospital in October 1917 but revised in July 1918:

Disabled

He sat in a wheeled chair, waiting for dark,
And shivered in his ghastly suit of grey,
Legless, sewn short at elbow. Through the park
Voices of boys rang saddening like a hymn,
Voices of play and pleasure after day,
Till gathering sleep had mothered them from him.

About this time Town used to swing so gay
When blow-lamps budded in the light blue trees,
And girls glanced lovelier as the air grew dim, -
In the old times, before he threw away his knees,
Now he will never feel again how slim
Girl's waists are, or how warm their subtle hands.
All of them touch him like some queer disease.

There was an artist silly for his face,
For it was younger than his youth, last year.
Now, he is old; his back will never brace;
He's lost his colour very far from here,
Poured it down in shell-holes till the veins ran dry,
And half his lifetime lapsed in the hot race
And leap of purple spurted from his thigh.

One time he liked a blood-smear down his leg,
After the matches, carried shoulder-high.
It was after football, when he'd drunk a peg,
He thought he'd better join. - He wonders why.
Someone had said he'd look a god in kilts,
That's why; and maybe, too, to please his Meg,
Aye, that was it, to please the giddy jilts
He asked to join. He didn't have to beg;
Smiling they wrote his lie: aged nineteen years.

Germans he scarcely thought of; all their guilt,
And Austria's, did not move him. And no fears
Of Fear came yet. He thought of jewelled hilts

For daggers in plaid socks; of smart salutes;
And care of arms; and leave; and pay arrears;
Esprit de corps; and hints for young recruits.
And soon, he was drafted out with drums and cheers.

Some cheered him home, but not as crowds cheer Goal.
Only a solemn man who brought him fruits
Thanked him, and then enquired about his soul.

Now, he will spend a few sick years in institutes,
And do what things the rules consider wise,
And take whatever pity they may dole.
Tonight he noticed how the women's eyes
Passed from him to the strong men that were whole.
How cold and late it is! Why don't they come
And put him to bed? Why don't they come?

Many former servicemen were unable to find jobs as they returned to take over the work which had been performed so ably by women during the war. Unemployment increased and industrial unrest fermented, culminating in the Great Strike of 1926. Not surprisingly, resentment festered against those who had stayed comfortably at home, a feeling captured by Vera Brittain in her poem *The Lament of the Demobilised*:

The Lament of the Demobilised

'Four years,' some say consolingly,
'Oh well,
What's that? You're young. And then it must have been
A very fine experience for you!' And they forget
How others stayed behind and just got on –
Got on the better since we were away
And we came home and found
They had achieved, and men revered their names,
But never mentioned ours;
And no one talked heroics now, and we
Must just go back and start again once more.
'You threw four years into the melting pot –

Did you indeed!' these others cry.
'Oh well,
The more fool you!'
And we're beginning to agree with them.

Vera Brittain saw it as her mission to ask why 'the many brave, uncom-
plaining men whom I had nursed and could not save' had been deceived
into fighting a war that had no moral justification. She became a pacifist,
seeing it as her 'job, now, to find out all about it, and try to prevent it, in so
far as one person can, from happening to other people in days to come'
(*Testament of Youth*, p.431).

Spanish Flu

While Europe tried to recover from the ravages of war, the winter of 1918-19
was hit by an outbreak of influenza, known colloquially as 'Spanish flu'.
Usually those most at risk from flu are the elderly, but Spanish flu dispro-
portionately attacked those in the 20-30 age group. The fever lasted for
three days, after which the sufferer would recover - if still alive. Before the
discovery of antibiotics there was no effective treatment and as many as
20 million are estimated to have died worldwide; ironically, more than had
died in the war. In Britain alone more than 200,000 are estimated to
have died from the disease.

THE IMPACT OF THE WAR ON SCOTLAND

One hundred and forty-eight thousand Scots had died on active service.
Many more suffered from permanent injury. Many families had been
scarred by the loss of a husband, a brother or a father, and many more
lived with the ever-present reminder of the scars left by war.

The effect on the Scottish economy was dramatic. At the outset of the
war the Scottish economy was in fine fettle, based mainly on the heavy
industries of the west coast, supported by coal. In 1913 the Clyde shipyards
had produced ships amounting to three quarters of a million tons, a third
of the total British output and more than the whole of the output of the
German shipbuilders. 'Clyde-built' had become synonymous with quality.
The North British Locomotive Company built steam railway engines which
were exported throughout the world, powering the railways of countries

within and outwith the empire. The American-owned Singer Sewing Machine Company was one of the largest industrial companies in the world, and its 10,000 employees in its Scottish plant produced 13,000 sewing machines every week. Fishing, jute in Dundee, coal, cotton in Paisley – the list was extensive.

The war demanded a rapid increase in output, particularly in shipbuilding – both fighting ships for the Royal Navy and merchant ships to expand Britain's Merchant Navy and replace those sunk by German U-boats. The Glasgow shipyard Beardmore's produced aircraft under licence, including the Sopwith Pup and Handley Page bombers, while the North British Locomotive Company built two new factories to produce artillery shells and mines, and also, later on in the war, for the manufacture of tanks. The jute industry of Dundee expanded to produce the millions of sandbags required for the trenches of Flanders.

Many Scottish men worked during the war in the heavy industries and by the end of the war there were 30,000 women working in munitions factories in Scotland alone, while throughout Britain there were hundreds of thousands more. (The girls who worked in the munitions factories were rather unkindly called `canary girls' because their continued exposure to the fumes of trinitrotoluene (TNT) caused their skin to acquire a rather nauseating yellow pallor (Royle, *Flowers*, pp.205-8).)

The end of the war brought massive adjustment. The shipbuilding industry had effectively been subsidised by the orders from the navy, which were not subject to international competition. The industry had become inherently uncompetitive and the profits of many of Scotland's heavy industrial manufacturers had been derived not from efficiency but by keeping wages low. This inevitably resulted in poor living conditions, ill health and industrial unrest, and the problem was compounded because low wages provided little purchasing power to encourage the growth of consumer-led industries. This dependence on heavy engineering would bedevil the Scottish economy for the next fifty years.

The effect of the end of the war upon female employment was harsh. The Restoration of Pre-War Practices Act gave returning solders their old jobs – an understandable reaction, but one at the expense of women. The jobs they had performed during the war in munitions, the jute industry and even as tram drivers evaporated when the men came home.

Home Rule

One of the political 'casualties' of the war was the embryonic Scottish Home Rule movement. For some years, the Liberals had supported the principle of Home Rule for Ireland; in Gladstone's words, 'to settle the great moral issue of Ireland.' In the general election held in 1910 the Liberals had not only won power but had secured 80 per cent of the parliamentary seats in Scotland, giving them a mandate to redesign the constitutional position of Scotland within the Union. On the basis of creating a new federal structure for the United Kingdom, a Scottish Home Rule Bill was introduced to mirror the structure proposed for Ireland, and in May 1914 it had passed the second reading in the House of Commons and was on the way to enactment. Scottish Home Rule had been a possibility 100 years before the 2014 referendum, but the outbreak of war brought an end to any such revolutionary thoughts.

'THE PITY OF WAR'

My Subject is War, and the Pity of War: The Poetry is in the Pity.

These words were used by Wilfred Owen as a preface for the collection of his poems which was published posthumously. The phrase was used by Owen in his disturbing poem *Strange Meeting*:

Strange Meeting

It seemed that out of battle escaped
Down some profound dull tunnel, long since scooped
Through granites which titanic wars had groined.

Yet also there encumbered sleepers groaned,
Too fast in thought or death to be bestirred.
Then, as I probed them, one sprang up, and stared
With piteous recognition in fixed eyes,
Lifting distressful hands, as if to bless.
And by his smile, I knew that sullen hall, –
By his dead smile I knew we stood in Hell.

With a thousand pains that vision's face was grained;
Yet no blood reached them from the upper ground,
And no guns thumped, or down the flues made moan.
'Strange friend,' I said, 'here is no cause to mourn.'
'None,' said that other, 'save the undone years,
The hopelessness. Whatever hope is yours,
Was my life also; I went hunting wild
After the wildest beauty in the world,
Which lies not calm in eyes, or braided hair,
But mocks the steady running of the hour,
And if it grieves, grieves richlier than here.
For by my glee might many men have laughed,
And of my weeping something had been left,
Which must die now. I mean the truth untold,
The pity of war, the pity war distilled.
Now men will go content with what we spoiled,
Or, discontent, boil bloody, and be spilled.
They will be swift with swiftness of the tigress.
None will break ranks, though nations trek from progress.
Courage was mine, and I had mystery,
Wisdom was mine, and I had mastery:
To miss the march of this retreating world
Into vain citadels that are not walled.
Then, when much blood had clogged their chariot-wheels,
I would go up and wash them from sweet wells,
Even with truths that lie too deep for taint.
I would have poured my spirit without stint
But not through wounds; not on the cess of war.
Foreheads of men have bled where no wounds were.

'I am the enemy you killed, my friend.
I knew you in this dark: for so you frowned
Yesterday through me as you jabbed and killed.
I parried; but my hands were loath and cold.
Let us sleep now ...'

(Written between January and March 1918)

'Lizzie and the Bairns'

The 'pity of war' is encapsulated in the letters and cards written by Charles Bowman to his wife Lizzie and the bairns. Bowman, who served in the 9th Battalion Gordon Highlanders, arrived in France in June 1916 and on 24 June wrote:

Dear Lizzie and the Bairns,

Owing to the censor I can only say that I am writing this somewhere in France. We arrived safely after a long journey and a good passage across. We had a bit of rain last night and the ground was a quagmire. It has cleared up a bit now and is a fine sunny night. We shifted up country a bit today by train. It is very pretty country very like the lowlands of Scotland with the green fields and trees.

I hope you and the bairns are well. Jean was just beginning to know me when I had to come away. Now dear I have some duties to do tonight I will stop. With love to you all and kisses.

Ever yours.

Dad

On 6 July he wrote:

Dear Willie, Irvine and Jean,

I hope that this will find you all well and that you are enjoying the summer weather and getting to the links and the sands every day. I was sorry I did not get spoken to you all when I was passing up King Street but never mind we'll all have some good times yet. I had a note from Miss Ganed and she was telling me that Irvine could play God Save the King on the piano. I was very pleased to hear that. I believe Willie would be a fine player on the Gramophone! Eh Bill – Jean's favourite instrument would I think be a ? sugar whistle. I will be very glad if you boys can spare time to write a few lines to me and if Irvine has had any sketches to send them on. Jean can ornament the letter with some of her pictures. Now I will stop and I hope that you will maybe get to Montrose before the end of your holidays.

With love to you all

Your loving Dad

He wrote again on 27 July:

Dear Lizzie

I have had no word from you since your letter dated 3rd July more than 3 weeks ago and am wearied to hear from you. It means so much out here to get a letter. ... We are getting good weather and I am keeping all right with the exception of my feet which are rather sore but they will get better through time. There was a hot time out here last night. Our artillery were at it all night and no one at home can imagine the scene. The sky was lit up almost continuously with the flack of the guns and the bursting of the shells. ... I hope you are keeping all right and not worrying. How is Jean getting on. She is a dear wee girl. I hope the boys are also keeping all right. They will soon be going back to school. Now dear, I will stop and I will write again at the first opportunity. With fondest love to you and the bairns.

Ever yours.

Chas

And on 6 August:

Dear Lizzie

I got your letter yesterday after I had written you and the bairns. I am very pleased to hear you were having a good time in Montrose ...

With love and kisses to the bairns and yourself.

Ever yours

Dad

Dear Irvine

I am writing this to wish you many happy returns on your birthday and hope you will be spared to see many of them and before your next one comes that I will be home beside you all. You will see by the above address that I have shifted [from the 9th to the 1st Battalion]. We have all got kilts again and were sent up to the front on Saturday. You would have laughed if you had seen us in cattle trucks lying on the floor and sitting with feet hanging out at the door. When we arrived at the end of our railway journey we had to march all night to get up here and you may be sure we were tired enough. We are just at the back of the firing line and the big guns are going night and day. ... Now as the man is waiting to take the letters I will stop. I will write you tonight.

With love to you all.

Ever your loving

Dad

On 18 August Bowman sent a postcard:

> Just a line or two to let you now I am OK we are up in the line having a hot
> time. Hope you are all keeping well and have benefitted by your holiday.
> Love and kisses you and the bairns.
>   Your loving
>   Dad

(Quoted in Young, *Scottish Voices*, pp.241-6)

Charles Bowman was shot and killed shortly after writing this postcard.
Lizzie and the bairns would never see him again.

That is the 'pity of war'.

Laurence Binyon - For the Fallen

Laurence Binyon wrote the words which are quoted at each Remembrance
Day service. Binyon was born in August 1869 and was nearly 45 when war
broke out. In 1893 he had joined the British Museum as an art historian and
he worked there until his retirement in 1933.

He was asked to join the government's Propaganda Department, which
had been set up by Lloyd George shortly after the outbreak of war, and
admirably, although too old for active service, volunteered in 1915 to work
as an orderly in a British hospital for French soldiers, returning in 1916 to
care for soldiers injured in the Battle of Verdun. He recorded his experiences
in his poem *Fetching the Wounded*. However, his enduring fame as a war
poet lies with his poem *For the Fallen*, which was first published in *The Times*
on 21 September 1914:

For the Fallen
[omitting the last three verses]

With proud thanksgiving, a mother for her children,
England mourns for her dead across the sea.
Flesh of her flesh they were, spirit of her spirit,
Fallen in the cause of the free.

Solemn the drama thrill: Death august and royal
Sings sorrow up into immortal spheres.

There is music in the midst of desolation
And a glory that shines upon our tears.

They went with songs to the battle: they were young,
Straight of limb, true of eye, steady and aglow.
They were staunch to the end against odds uncounted:
They fell with their faces to the foe.

They shall not grow old, as we that are left grow old:
Age shall not weary them, nor the years condemn.
At the going down of the sun and in the morning
We will remember them.

J.B. Salmond – Twenty Years Ago

The final words should belong to a Scot, J.B. Salmond, who wrote the bitter poem *Twenty Years Ago* in August 1934. Salmond was born in Arbroath in 1891. Writing was in his blood, as his father was editor of the *Arbroath Herald*. He enlisted in the Black Watch in 1915 as a second lieutenant and was promoted to lieutenant in 1917. He suffered from trauma and was a patient at Craiglockhart Hospital where he edited the hospital magazine. After the war he became editor of the *Scots Magazine*.

Twenty Years Ago

There's a thin rain of music comes across the poppied corn,
    Across the poppied corn and the sun-splashed sea,
Crying, 'Who's a-going venturing, a-venturing, a-venturing,
    Who's going a-venturing with all a man can be?'
O. listen, listen, listen, for it's far, far away,
    The dim remembered country where the ghostly pipers blow,
Across a world of sorrows to a green blue day
When boyhood went a-soldiering, a-soldiering, a-soldiering,
    When boyhood went a-soldiering, twenty years ago.

    So off the white starched collar
        And the neat grey suit,
    The crease in the trousers
        And the pointed boot,

The rolled umbrella
    And the bowler hat
Make them in a bundle –
    That's the end of that.
For it's polish for the buttons
    And dubbin for the boots,
And a D.P. rifle
    For the new recruits.
We're learning 'Tipperary'
    And the squad drill back,
And we're breaking faulty bayonets
    In a straw-filled sack.
We're studying the language
    That the bugles blow.

Lad, can it be twenty years, twenty years, twenty years,
Lad, can it be twenty years, twenty years ago?

They made the boy a soldier in the passing of a day,
    And Agamemnon's warriors on the windy plains of Troy,
And Caesar's legionaries and the guards of Marshal Ney,
    Ay, even the Crusaders had nothing on the boy;
For he fought in France and Flanders mud, in Macedonian sand,
    In Africa's green jungle, and in the Russian snow,
And he marched against Jerusalem, and made the Promised Land –
The boy that went a-soldiering, a-soldiering, a-soldiering,
    The boy that went a-soldiering, twenty years ago.

With poisoned gas they choke him,
    With shell and shock and flame
The beauty of his body
    They mangle and they maim.
And when it all was over,
    They worship for an hour,
And build him a memorial,
    And bring to him a flower.
And as the years piled higher,
    They dipped a bloody pen

Into a well of filthiness
    And killed the boy again.
They branded him a libertine,
    A coward and a sot.
The wrong things were remembered,
    And the promises forgot.
Yes, round his grave they watched unmoved
    The weeds of horror grow,
The boy they swore they'd ne'er forget
Just twenty years ago, just twenty years ago, just twenty years ago.

The boy is dead in all of us, and War's an ugly thing,
    And the pacifist is right no doubt, and the service man is ex.,
And 'Tipperary' nowadays is no great song to sing,
    And there isn't much romance about shell-shock and nervous wrecks.
But still we hear the music across the poppied corn,
    Across a world of sorrow the ghostly pipers blow.
And thank God we went soldiering, a-soldiering, a-soldiering,
    With that boy that went a-soldiering twenty years ago!

SOURCES

WAR POETRY

Bostridge, Mark (ed.), *Because You Died: Poetry and Prose of the First World War and After*. Virago Press, London, 2008.

Brooke, Rupert, *Collected Poems of Rupert Brooke*. Sidgwick and Jackson, London, 1928.

Frissardi, Andrew (ed.), *Giuseppe Ungaretti: Selected Poems*. Farrar, Strauss and Giroux, New York, 2002.

Goldie, David, and Roderick Watson (eds), *Scottish War Poetry 1914–45 (From the Line)*. The Association for Scottish Literary Studies, Glasgow, 2014.

Graves, Beryl, and Dunstan Ward (eds), *Robert Graves: The Complete Poems*. Penguin Books, London, 2003.

Hart-Davis, Rupert (ed.), *Siegfried Sassoon: The War Poems*. Faber and Faber, London, 1983.

MacDonald, Lyn (ed.), *Anthem for Doomed Youth: Poets of the Great War*. The Folio Society, London, 2000.

Mackintosh, Ewart Alan, *A Highland Regiment*. John Lane, London, 1918.

Mackintosh, Ewart Alan, *War, the Liberator and Other Pieces*. John Lane, London, 1918.

O'Prey, Paul (ed.), *Poems from the Front*. IWM, London, 2014.

Reilly, Catherine (ed.), *Scars Upon My Heart: Women's Poetry of the First World War*. Virago Press, London, 2006.

Seeger, Alan, *Poems*. Charles Scribener, New York, 1919.

Silkin, John (ed.), *The Penguin Book of First World War Poetry*. Penguin Books, London, 1979.

Spear, Hilda D. (ed.), *The Poems and Selected Letters of Charles Hamilton Sorley*. Blackness Press, Dundee, 1978.

Stallworthy, John (ed.), *Wilfred Owen: The War Poems*. Chatto & Windus, London, 1994.

BACKGROUND READING AND PROSE SOURCES

Bell, John (ed.), *Wilfred Owen: Selected Letters*. Oxford University Press, Oxford, 1985.

Blunden, Edmund, *Undertones of War*. Oxford University Press, Oxford, 2015.

Brittain, Vera, *Testament of Youth*. Virago Press, London, 1978.

Brown, Malcolm, *The Imperial War Museum Book of the First World War*. Sidgwick & Jackson, London, 1991.

Buchan, John, *A History of the Great War*. Houghton Mifflin Company, Boston, 1923.

Campbell, Colin, *Engine of Destruction: The 51st (Highland) Division in the Great War*. Argyll Pblishing, Glendaruel, Scotland, 2013.

Campbell, Colin, and Green, Rosalind, *Can't Shoot a Man with a Cold*. Argyll Publishing, Glendaruel, Scotland, 2004.

Clark, Christopher, *The Sleepwalkers*. Penguin Books, London, 2013.

Crofton, Eileen, *The Women of Royaumont*. Tuckwell Press, East Linton, Scotland, 1997.

Evans, Martin Marix, *Somme 1914-1918: Lessons in War*. The History Press, Stroud, Gloucestershire, 2010.

Ewing, John, *The History of the Ninth (Scottish) Division 1914-1919*. John Murray, London, 1921.

Faulkner, Neil, *Lawrence of Arabia's War*. Yale University Press, New Haven, 2016.

Ferguson, Andrew, *Scots Who Enlightened the World*. Polwarth Publishing, Edinburgh, 2013.

Ferguson, Niall, *The Pity of War*. Penguin Books, London, 1998.

Freeman, Richard, '*Unsinkable*': *Churchill and the First World War*. The History Press, Stroud, Gloucestershire, 2013.

Gilbert, Martin, *First World War*. BCA, London, 1994.

Gooch, John, *The Italian Army and the First World War*. Cambridge University Press, Cambridge, 2014.

Graves, Robert, *Goodbye to All That*. Penguin Books, London, 1960.

Hamilton, Sir Ian, *Gallipoli Diary*. George H. Doran Company, New York, 1920.

Hastings, Max, *Catastrophe*. William Collins, London, 2013.

Keegan, John, *The First World War*. The Bodley Head, London, 2014.

Lawrence, T.E., *Seven Pillars of Wisdom*. Jonathan Cape, London, 1928.

Lussu, Emilio, *A Soldier on the Southern Front: The Classic Italian Memoir of World War 1*. Rizzoli Ex Libris, New York, 2014.

MacDonald, Catriona, and E.W. McFarland (eds), *Scotland and the Great War*. Birlinn, Edinburgh, 2014.

Mackenzie, Compton, *Gallipoli Memories*. Cassell, London, 1929.

MacMillan, Margaret, *The War that Ended Peace*. Profile Books, London, 2013.

McLaren, Eva Shaw, *A History of the Scottish Women's Hospitals*. Macmillan, London, 1920.

McLaren, Eva Shaw, *Elsie Inglis: The Woman with the Torch*. London, 1929.

Munro, Kevin, *Scotland's First World War*. Historic Scotland, Edinburgh, 2014.

Roberts, David (ed.), *Minds at War: Poetry and Experience of the First World War*. Saxon Books, Burgess Hill, England, 1996.

Rorie, Colonel David, *A Medico's Luck in the War*. Milne and Hutchinson, Aberdeen, 1929.

Royle, Trevor (ed.), *In Flanders Fields: Scottish Poetry and Prose of the First World War*. Mainstream Publishing, Edinburgh, 1990.

Royle, Trevor (ed.), *Isn't all this Bloody?* Birlinn, Edinburgh, 2014.

Royle, Trevor (ed.), *The Flowers of the Forest*. Birlinn, Edinburgh, 2007.

Sassoon, Siegfried, *Memoirs of a Fox-Hunting Man*. Faber and Faber, London, 1928.

Sassoon, Siegfried, *Memoirs of an Infantry Officer*. Faber and Faber, London, 1930.

Sassoon, Siegfried, *The Complete Memoirs of George Sherston*. Faber and Faber, London, 1937.

Stallworthy, Jon, *Wilfred Owen*. Oxford University Press, Oxford, 1974.

Stewart, Lieutenant Colonel J., and John Buchan, *Fifteenth (Scottish) Division 1914–19*. William Blackwood, Edinburgh, 1926.

Strachan, Hew, *The First World War*. Simon & Schuster, London, 2003.

Young, Derek, *Scottish Voices from the Great War*. The History Press, Stroud, Gloucestershire, 2008.

INDEX OF POEMS